The Afterlives of Roland Barthes

Also Available from Bloomsbury

Benjamin, Barthes and the Singularity of Photography,
Kathrin Yacavone
Literary Criticism in the 21st Century: Theory Renaissance,
Vincent B. Leitch

The Afterlives of Roland Barthes

Neil Badmington

BLOOMSBURY ACADEMIC
LONDON • NEW YORK • OXFORD • NEW DELHI • SYDNEY

BLOOMSBURY ACADEMIC
Bloomsbury Publishing Plc
50 Bedford Square, London, WC1B 3DP, UK

BLOOMSBURY, BLOOMSBURY ACADEMIC and the Diana logo are
trademarks of Bloomsbury Publishing Plc

First published in Great Britain 2016
Paperback edition first published 2018

© Neil Badmington, 2016

Neil Badmington has asserted his right under the Copyright, Designs and Patents
Act, 1988, to be identified as Author of this work.

For legal purposes the Acknowledgements on p. viii constitute
an extension of this copyright page.

Cover design: Anna Berzovan
Cover image © Getty Images

All rights reserved. No part of this publication may be reproduced or transmitted in any
form or by any means, electronic or mechanical, including photocopying, recording, or
any information storage or retrieval system, without prior permission in writing from
the publishers.

Bloomsbury Publishing Plc does not have any control over, or responsibility for,
any third-party websites referred to or in this book. All internet addresses
given in this book were correct at the time of going to press. The author and
publisher regret any inconvenience caused if addresses have changed or
sites have ceased to exist, but can accept no responsibility for any such changes.

A catalogue record for this book is available from the British Library.

A catalog record for this book is available from the Library of Congress.

ISBN: HB: 978-1-4742-9745-5
PB: 978-1-3500-6699-1
ePDF: 978-1-4742-9747-9
ePub: 978-1-4742-9746-2

Typeset by RefineCatch Limited, Bungay, Suffolk

To find out more about our authors and books visit
www.bloomsbury.com and sign up for our newsletters.

For Maria, Dylan and Felix, who will be glad to see the back of this.

Contents

Acknowledgements	viii
Note on Translations and Abbreviations	x
1 Introduction: The Afterlives of Roland Barthes	1
2 For Henriette's Tomb: Mourning with Mallarmé	13
3 *Punctum Saliens*: Mourning, Film, Photography	41
4 The 'Inkredible' Roland Barthes	61
5 Bored with Barthes: Ennui in China	83
6 Hitchcock *Hapax*: Realism Revisited	109
Postscript: Afterlives' Afterlives	137
Bibliography	139
Index	151

Acknowledgements

Readers of Roland Barthes know all too well that a text is 'a fabric of quotations'. This book is no exception, but its fabrication is also in part the product of conversations of different kinds with a number of people over the years. I am particularly indebted to the following:

David Avital, Tom Baldwin, Bill Bell, Catherine Belsey, Chu-chueh (Cherry) Cheng, Claude Coste, Martin Coyle, Carl Distefano, Sam Ferguson, Reshmi Dutta-Flanders, Juliet Gardner, Calum Gardner, Katie Gramich, Katja Haustein, Ann Heilmann, Merv Honeywood, Julia Jordan, Lawrence D. Kritzman, Diana Leca, Jean-Jacques Lecercle, Anthony Mandal, Éric Marty, Emma Mason, Laurent Milesi, Iain Morland, Irene Morra, John McKeane, Becky Munford, Magali Nachtergael, Lucy O'Meara, Carl Phelpstead, Jürgen Pieters, Kris Pint, Jean-Michel Rabaté, Graham Riach, Mark Richardson, Nicholas Royle, Carrie Smith, Andy Stafford, Julia Thomas, Laurence Totelin, Hiroyuki Tsuruta, David Tucker, Richard Vine, Damian Walford Davies, Adam Watt, Shane Weller, Richard Wilson, Michael Wood, Mikkel Bruun Zangenberg.

Some of the material in this book was presented in earlier forms at Cardiff University, Universiteit Gent, University of Cambridge, Kent University and University of Leeds. I thank all those who commented. I also learnt a great deal from an afternoon's discussion of my work hosted by the Group for Early Modern Studies at Universiteit Gent in December 2015.

An earlier version of Chapter 3 appeared as '*Punctum Saliens*: Barthes, Mourning, Film, Photography' in *Paragraph* in 2012. The version published here has been updated to take account of research that was not available to me when I was writing the original essay in 2010 and 2011. A far shorter, lighter version of Chapter 4 was published in *Paragraph* in 2008. I have made extensive conceptual revisions here, and the piece is now around twice as long as its rather immature predecessor. Chapter 5 first appeared in briefer form in 2016, as part of a special issue of *Textual Practice* entitled 'Deliberations: The Journals of Roland Barthes'. I am grateful in each case for permission to reprint here.

The Afterlives of Roland Barthes could not have been written without a year-long research fellowship awarded to me by Cardiff University. I thank the institution for its support.

N.B.
Cardiff, February 2016

Note on Translations and Abbreviations

As this book is in English, texts by Roland Barthes will be quoted in translation, with references to the original French where necessary. Where published translations exist, I have used these, occasionally modifying the English (and indicating where I have done so). Where translations do not exist, the English renderings given are my own.

The following abbreviations for works by Roland Barthes are used throughout this book:

ADP   'On Robert Bresson's Film *Les Anges du péché*'. Trans. Richard Howard. In *Robert Bresson*, ed. James Quandt, 211–13. Toronto: Toronto International Film Festival Group, 1998.

AL   *Album: Inédits, correspondances et varia.* Eds Éric Marty and Claude Coste. Paris: Seuil, 2015.

CE   *Critical Essays.* Trans. Richard Howard. Evanston, IL: Northwestern University Press, 1973.

CL   *Camera Lucida: Reflections on Photography.* Trans. Richard Howard. Rev. edn. New York: Hill and Wang, 2010.

CVC   *Carnets du voyage en Chine.* Paris: Christian Bourgois, 2009.

DA   *Le Discours amoureux: Séminaire à l'Ecole pratique des hautes études 1974–1976.* Ed. Claude Coste. Paris: Seuil, 2007.

DAN   'Dear Antonioni'. Trans. Geoffrey Nowell-Smith. Appendix to Geoffrey Nowell-Smith, *L'avventura*, 63–8. London: BFI, 1997.

EL   *Elements of Semiology.* Trans. Annette Lavers and Colin Smith. New York: Hill and Wang, 1973.

ES   *Empire of Signs.* Trans. Richard Howard. New York: Hill and Wang, 1983.

ET   *The Eiffel Tower and Other Mythologies.* Trans. Richard Howard. Berkeley and Los Angeles: University of California Press, 1979.

FS   *The Fashion System.* Trans. Matthew Ward and Richard Howard. Berkeley and Los Angeles: University of California Press, 1990.

GV   *The Grain of the Voice: Interviews 1962–1980.* Trans. Linda Coverdale. Berkeley and Los Angeles: University of California Press, 1991.

HTLT *How To Live Together: Novelistic Simulations of Some Everyday Spaces.* Trans. Kate Briggs. New York: Columbia University Press, 2013.

IN   *Incidents.* Trans. Teresa Lavender Fagan. London and New York: Seagull Books, 2010.

JD   *Journal de deuil: 26 octobre 1977 – 15 septembre 1979.* Ed. Nathalie Léger. Paris: Seuil/IMEC, 2009.

L   'Lecture: In Inauguration of the Chair of Literary Semiology, Collège de France, January 7, 1977'. Trans. Richard Howard, *Oxford Literary Review* 4, vol. 1 (1979): 31–44.

LA   *Le Lexique de l'auteur: Séminaire à l'École pratique des hautes études 1973–1974, suivi de fragments inédits du Roland Barthes par Roland Barthes.* Ed. Anne Herschberg Pierrot. Paris: Seuil, 2010.

LD   *A Lover's Discourse: Fragments.* Trans. Richard Howard. Harmondsworth: Penguin, 1990.

LF   *The Language of Fashion.* Eds Andy Stafford and Michael Carter. Trans. Andy Stafford. Oxford and New York: Berg, 2006.

LN   *Le Neutre: Notes de cours au Collège de France 1977–1978.* Ed. Thomas Clerc. Paris: Seuil/IMEC, 2002.

MD   *Mourning Diary: October 26, 1977 – September 15, 1979.* Ed. Nathalie Léger. Trans. Richard Howard. New York: Hill and Wang, 2010.

MI   *Michelet.* Trans. Richard Howard. Oxford: Basil Blackwell, 1987.

MY	*Mythologies*. Rev. edn. Ed. Annette Lavers. Trans. Annette Lavers and Siân Reynolds. London, Vintage, 2009.
N	*The Neutral: Lecture Course at the Collège de France (1977–1978)*. Ed. Thomas Clerc. Trans. Rosalind E. Krauss and Denis Hollier. New York: Columbia University Press, 2005.
OC	*Oeuvres complètes*. Rev edn. Ed. Eric Marty. Paris, Seuil, 2002. 5 vols. Abbreviated references to the *Oeuvres complètes* will take the form of OC I, OC II, OC III, OC IV, and OC V to indicate volume numbers. OC IV, 432, for example, would therefore refer to page 432 of the fourth volume.
OCS	'On CinemaScope'. Trans. Jonathan Rosenbaum, *Jouvert* 3, vol. 3 (1999). Online publication, available online at http://english.chass.ncsu.edu/jouvert/v3i3/barth.htm.
PDT	*Le Plaisir du texte* précédé de *Variations sur l'écriture*. Paris: Seuil, 2000.
PN	*The Preparation of the Novel: Lecture Courses and Seminars at the Collège de France (1978–1979 and 1979–1980)*. Ed. Nathalie Léger. Trans. Kate Briggs. New York: Columbia University Press, 2011.
PR	*La Préparation du roman I et II: Notes de cours et de séminaires au Collège de France 1978–1979 et 1979–80*. Ed. Nathalie Léger. Paris: Seuil/IMEC, 2003.
PRN	*La Préparation du roman: Notes de cours et de séminaires au Collège de France 1978–1979 et 1979–80*. New edn. Eds Nathalie Léger and Éric Marty. Transcriptions by Nathalie Lacroix. Paris: Seuil, 2015.
PT	*The Pleasure of the Text*. Trans. Richard Miller. New York: Hill and Wang, 1975.
RB	*Roland Barthes by Roland Barthes*. Trans. Richard Howard. London: Papermac, 1995.
RF	*The Responsibility of Forms: Critical Essays on Music, Art, and Representation*. Trans. Richard Howard. Berkeley and Los Angeles: University of California Press, 1991.

RL   *The Rustle of Language*. Trans. Richard Howard. Oxford: Blackwell, 1986.

SC   *The Semiotic Challenge*. Trans. Richard Howard. Berkeley and Los Angeles: University of California Press, 1994.

SDB   Sarrasine *de Balzac: Séminaires à l'École pratique des hautes études 1967–1968, 1968–1969*. Eds Claude Coste and Andy Stafford. Paris: Seuil, 2011.

SFL   *Sade, Fourier, Loyola*. Trans. Richard Miller. Baltimore and London: Johns Hopkins University Press, 1997.

SM   'The "Scandal" of Marxism' *and Other Writings on Politics*. Trans. Chris Turner. London and New York: Seagull Books, 2015.

SPC   'Simply a Particular Contemporary': *Interviews, 1970–79*. Trans. Chris Turner. London and New York: Seagull Books, 2015.

SW   *Sollers Writer*. Trans. Philip Thody. London: Athlone Press, 1987.

SZ   *S/Z*. Trans. Richard Miller. Oxford: Blackwell, 1990.

TC   *Travels in China*. Trans. Andrew Brown. Cambridge: Polity, 2011.

VFG   'A Very Fine Gift' *and Other Writings on Theory*. Trans. Chris Turner. London and New York: Seagull Books, 2015.

WDZ   *Writing Degree Zero*. Trans. Annette Lavers and Colin Smith. London: Jonathan Cape, 1967.

1

Introduction: The Afterlives of Roland Barthes

There were lights on the side of the bridge over the railway line. They formed letters, words, a phrase: 'Commence alors la grande lumière du Sud-Ouest'. *Then the great light of the South West begins.*

The text came from an essay by Roland Barthes and had been installed on Pont de Birambits in Bègles, a suburb of Bordeaux, by the artist Pascal Convert to mark the centenary of Barthes's birth in 2015.¹ The location was not neutral: as Magali Nachtergael has explained, the crossing over the tracks marks the point of entry into the southern region formerly known as Aquitaine – a part of France in which Barthes had lived as child, where he would later spend much of his time when he was not in Paris and which he celebrated at length in 'The Light of the South West'.²

I am writing these introductory pages in early 2016. If I allow my memory to drift back to the other side of the new year, I feel weary, overwhelmed; my body tenses and prickles. Trying to keep up with all of the commemorative events and publications during 2015 was exhausting, perhaps impossible, but nonetheless intellectually thrilling. I feel privileged to have lived through those twelve months and it saddens me to think that I will not be here to enjoy the festivities which will no doubt surround the second centenary. (Should an as-yet-unborn Barthesian happen to be reading these lines in 2115, I salute from beyond the grave and apologize for my absence. It is now your turn, as Chateaubriand puts it at the end of his *Mémoires d'outre-tombe*.³) The late Michael Sheringham was right, I think, when opening the 'Roland Barthes and Poetry' conference at Leeds University in March 2015, to say that a 'Barthes-athon' was underway.⁴ Celebratory events were staged in, among other places: Paris, Bordeaux, Orthez, London, Providence, Delhi, Tucumán, Cherbourg, Manchester, Lisbon, Tartu, Cardiff, La Paz, Londrina, Zagreb, New York, São

Paulo, Lancaster, Bucharest, Arles, Bayonne, Kaslik, Boston, Saint Petersburg, Budapest, Mexico City, Valencia (Venezuela) and Buenos Aires. (I remember a bright and busy day in late June on which Twitter was describing simultaneous Barthes events in Cardiff, Zagreb and São Paulo.) Elsewhere in the year, the fashion house Hermès unveiled a luxurious silk *carré* inspired by Barthes's bestselling *A Lover's Discourse*, the French postal service produced a stamp bearing the author's face, and the southern town of Bayonne gave a new name to one of its public spaces: 'Esplanade Roland Barthes'.[5]

Then there was the mighty wave of publications – 'the ultimate tyranny of paper', to take a phrase from Ian McEwan.[6] Among these were: a large and elegant volume of previously unpublished writings by Barthes entitled *Album: Inédits, correspondances et varia* (AL), along with a new edition of *La Préparation du roman* (PRN); Tiphaine Samoyault's monumental *Roland Barthes: Biographie*; Fanny Lorent's *Barthes et Robbe-Grillet: Un dialogue critique*; Magali Nachtergael's *Roland Barthes contemporain*; Chantal Thomas's *Pour Roland Barthes*; Philippe Sollers's *L'Amitié de Roland Barthes*; Antoine Compagnon's *L'Âge des lettres*; Dimitri Lorrain's *Roland Barthes, la mélancolie et la vie*; Guillaume Cassegrain's *Roland Barthes ou l'image advenue*; Jean-Marie Schaeffer's *Lettre à Roland Barthes*; a special issue of *Critique* entitled 'Une année avec Roland Barthes'; Jean Narboni's *La Nuit sera noire et blanche: Barthes,* La Chambre claire*, le cinéma*; and, somewhat controversially, a novel by Laurent Binet, *La Septième fonction du langage*, which reimagined the traffic accident that led to Barthes's death as an assassination attempt linked to a bizarre global conspiracy.[7] At the same time, anglophone readers were treated to: three volumes of hitherto untranslated material by Barthes; Andy Stafford's *Roland Barthes* in Reaktion's 'Critical Lives' series; a special number of *L'Esprit créatur* entitled 'What's So Great About Roland Barthes?'; and, if I may be permitted to refer to a modest contribution of my own, the first issue of the new journal *Barthes Studies*.[8]

A prominent Barthes scholar emailed me on 1 January 2016 to say that she was rather relieved to have a quieter year ahead. Things will be calmer, no doubt, but new publications and events have continued to appear while I have been putting the finishing touches to this book. In February 2016, for instance, the John Hansard Gallery in Southampton unveiled a selection of Barthes's drawings for the first time in the United Kingdom as part of its *Barthes/Burgin* exhibition.[9] A couple of weeks later, a special issue of the journal *Textual Practice* entitled 'Deliberations: The Journals of Roland Barthes' was published and two more volumes of previously untranslated material by Barthes will be released by Seagull Books in the spring.[10] In the summer, meanwhile, the Centre Culturel International de Cerisy will host a week-long conference on Barthes's work, thirty-nine years on from the famous event of 1977 attended by, among others, Alain Robbe-Grillet, Antoine Compagnon, Jacques-Alain Miller and François Wahl.[11] Barthes, as ever, lies ahead.

Afterlives, structure

When Roland Barthes died in March 1980, he had published a vast amount of work and was one of the key intellectuals of the twentieth century. But death was by no means the end. As Dora Zhang put it in 2012: 'Lately the posthumous corpus of Roland Barthes has been growing at a rate that rivals Tupac Shakur's. (Can a hologram Barthes be far behind?).'[12] This 'posthumous corpus' includes: the five-volume *Oeuvres complètes*, which featured previously unseen material (such as the sketches for the unrealized *Vita Nova*); the 'outing' *Incidents*; six full collections of teaching notes; two diaries; notes and drafts for *Roland Barthes by Roland Barthes*, *A Lover's Discourse* and *Camera Lucida*; and the letters, notes and short texts of the recently published *Album*. In short, in recent years we have witnessed Barthes enjoying a remarkable afterlife – or, to be more precise, given the range of the posthumous publications, a series of remarkable afterlives. When I glance now at early studies in the field – Annette Lavers's *Roland Barthes: Structuralism and After* or Philip Thody's *Roland Barthes: A Conservative Estimate*, for example – I am struck above all by how small, comparatively speaking, a body of work such critics faced.[13] Looking back in this way is like studying Roland Barthes through the wrong end of a telescope.

In the immediate aftermath of the centenary celebrations, while the scent of the fireworks still lingers, this book seizes the day to ask a series of questions about the afterlives of Roland Barthes. How do the many publications bearing Barthes's name which have appeared since his death affect our understanding of his work? What difference do these posthumous offerings make? What is the relationship between then and now? Why, in short, might we need to consider the afterlives of Roland Barthes? I want to ask these questions, and I want to ask them by moving freely across the posthumous body, because it seems to me that they have not been asked to date with sufficient sweep. There are several fine studies specifically of Barthes's lecture notes from the Collège de France, for example, but those notes represent just a part of the much larger posthumous corpus.[14] There are other afterlives, other stories to tell, and I want in what follows to pursue these closely and rigorously by reading the recent publications which carry Barthes's name with a careful eye for what they reveal and what they rewrite. My aim is not to offer a masterful encyclopedia which says everything about everything published since 1980. I wish, rather, merely to intervene in a timely manner with a new approach to, and new observations about, the work of Roland Barthes. While this book is in English, it engages often with recent texts by and about Barthes which have yet to be translated from French, as another of my aims in these pages is to expand the knowledge of readers who are curious but unable to read such works in their original language. (The afterlives do not wait for translators.)

Because Barthes's posthumous publications differ so notably from each other – in terms of form, purpose, mode of address and date of composition, for example – it would be naive to argue that a single thread binds them all together, and therefore that a single theme in the posthumous Barthes can unite the chapters of this book. Such an indifferent approach would also be at odds with Barthes's later writings, in fact, where the old certainties of structuralism, of underlying systems, came to be treated with great suspicion. 'Seeing a landscape in a bean', as the opening paragraph of *S/Z* so memorably proposed in 1970, is 'a task as exhausting . . . as it is ultimately undesirable, for the text thereby loses its difference' (*SZ*, 3). I have no interest in 'an in-different science' (*SZ*, 3), and this book is driven by a respect for the differences which distinguish one posthumous text bearing Barthes's name from another. This is why I have chosen as my title *The Afterlives of Roland Barthes*, not *The Afterlife of Roland Barthes*.

Each of the following chapters isolates part of the posthumous body in order to ask: what does this mean for our established understanding of Barthes's work? How, moreover, does it invite us to reread and rethink the work published by Barthes during his lifetime? Or, to put things another way, how is the established body reshaped repeatedly by the posthumous body, by the afterlives of Roland Barthes? It is this repeated re-evaluation, this consideration of a shifting legacy, which acts as the book's guiding thread. The internal coherence lies in my approach, in other words, and not in the texts under consideration. Readers who want a neat account of a neat body of work will need to look elsewhere for their landscape in a bean.

The book opens properly with chapters (Chapters 2 and 3) on the *Mourning Diary* – a journal kept by Barthes for nearly two years following the death of his mother in 1977 but not actually published until 2009. While writing this book I have often asked myself if devoting two chapters to this single posthumous text is wise or necessary, particularly when we are faced with so many other recent publications bearing Barthes's name. I have wondered, too, if this lengthy engagement with the writing of grief has been led unnecessarily by a recent loss within my own life, by an event whose echo endures and has, I can now see as I look back across the final typescript, left its mark upon my pages and made them at times a kind of cryptic mourning diary. I remain convinced, however, that these two distinct chapters are needed and that they differ from each other to such an extent that they could not have been one. I remain equally convinced that the *Mourning Diary* is, because of the range of questions that it raises and the constellation of connections that it cradles, one of the most richly significant of Barthes's posthumous publications. It is a sparse, scattered, slender text, but its entries resonate with reach.

Chapter 2 addresses the relationship between Barthes's *Mourning Diary* and the notes which were written by Stéphane Mallarmé for a work in response to the death of his young son in 1879, but not published until 1961 (as *Pour un tombeau d'Anatole*). There are obvious points of connection – each text is fragmentary, articulates grief, reaches towards a work in honour of the lost one and was published after the death of its author – but we might go further. While some critics have already addressed the primary place of Proust in Barthes's diary, no one has considered at length the echoes of Mallarmé's fragments, which we know that Barthes had read and had even performed. I first address the traces of Mallarmé by looking at how the *Mourning Diary* mirrors the manner in which *Pour un tombeau d'Anatole* links the experience of grief to the physical surroundings of grief, to living space. The chapter proceeds to argue that Mallarmé's failure to develop his notes into an actual work – a literary '*tombeau*' – foreshadows Barthes's failure to develop into a completed work his plans for *Vita Nova* (a 'grand project of writing' imagined in his final years). Like Anatole, Barthes's mother receives no gift of a *tombeau*. Both figures are remembered elsewhere, otherwise, in posthumously published fragments that reach for words and works which will not come. Barthes's journal of grief might at first glance seem to be a profoundly personal, private response to the loss of a loved one; it turns out, however, to be a fabric of quotations. Intertextuality – a concept so often associated (sometimes loosely, casually) with Barthes's name – finds a new form in the *Mourning Diary*.

Chapter 3 returns to the journal of grief, but with a different set of questions in mind. Here I read the diary closely to rethink the origin of *Camera Lucida*'s influential theory of the *punctum*. Where does life really begin for the concept of the photographic detail that 'rises from the scene, shoots out of it like an arrow, and pierces' perception (CL, 26)? Between 1980 and 2009, the answer tended to go without saying: in the photographic analyses of *Camera Lucida*. However, the publication in 2009 of the *Mourning Diary* complicated matters by casting new light on the development of the *punctum* and, more generally, on *Camera Lucida*. By examining the journal's series of unsettling filmic encounters, I argue that the *punctum* has cinematic roots which are repressed in *Camera Lucida* and which did not become visible until the publication of the *Mourning Diary*. The 'most quoted book in the photographic canon' is not quite what it once was; an aspect of the afterlives of Roland Barthes has unearthed new elements, new vistas.[15]

Chapter 4 considers the way in which Barthes's body of work is covered with what might be called 'ink blots', by which I mean points at which an obsession with the materials and materiality of writing leaves its mark. Tracing Barthes's 'almost obsessive relation to writing instruments' and interest in the material act of inscription, I relate the ink blots to the development of a non-arrogant, non-expressive, non-idealistic theory of language in *The Neutral* and related posthumous texts (such as *The Preparation of the Novel* and 'Variations sur l'écriture'). My argument here is that this understanding of language had long been present in the post-Saussurean work of Roland Barthes, but that its precise nature only became apparent in the light of the posthumous publications.

In Chapter 5 I examine the overwhelming sense of *ennui* articulated in *Travels in China* – a collection of diary-like notebooks filled by Barthes during a disappointing trip to Mao's China in 1974 and published only in 2009. If Barthes is, as Steven Ungar argued many years ago, a professor of desire, he is also a professor of boredom. This is nowhere more apparent than in *Travels in China*, but the chapter begins by tracing the neglected history of boredom in Barthes more generally. Boredom is there very early, in fact – a letter written by the sixteen-year-old Barthes in 1932, but not made public until 2015, worries about the condition – and I show how ennui goes on to surface repeatedly throughout the rest of his work, reaching a weary peak in the 1970s during the trip to China. What the posthumously published notebooks from the visit allow us to see – especially if we read them alongside the related 'Compte rendu du voyage en Chine', another text about the trip which was published long after Barthes's death – is the significance of Barthes's discussions of ennui and the relationship between boredom and the familiar Barthesian theme of *doxa*. Scholarly accounts of boredom tend to overlook Barthes or reduce him to a single line from *The Pleasure of the Text*, but I propose in this chapter that we might correct this oversight and begin at last to read Barthes as a remarkable, playful professor of boredom.

Chapter 6 brings the book to a close by looking and moving in a different direction. At the moment of Barthes's death, his published work contained references to many directors and their films, but nowhere was there a mention of Alfred Hitchcock, even though Hitchcock had been the most famous director of all for most of Barthes's writing life. This silence survived the publication of many of the posthumous texts and remained intact until 2009, when the *Mourning Diary* exposed a very brief discussion of Hitchcock's *Under Capricorn*. This is still the sole reference to Hitchcock in the published work of Roland Barthes.

Meanwhile, the publication in 2011 of the teaching notes from 1967 to 1969 which gave rise to Barthes's *S/Z* invited us to reopen the question of realism. While many of the discussions in *Sarrasine de Balzac* have counterparts in *S/Z*, the seminars contain intriguing propositions which did not survive to the completed book. Chapter 6, accordingly, revisits Barthes's approach to realism with the Hitchcock *hapax* in mind. Why, I ask, did Barthes discuss many other filmmakers but avoid Hitchcock? After considering Barthes's writings on cinema and examining their distrust of realism, I argue that Barthes's gaze, had it lingered, had it treated Hollywood like it treated Balzac, might have discovered that Hitchcock's work is not quite what it seems, not quite a straightforward case of realism. To make my case, I turn to *Under Capricorn* in the light of Sarrasine *de Balzac*. While Hitchcock's film, as a Hollywood production, is at first glance a classic case of a 'readable' text (to use the vocabulary of Sarrasine *de Balzac* and *S/Z*), there are subtle ways in which it undoes the conventions of the 'readable'. The choice for the critic need not be a simple one between Hollywood realism and the non-Hollywood avant-garde; there is, rather, what Sarrasine *de Balzac* calls 'a third way'.

Above all, this final chapter unfolds on two fronts: it reads Barthes and it puts Barthes to work in the analysis of a text. There are, in other words, two different types of text under consideration here: the work of Roland Barthes and a case of cinematic realism directed by Alfred Hitchcock. This is not to lose sight of the posthumous publications and the afterlives around which this book revolves. I merely want, once I have attended to Barthes's work, also to remember that Roland Barthes was primarily an analyst of cultural forms (literature, film, theatre, architecture, photography and so on). His work offers not abstract philosophical propositions but careful, innovative *readings* (of Balzac, of Eisenstein, of Brecht, of the Eiffel Tower, of Mapplethorpe, of advertising, of everyday life and so forth). If we forget this, if we look only for a body of theoretical work to master and summarize, we do Roland Barthes a profound disservice. We miss the point.

Style

My aim with *The Afterlives of Roland Barthes* was to write a book that is both scholarly and accessible. There are extensive academic endnotes, then, and close engagements with a range of Barthes's writings; there is detailed argument, intellectual rigour, textual evidence, and, particularly in the readings of the *Mourning Diary*, a sense of seriousness. But there is also a commitment throughout the book to writing which is alert, engaging, playful and always aware of itself *as writing*. This is not meant to be a dry, dusty monograph with an imagined audience of around fifteen other academics.

In this respect, I was heartened to read in *Times Higher Education* when this book was nearly finished an article which observed that 'academic writers who succeed in engaging with their readers often do so by writing texts that are lively, enthusiastic and frequently irreverent, encompassing the odd anecdote, colloquialism and venture into the personal'.¹⁶ This description of successful academic writing applies very well, in fact, to the work of Roland Barthes, who opened his first book in 1953 with the words: 'Hébert never began an issue of *Père Duchêne* without introducing the odd "fuck" and "bugger".'¹⁷ *Writing Degree Zero* soon settles down and develops a serious, documented, scholarly academic argument, of course, but that opening line, like so many other phrases in Barthes, serves a purpose: it catches the eye of the reader and encourages him or her to carry on reading. The signifier seduces. I have written in the firm belief that producing a stylistically sombre book about Roland Barthes would be to have learnt nothing from his work.

* * *

'We thought we knew everything about Roland Barthes,' wrote Sylvère Lotringer at the beginning of a review of *The Preparation of the Novel* in 2011, before going on to show how the posthumous publication of that particular set of Barthes's teaching notes invited us to recognize what we did *not* know about the author and his work.¹⁸ When reading texts imprinted with a name as familiar as that of Roland Barthes, it is easy – seductively so – to be lured towards comfortable mastery, towards a sense of knowledge which allows us to settle into ourselves and our ways. Writing this book and reading each 'new' posthumous publication when the ink has been still warm, I have found myself having repeatedly to revise my understanding of Barthes's *oeuvre*. It grows, it shifts. New texts call for new readings and new rereadings. 'We thought we knew everything about Roland Barthes', yes, but we need to think again and read again. This is the call of the afterlives of Roland Barthes.

Notes

1 For a photograph and discussion of Convert's installation, which was simply entitled *Commence alors la grande lumière du Sud-Ouest*, see Magali Nachtergael, *Roland Barthes contemporain* (Paris: Max Milo, 2015), 108–9. The phrase by Barthes can be found in 'The Light of the South West' (IN, 7). (I have modified Teresa Lavender Fagan's translation slightly here, as she has 'Then the great light of the South West appears'.)

2   Nachtergael, *Roland Barthes contemporain*, 108. Aquitaine became part of a new region with the temporary name of Aquitaine-Limousin-Poitou-Charentes in January 2016, with an official renaming to follow. (This occurred after the publication of Nachtergael's book, of course.) Barthes called the South West his "'homeland'" (the quotation marks are his) in the long interview with Jean Thibaudeau published as 'Answers' (SPC, 4). For a fictionalized account of Barthes's life in the southern village of Urt, where he had a second home, see Jean Esponde, *Roland Barthes, un été (Urt 1978)* (Bordeaux: Éditions Confluences, 2009).

3   Available in English in abridged form as François-René de Chateaubriand, *Memoirs of Chateaubriand*, trans. by Robert Baldick (Harmondsworth: Penguin, 1965), 405.

4   For a selection of papers from the Leeds conference, see *Barthes Studies* 2 (2016), guest-edited by Calum Gardner.

5   I call *A Lover's Discourse* 'bestselling' because it sold 70,000 copies in its year of publication alone. See Tiphaine Samoyault, *Roland Barthes: Biographie* (Paris: Seuil, 2015), 618.

6   Ian McEwan, *Sweet Tooth* (London: Vintage, 2013), 47.

7   Samoyault, *Roland Barthes: Biographie*; Fanny Lorent, *Barthes et Robbe-Grillet: Un dialogue critique* (Paris: Les Impressions Nouvelles, 2015); Nachtergael, *Roland Barthes contemporain*; Chantal Thomas, *Pour Roland Barthes* (Paris: Seuil, 2015); Philippe Sollers, *L'Amitié de Roland Barthes* (Paris: Seuil, 2015); Antoine Compagnon, *L'Âge des lettres* (Paris: Gallimard, 2015); Dimitri Lorrain, *Roland Barthes, la mélancolie et la vie* (Paris: Lemieux Éditeurs, 2015); Guillaume Cassegrain, *Roland Barthes ou l'image advenue* (Vanves: Hazan, 2015); Jean-Marie Schaeffer, *Lettre à Roland Barthes* (Vincennes: Éditions Thierry Marchaisse, 2015); *Critique* 822 (2015) ('Une année avec Roland Barthes'); Jean Narboni, *La Nuit sera noire et blanche: Barthes,* La Chambre claire, *le cinéma* (Paris: Les Prairies Ordinaires / Capricci, 2015); Laurent Binet, *La Septième fonction du langage* (Paris: Grasset, 2015).

8   Barthes, VFG, SM, and SPC; Andy Stafford, *Roland Barthes* (London: Reaktion, 2015); *L'Esprit créateur* 55, vol. 4 (2015); *Barthes Studies* 1 (2015).

9   For the catalogue of the exhibition, see Ryan Bishop and Sunil Manghani, ed., *Barthes/Burgin: Research Notes for an Exhibition* (Edinburgh: Edinburgh University Press, 2016).

10 Neil Badmington, ed., 'Deliberations: The Journals of Roland Barthes', special issue of *Textual Practice* 30, vol. 2 (2016).

11 For the proceedings of the 1977 conference, see Antoine Compagnon, ed., *Prétexte: Roland Barthes: Colloque de Cerisy* (Paris: Christian Bourgois, 2003).

12 Dora Zhang, 'The Sideways Gaze: Roland Barthes's Travels in China', *Los Angeles Review of Books*, 23 June 2012. Available online at https://lareviewofbooks.org/essay/the-sideways-gaze-roland-barthess-travels-in-china. Accessed on 24 February 2016. For a thoughtful discussion of the very concept of Barthes's 'posthumous life', see the introduction to Stafford, *Roland Barthes*.

13 Annette Lavers, *Roland Barthes: Structuralism and After* (London: Methuen, 1982); Philip Thody, *Roland Barthes: A Conservative Estimate* (London: Macmillan, 1977).

14 Lucy O'Meara, *Roland Barthes at the Collège de France* (Liverpool: Liverpool University Press, 2012); Guillaume Bellon, *Une Parole inquiète: Barthes et Foucault au Collège de France* (Grenoble: ELLUG, 2012); Sémir Badir and Dominique Ducard, ed., *Roland Barthes en Cours (1977–1980): Un style de vie* (Dijon: Éditions Universitaires de Dijon, 2009); and Nathalie Léger, ed., *Roland Barthes au Collège de France 1977–1980* (Paris: Éditions de l'IMEC, 2002); Kris Pint, *The Perverse Art of Reading: On the Phantasmatic Semiology in Roland Barthes' Cours au Collège de France*, trans. Christopher M. Gemerchak (Amsterdam and New York: Rodopi, 2010).

15 Geoffrey Batchen, 'Palinode: An Introduction to *Photography Degree Zero*', in *Photography Degree Zero: Reflections on Roland Barthes's Camera Lucida*, ed. Geoffrey Batchen (Cambridge, MA and London: MIT Press, 2009), 3.

16 Karen Harris, 'This Essay is a 1000-word Bore: Discuss', *Times Higher Education*, 3 September 2015. Available online at https://www.timeshighereducation.com/opinion/the-essay-is-a-one-thousand-word-bore-discuss. Accessed 24 February 2016.

17 WDZ, 1. I have modified the published English translation extensively here, as it offers the far more polite: 'Hébert, the revolutionary, never began a number of his news-sheet *Le Père Duchêne* without introducing a sprinkling of obscenities.' For the original French, see OC I, 171.

18 Sylvère Lotringer, 'Barthes After Barthes', *Frieze* 136 (January–February 2011). Available online at http://www.frieze.com/issue/article/barthes-after-barthes. Accessed 24 February 2016.

2

For Henriette's Tomb: Mourning with Mallarmé

'We grieve in character.'

Julian Barnes, *Levels of Life*.[1]

The loved one, born in July, dies in October after a period of illness. The writer, he who lives on, puts words to paper in grief, using not full sheets but hundreds of small slips. The fragments reach for a work which will honour the one who has been lost and yet who is nonetheless never identified by name. But no work comes, comes out of the mourning, and the notes remain unpublished until long after the writer himself has gone to the same tomb. Some years later there is uncertainty over plans to publish the sheets – are they too intimate, too raw to see the light of day? – but it is decided eventually to proceed.

It is not clear to whom my opening paragraph refers: Roland Barthes or Stéphane Mallarmé. In October 1879, Mallarmé's son, Anatole, died of ascites – an excessive accumulation of fluid in the abdominal cavity.[2] His eighth birthday had been on 16 July.[3] Mallarmé recorded his grief and gestured towards a commemorative work on over two hundred small slips of paper, all but one of which measured 13cm by 7.5cm.[4] As Raymond Bach has pointed out, Anatole is never named in the sketches, and Mallarmé ceased mentioning him altogether in letters not long after the boy's death.[5] The projected work was never completed, and the preparatory notes did not come to light until 1961, over sixty years after Mallarmé's own passing.[6] Jean-Pierre Richard, who prepared them for publication, reported feeling contradictory emotions on opening for the first time the soft red box containing the small, desperate sheets: exaltation, yes, but also discomfort and indiscretion.[7] Exaltation because of the writing and its significance; indiscretion in the face of intimate grief, of phrases which had not been polished for publication, and which Mallarmé had even asked to be burnt after his death.⁸

On 25 October 1977, Henriette Barthes, born on 18 July 1893, passed away. The following day, her son, Roland, began to keep a mourning diary. For nearly two years he amassed 330 small slips of paper – regular sheets quartered – upon which he inscribed his grief.⁹ While he often refers to 'maman' – or, to be more precise, 'mam.' – nowhere does the name 'Henriette' figure. When Barthes died and was buried alongside his mother in Urt in 1980, the mourning diary had not been published; it would not appear for another twenty-nine years. In early 2009, on the eve of unveiling, a public dispute broke out when François Wahl, who had been Barthes's friend and his editor at Seuil, denounced the decision to open the journal to the eyes of the world. Its publication, he told *Le Monde*, 'would have positively disgusted him' as a violation of privacy.¹⁰ In the pages of *Libération*, meanwhile, Éric Marty defended the publication by arguing that Barthes had gone so far as to give it a title and that the text was 'not an outpouring of feelings; there is a real writing project'.¹¹ One year later, Marty developed his point by arguing that Barthes had imagined a future in print for the diary, 'a precise place in the book to come, *Vita Nova*' – a project and a possibility to which I will turn later in the present chapter.¹²

While there are similarities, curious connections, between the *Mourning Diary* and *For Anatole's Tomb*, there are, of course, also significant differences, and these should not be forgotten. ('It is easy to see superficial resemblances between things. It takes a first-rate mind to perceive the differences underneath,' as Walter Berry told the young Edith Wharton.¹³) Anatole, for example, was a young child with no sense of his coming death, whereas Henriette was a woman in her eighties who cannot have been unaware of mortality.¹⁴ Meanwhile, Mallarmé's fragments bore no title when they were discovered: *Pour un tombeau d'Anatole* was chosen in 1961 by Jean-Pierre Richard, presumably to echo the famous '*tombeau*' poems published by Mallarmé during his lifetime.¹⁵ Barthes's observations, however, as I have already noted, were named by him in a pencilled addition to one of his sketches for the unwritten *Vita Nova*.¹⁶ And in spite of their *material* formal similarity – brief bursts of grief on hundreds of slips of paper – Mallarmé's notes and Barthes's journal differ from each other on another *formal* level: Mallarmé was not keeping a diary.¹⁷

I want nonetheless to devote this chapter to the threads of threnody that bind the *Mourning Diary* to *For Anatole's Tomb*. (Éric Marty notes the 'fascinating proximity' of these two texts, but does not have the space in his short book to develop the point.[18]) Barthes reminded his audience at the Collège de France on 1 December 1979 that there is 'no text without filiation' (PN, 137), and my interest here is textual filiation beyond difference. To be more precise, I want to touch upon the traces of Mallarmé's notes in Barthes's journal. As Adam Watt has argued persuasively, Proust is clearly the most obvious literary influence in the *Mourning Diary*, whose pages incant his name on many occasions.[19] Mallarmé, by way of contrast, is never mentioned in the journal. There is, however, plenty of evidence that Barthes knew *For Anatole's Tomb* when he came to write his fragments of grief: he refers to it in 1977 in *A Lover's Discourse* (LD, 99) and in his seminar notes of both 1973–4 (LA, 365) and 1974–6 (DA, 283), and he was even recorded reading extracts from Mallarmé's text for André Boucourechliev's composition *Thrène* in 1974.[20] What is more, Boucourechliev would have been in Barthes's thoughts while he was writing the *Mourning Diary* between October 1977 and September 1979, for an issue of *L'Avant-scène opéra* published in late 1978 carried his short commentary on the composer's *Oedipe*, which had been staged in Avignon some months earlier (OC V, 484).[21]

My point is not that Barthes had Mallarmé uppermost in his mind or open on his desk when he was writing about his mother; Proust, clearly, is the *conscious* literary point of reference in the diary. But Mallarmé's fragments, I want to suggest, nonetheless inflect and inform the *Mourning Diary*. They flicker between the lines; they sigh in the sighs.[22] To speak to these pale, passing ghosts is, building upon the work of Éric Marty, Antoine Compagnon and Adam Watt, to speak further to the ways which Barthes's grief is written upon writing, as textual as the passion of *A Lover's Discourse*.[23] 'We grieve in character,' Julian Barnes writes in his moving account of the death of his wife; Barthes does precisely this. What might at first glance seem to be a profoundly personal, private response to the loss of a loved one – Barthes's mother – turns out to be a tissue of quotations. There is at work an intertextuality which is not about quotation or open naming, but which involves mute gesture, hint and echo. The intimate is already inscribed.[24] Barthes grieves in character.

'The time of the empty room': The place of grief

I

The apartment at 11 rue Servandoni which Barthes shared with his mother is, it seems to me, one of the principal characters in the *Mourning Diary*. It appears explicitly by name, so to speak, on nine occasions in the journal, more than any one of Barthes's acquaintances who grace the pages. In other entries which do not actually house the term 'apartment', meanwhile, the contents and the qualities of the living space occupy Barthes's writing of grief. Mourning, in short, is inhabited.

The first reference to living space – and 'living' should be understood here in every sense of the term – occurs in the fifth entry, just two days after the death of Barthes's mother. The apartment is not named as such, but there is a mention of 'shifting furniture' as part of a 'frenzied construction of the future' in the wake of loss (MD, 6). (In *Empire of Signs* some years earlier, Barthes had remarked that the French term for 'furniture', 'meuble', was paradoxical because, while its etymology implies movement, the signifier 'generally designates a property anything but mobile' [ES, 108]. Furniture, moreover, he adds, is meant to endure, to survive.) Four days later, Barthes returns from the funeral in Urt and writes: 'Back alone for the first time in the apartment. How am I going to manage to live here all alone? And at the same time, it's clear that there's no other place' (MD, 24). These first two references to the dwelling on rue Servandoni establish one of the threads of threnody in the text: the flat which Barthes occupied with his mother still exists, as do its contents, but the living space is now also a non-living space, a space of absence, of the lost, of a demand to dwell differently. What was once shared – and an apartment, with its foundations in the Latin 'partire', involves sharing – is now suffered in solitude, and Barthes's poignant question, 'How am I going to manage to live here all alone?', acts as a counterpart to the title of the course given at the Collège de France when his mother was still alive: *How to Live Together*. Here, later, in mourning, there is no need for idiorrythmy. 'Comment vivre sans elle?' as Tiphaine Samoyault puts it: how to live without her?[25] Barthes's desperate wondering about living alone resonates throughout the diary as he attempts to come to terms not just with his mother's absence, but also with her absence from a space containing memoried objects that live on. Repeatedly the text records Barthes's arranging of the apartment, his cleaning and ordering of the living space in the deranging shadow of dying; Samoyault calls this his 'hypersensitivity to what surrounds him'.[26] At around 5pm on 4 November 1977, for example, his distress leads to the clearing-away of an object (*à ranger un objet*) and the subsequent sense that 'horribly enough, I *enjoyed* the tidied apartment [*l'appartement rangé*]' (MD, 35; translation modified). The next entry in the diary records how, roughly one hour later, 'the apartment is warm, clean, well-lit, pleasant' (MD, 36). This prosaic picture is haunted by the (house)work of mourning, however, for the journal continues, 'I make it that way, energetically, devotedly (enjoying it *bitterly*): henceforth and forever I am my own mother' (MD, 36).[27] When Barthes attends to the living space, in other words, when he arranges and cares for it, he is continuing the work of his now-absent mother – the work to which the diary alludes in its later description of how she organized the flat while she was alive (MD, 190).[28] Towards the end of the text, in fact, Barthes writes of the depression caused by the possibility of finding a '*substitute*' for his mother, but adds immediately that 'where it proceeds least badly is when I'm in a situation where there is a sort of *extension* of my life with her (the apartment)' (MD, 193). Death shall have no dominion in a domain where time stands still, where domestic duties allow the lost to rise again in the body of the one who lives on. As an entry from August 1978 explains:

> To share the *values* of the silent dailiness (to manage the cooking, the cleaning, the clothes, the choice and something like the past of objects), this was my (silent) way of conversing with her. – And this is, her no longer being here, how I can still do it.
>
> (MD, 192)

But however much the apartment brings 'comfort' (MD, 39), light and warmth – however much it enables a certain resurrection – it is also 'silent' in a more upsetting and irreversible way (MD, 37), and the diary elsewhere abandons illusion, magical thinking, to acknowledge the absence of the individual to whom the rites and objects refer. The entry dated 9 July 1978 reveals, for example, that the living space now contains a conventional *memento mori*, as if the earlier simulations of life, of an irretrievable past, have withered away:

> Leaving the apartment for Morocco, I remove the flower left on the spot where *maman* was ill – and once again the horrible fear (of her death) overwhelms me: cf. Winnicott: how true: *the fear of what has happened*. But stranger still: *and cannot recur.* Which is the very definition of the *definitive*.
>
> (MD, 158; translation modified)

With time, time itself has returned from suspension. (In 'Writing Mourning', Antoine Compagnon discusses with persuasive force the desire to stop time and the denial of temporality which are articulated repeatedly in the diary.) If Barthes once became his mother and thus in a sense negated her death, here the flower admits to her disappearance; Winnicott's fear, after all, is the fear of *what has happened*, not what will happen. This solitary flower becomes, a little later, a vigilant bouquet marking a kind of tomb or shrine within the apartment:

> The locality of the room where she was ill, where she died, and where I now live, the wall against which the head of her bed rested where I have placed an icon – not out of faith – and still put flowers on a table next to it. I have reached the point of no longer wanting to travel in order to be here, so that the flowers here will never be wilted.
>
> (MD, 191)

In February 1979, in the last of the diary's entries to name the apartment, Barthes concludes:

> What separates me from *maman* (from the mourning that was my identification with her) is the density (enlarging, gradually accumulating) of the time when, since her death, I have been able to live without her, inhabit the apartment, work, go out, etc.
>
> (MD, 228)

This sense of separation, this long and slow acceptance of dwelling alone, this work of mourning, is bound to the apartment, to the living space where death is admitted.

II

In his sustained struggle with the surroundings of grief, Barthes recalls Mallarmé. As Patrick McGuinness observes, in the afterword to his wonderful English translation of *Anatole*, '[o]ne of Mallarmé's many struggles in his projected poem is with the world of things, of matter – the boy's clothes, his room, his bed, toys left in mid-play, the flat.'[29] The family apartment, McGuinness continues, becomes 'a different kind of cemetery, one in which the child is not in fact "buried" but constantly referred to' (82). As fragment 186 of *Anatole* states simply: 'true mourning [*vrai deuil*] in the apartment – furniture – not cemetery' (69; translation modified). These words, it seems to me, might have been written by Barthes, who does actually use the term 'true mourning [*vrai deuil*]' at one point in the diary (MD, 50; JD, 60).

Although the living space is the site of 'true mourning', there is nonetheless an invocation of the funeral ceremony at the cemetery in Mallarmé's notes. Fragment 31, for example, describes the 'moment when we must break with the living memory, to bury him – put him in the coffin, hide him – with the brutalities of the laying in the coffin rough contact, etc.' (15). Fragments 43 and 44, meanwhile, read:

> ceremony – coffin – etc.
> there we saw (the father) the whole material side – which lets us tell ourselves at need – ah! well yes! it is all there – no fear for me thinking of something else (the reformation of his spirit, which is eternal – can wait (granted but eternity through my life).
>
> (17)

These lines are preceded, in fragment 41, by a desperate declaration, possibly voiced at the open grave itself:

> You can, with your little hands, drag me into your tomb – you have the right – I myself who am joined with you, I let myself go.
>
> (17; translation modified)

Scenes of this kind appear nowhere in Barthes's diary, which is strangely silent about his mother's burial. The entry of 28 October 1977 describes the conveyance of her corpse from Paris to Urt, where she would be interred, but nothing in the entries for that day, for 29 October, or for 30 October refers to the funeral itself; by 31 October, Barthes is back in Paris. In short, Mallarmé and Barthes differ considerably from each other when it comes to what the former calls 'the whole material side' of the funereal: Mallarmé takes readers to the grave in terrible detail, but Barthes steps back, holds back, even though late October 1977 is a period during which he is writing regularly in his journal.[30]

I am nonetheless struck by how a sequence of four fragments found near the end of Mallarmé's text foreshadows Barthes in its rapid turning away from the grave to the domestic space of mourning:

> perhaps imply the cemetery – funeral etc. – in short what the world saw – (burial mass? to bring it all back to intimacy – the room – empty – absence – open – the moment when his absence ends, so he can be in us –
> – that would be this 3rd part – after he has been taken away, left the room –
> – then see how II – 'the sickness and the little ghost' – would be framed –
> – III returning over, towards end of II – death – thus furniture immortality and background of nature
> I – he will no longer play – mingling with the countryside he rests in?
>
> (61)

What occurs in public ('what the world saw') lacks the lacerating intensity of what takes place at home, behind closed doors, surrounded again by familiar furniture. True mourning in the apartment, indeed, for it is *there* that the absence of Anatole – like the absence of Henriette – is at its most apparent, its most intimate. Anatole should be at home – it is *his home* and he is too young to live alone – but he is not, and when his clothes are encountered they underscore his death: 'to find *absence only* – in presence of little clothes – etc. – mother' (71). What remains, what remains present, reminds the living of what is now absent. This could explain why an earlier passage, referring to a time when Anatole was still alive, yet ill, invokes the decision to hide from view material objects associated with the child:

> sick considered dead
> already we love this or that object 'which reminds us of him'
> put away.
>
> (55)

The final verb enlisted by Mallarmé at this point is precisely the one that Barthes will use on four occasions in his diary when discussing daily life in the apartment, in the space of mourning, without his mother: *ranger* (to put away or to tidy up).[31]

Chez Barthes, chez Mallarmé, death deranges, stills time and speaks from the surroundings of grief – where, paradoxically, it mimics life, even to the point of cruel immortality. And in each case there is an attempt to move from passivity before death to activity, to order living space, the space of the living, beneath the weight of the dead.

'The ideal tomb': The work of mourning

I

Threaded through Mallarmé's notes as they struggle with the surroundings of grief are many explicit references to the shape of the projected work of mourning. Little is lucid, but the scattering of Roman numerals sketches a work in three main parts, 'perhaps in verse' (11), and perhaps entitled 'poetry of sickness' (11) or 'true return into the ideal' (15).[32] Anatole is described at one point, in a passage actually spoken by Barthes in Boucourechliev's *Thrène*, as the 'child of the w[or]k.' (*l'enfant de l'oe*):

> with gift of words I could have made you king you, made you the child of the wk. instead of the son in us[33]

Death has shown its power in 'abolishing this little child "self"' (3), but the defiant father, apparently addressing death directly ('no death – you will not deceive him'), declares that he will 'take him back from you for the ideal tomb' (49).[34] Refusing to 'believe in all that has happened', Mallarmé vows to 'rebegin him in spirit beyond – the burial etc.' (55). Blaming himself for a fatal genetic inheritance, 'cursing his blood', the 'father will redeem everything later by prolonging his being, reabsorbing etc.' (43).

This redemption or 'rebeginning' calls for writing, calls to be written, calls for a work, because Anatole can only live on in his parents 'so long as we ourselves live' (19). When death returns for them, the son 'in us' will be taken too. But inscription, a work, will deny death that further victory, for the stubborn signifier outlasts even the one who writes, the one who writes of loss, the one whose own dying must come in time. And in that projected writing, as Éric Benoit has discussed so poignantly, the poet will be able to imagine the life, the adult life, that Anatole was denied in reality.[35] The child of the work enjoys privileges taken from the child of the world.

There are complications, however – complications articulated in the notes themselves. The work is not innocent, pure. Analysing the way in which Mallarmé moves, in the same fragment, from stating 'I cannot believe in all that has happened' to vowing to 'rebegin him in spirit beyond – the burial etc.', Patrick McGuinness writes:

> There are two contradictory impulses struggling here: on the one hand, the father refusing to believe, in the sense of believing *in*, what has happened (that Anatole has died); on the other, an attempt to *rebegin* Anatole beyond ('au delà'), for which he as poet knows he *must* believe in what has happened, in order to undertake the child's continuation. This too is part of a drama, often figured as a struggle *with* the child, that dominates the attempted poem. The boy fights against death, wants to live an earthly life, while the poet, designing the tomb, is complicit with death by trying to ensure him an afterlife.[36]

This 'conflict', McGuinness continues (91), is described explicitly in one of Mallarmé's sketches for the second part of the projected work:

> struggle of the two father and son the one to preserve son in thought – ideal
>   – the other to live, rising up etc. –
> – interruptions lack) –
> so
> and mother tend him well – mother's cares interrupting thought – and child
>   between father who thinks him dead, and mother life.
> (75)

Writing, which ought to labour on the side of life, eternal life beyond speech and parental memory, has dealings with death. If the signifier is to preserve Anatole, it first agrees, in the very composing of a *tombeau*, that the body of the child is decomposing in the ground, 'mingling with the countryside he rests in' (61). It is little wonder, then, that Mallarmé – he 'who built the tomb' (71) – appears at one point to cast and castigate himself as one of 'death's accomplices' (67).

Had the projected work been completed, it would thus have been duplicitous. On the one hand, it would have prolonged Anatole's being, to invoke *feuillet* 119, and undone death with resurrection. But on the other hand, *as a tomb*, even an 'ideal tomb', it would have been raised upon an acceptance of death. In the end, however, Mallarmé's *tombeau* for Anatole was never completed; all that exists are the troubled fragments which imagine and interrogate the work which never comes.[37]

II

As I will discuss at length in Chapter 3 of this book, there is a sense in which the *Mourning Diary* is a form of faltering preparation for *Camera Lucida*, the book about photography and loss which was published shortly before Barthes's own death. Scattered like ashes through Barthes's journal, however, are gestures towards another work – a work which, unlike *Camera Lucida*, yet like Mallarmé's *tombeau* for Anatole, was never completed: *Vita Nova*. Although Barthes had alluded to this project towards the end of his life, it was not until 1995 that written plans emerged in the third volume of the posthumous *Oeuvres complètes*.[38] These outlines are sparse and enigmatic: just eight handwritten sheets produced between August and December 1979 and filed away in a red cardboard folder marked with the words 'VITA NOVA'. The publication of *Album* in mid-2015 brought to light a number of further *fiches* – usually less detailed, more *romanesque* – on which Barthes made additional notes towards the project.[39]

I do not wish to speculate wildly here about why Barthes failed to develop these plans into a work.[40] What interests me, rather, is a simple fact: while no completed text by Barthes entitled *Vita Nova* exists, there are allusions to it in the *Mourning Diary*, and vice versa. These intertextual twinklings will be my concern in what follows, as will an attention to what links Barthes to Mallarmé. If the diary of death is, as Marie Gil has proposed, at once a 'journal of the new life', perhaps it is also a record of failure touched by traces of Anatole.[41]

The first of the eight *Vita Nova* sketches is dated 21 August 1979 – the day on which, as Nathalie Léger has reminded us, *Camera Lucida* was finally submitted to the publisher.[42] There were, however, earlier gestures towards the 'new life'. In a lecture given at the Collège de France on 19 October 1978 under the title 'Longtemps, je me suis couché de bonne heure. . .', for instance, Barthes began by discussing Proust before turning to Dante in a meditation on age, mortality, mourning and writing:

> And then a time also comes . . . when what you have done, worked, written, appears doomed to repetition: What! Until my death, to be writing articles, giving courses, lectures, on 'subjects' which alone will vary, and so little! . . . [T]here occurs all of a sudden this obvious situation: on the one hand, I no longer have time to try several lives: I must choose my last life, my new life, '*Vita Nova*' . . .; and on the other hand, I must emerge from that shadowy state (medieval theory called it *acedie*) to which the attrition of repeated tasks and mourning dispose me. Now, for the subject who writes, who has

chosen to write, there can be no 'new life', it seems to me, except in the discovery of a new practice of writing.

(RL, 285–6)

A little under two months later, Barthes repeated some of the formulations and phrases of 'Longtemps ...' in the opening lecture of his course entitled *The Preparation of the Novel*, again at the Collège de France.⁴³ But then, having described the desire for a *Vita Nova*, he added what he called 'a little personal anecdote':

> When was this decision 'to change' taken? – April 15, 1978. Casablanca. The sluggishness of the afternoon. The sky clouds over, a slight chill in the air. A group of us go in two cars to the Waterfall (a pretty little valley on the way to Rabat). *The same, uninterrupted* sadness, a kind of listlessness that (since a recent bereavement) bears upon everything I do, everything I think (lack of investment). Return, an empty apartment; a difficult time: the afternoon (I'll speak of it again). Alone, sad → Marinade; I reflect with enough intensity. The beginnings of an idea: something like a 'literary' conversion – it's those two very old words that occur to me: to enter into literature, into writing; *to write*, as if I'd never written before: to do only that → First, all of a sudden, the idea of resigning from the Collège in order to settle into a life of writing (for the lecture course often comes into conflict with writing). Then, the idea of investing the Course and Work in the same (literary) enterprise, of putting a stop to the division of the subject, in favor of a single Project, the Grand Project: joyous image: what if I were to assign myself a single task, such that I'd no longer have to keep up with all the work to be done (lectures, demands, commissions, constraints), and that each moment of my life would henceforth be integrated into the Grand Project? → That April 15: basically a kind of *Satori*, a kind of bedazzlement, analogous to (no matter if the analogy is naive) the sudden realization that Proust's narrator experiences at the end of *Time Regained* (although *his* book is *already written!*).
>
> (PN, 7–8)⁴⁴

This long passage again connects the writing of the new life to grief: the 'recent bereavement' mentioned here on 2 December 1978 recalls the 'cruel bereavement' and mourning named in 'Longtemps ...' some months earlier (RL, 286), and in the reference to returning from a trip to an 'empty apartment' in Casablanca there is an echo of the passage in the *Mourning Diary* which sees Barthes, following the funeral in Urt, '[b]ack alone for the first time in the apartment' (MD, 24).

It is not surprising, then, that when Barthes came to write the plans for *Vita Nova* the following year, he invoked repeatedly the 'decision of April 15, 1978' and the period of mourning following the death of his mother.[45] More importantly, as far as the present chapter is concerned, the plans for *Vita Nova* refer specifically to the *Mourning Diary*.[46] In the final of the eight outlines which appeared in 1995, alongside the bracketed words '[Mam. as guide]', which are written in ink, Barthes adds, in pencil, 'Mourning Diary'.[47] The plan is dated 12 December 1979, by which time he had stopped writing the text which is now known as the *Mourning Diary* and had also, in August and September 1979, produced another short journal which appeared posthumously as 'Evenings in Paris' (IN, 131–72).[48] Meanwhile, Éric Marty's introduction to the *fiches* relating to *Vita Nova* published for the first time in *Album* explains that a slip from October 1977 (but not actually reproduced in *Album*) sees Barthes considering a suitable point at which to 'insert' the *Mourning Diary* (AL, 372).

If the *Mourning Diary* and 'Evenings in Paris' both have what Marty calls 'a precise place in the book to come, *Vita Nova*', then *Vita Nova* also has a precise place in the *Mourning Diary*.[49] The journal's first explicit reference to the desire for a new life, in fact, changes significantly the general understanding of Barthes's unrealized 'Grand Project'. Until the publication of the diary in 2009, the longing for a *vita nova* in the wake of loss appeared to begin with the enigmatic 'decision' of 15 April 1978, then actually acquire the name '*Vita Nova*' in October 1978 (with the delivery of 'Longtemps . . .'), before taking shape in more detail with the beginning of the course on the preparation of the novel two months later.[50] But the diary reveals that the roots of the 'new life' go back considerably further than 15 April 1978, for on 30 November 1977 – a little over a month after the death of Henriette Barthes, and nearly a whole year before the delivery of 'Longtemps . . .' at the Collège de France – Barthes writes in his journal:

> *Vita nova* as a radical gesture: (discontinuous – necessity of discontinuing what previously continued on its own momentum).
>
> (MD, 74)

This brief entry anticipates the way in which 'Longtemps . . .' and *The Preparation of the Novel* articulate what the former calls a 'desire for a mutation' when daily life 'appears doomed to repetition' (RL, 284, 285). It also, crucially, situates the longing for the *vita nova* much closer to the death of Barthes's mother – the death which is invoked in 'Longtemps ...' and *The Preparation of the Novel* in 1978. Just a few weeks into his mourning, and months before the mystical 'decision' of 15 April 1978, Barthes is imagining the new life and has already borrowed a title from Dante, whose own *Vita Nuova* was in part a work of mourning.[51]

This is the sole explicit reference to the *Vita Nova* in the *Mourning Diary*. However, although the phrase appears nowhere else in the text, there are several notable allusions to it, and it is in these allusions, I think, that the Mallarméan quality of the unfinished work becomes apparent.[52]

Near the end of the diary, on 22 July 1979, Barthes, having written nothing in his journal for over a month, offers a profoundly pessimistic assessment of his situation:

> All the 'rescues' of the Project fail. I find myself with nothing to do, without any work (*oeuvre*) ahead of me – except for the repeated tasks of routine. Any form of the Project: limp, nonresistant, weak coefficient of energy. 'What's the use?'
>
> (MD, 237; translation modified)

Barthes does not specify which 'Project' has failed, but he cannot mean *Camera Lucida* because the end of that text locates its own composition between 15 April and 3 June 1979. An editorial note in the *Mourning Diary* concludes instead that Barthes is alluding to *Vita Nova*, which makes perfect sense, as the diary has already identified this project by name.[53]

It seems to me that the early pages of the *Mourning Diary* offer a hint of an explanation of the failure to bring the 'grand project of writing' into being. This hint, I want to argue, is at once a hint of Mallarmé's *Anatole*. On 31 October 1977, less than a week into his period of mourning, Barthes writes: 'I don't want to talk about it, for fear of making literature out of it – or without being sure of not doing so – although as a matter of fact literature originates within these truths' (MD, 23). Twenty entries in the diary precede this one, which raises for the first time in the text a problem which has echoes of the anxiety articulated in Mallarmé's notes for Anatole's *tombeau*: to write loss is to honour love and what has been lost, but 'making literature out of it' involves accepting death, accepting the time of the empty room, and accepting this, moreover, in language which, as language, honours no singularity.⁵⁴ (Is this the Mallarméan fear of being one of 'death's accomplices'?) If Barthes turns loss into literature with what Antoine Compagnon calls 'the reductive and generalising force' of language, then the particularity of his mother is at risk of transformation into something generic – something recognizable, precisely, as 'literature'.⁵⁵ If the obsession with a '*vita nova*' is, as Diana Knight has proposed, underpinned by a 'conversion narrative', then it is at once marked by an anxiety about converting the singular into the general.⁵⁶ As Barthes notes on 29 November 1977, in fact, in response to a comment made by 'AC' (Antoine Compagnon himself⁵⁷), 'I can't endure seeing my suffering being *reduced* – being *generalized* – (à la Kierkegaard): it's as if it were being stolen from me' (MD, 71).⁵⁸ Or, as he would put it in a lecture at the Collège de France some months later, 'one never thinks anything about death but banal thoughts' (N, 83).⁵⁹

In spite of this tension, the diary records a subsequent commitment of sorts to what it calls a 'monument' for Henriette.⁶⁰ On 5 June 1978, Barthes produces an entry which anticipates the concerns of 'Longtemps ...' and the beginning of *The Preparation of the Novel*:

> For me, at this point in my life (when *maman* is dead) I was *recognized* (by books). But strangely – perhaps falsely? – I have the obscure feeling, now she's no longer here, that I must gain recognition all over again. This cannot be by writing any book: the idea of *continuing* as in the past to proceed from book to book, course to course, immediately struck me as mortiferous (this I saw *to my dying day*).
> (Whence my present efforts of resignation).
> Before resuming *sagely and stoically* the course (quite unforeseen moreover) of the work, it is necessary for me (I feel this strongly) to write this book around *maman*.
>
> (MD, 133)

The reference here to 'this book' is, as I will discuss in Chapter 3, probably to *Camera Lucida*, which appears as a work in troubled development – 'the book about Photography' – earlier in the journal (MD, 105). But the entry dated 5 June 1978 proceeds to discuss in more general terms the question of a work to honour and bring recognition for the one who has been lost:

> In a sense, therefore, it is as if I had *to make* maman *recognized*. This is the theme of the 'monument'; but:

> For me, the Monument is not the *durable*, the *eternal* (my doctrine is too profoundly *Everything passes*: tombs die too), it is an act, an action, *an activity* that *brings* recognition.[61]

A certain distance arises between Barthes and Mallarmé at this point – a distance that is signalled at the level of the signifier when the journal refers, in the original French, to the dying of '*tombes*', not the more monumental and literary '*tombeaux*' (JD, 145).[62] Recognition is what matters here – incarnations of the term in question appear on five occasions in this single day's entry – and this recognition is perhaps passing ('tombs die too').[63]

The troubled 'monument' surfaces again in the journal in August 1978, when Barthes asks why he would want 'the slightest posterity' when those most dear to him 'will leave none':

> What would it matter for me to outlive myself in History's cold and mendacious unknown, since the memory of *maman* will not outlive me and those who have known her and who will one day die in their turn? I would not want a monument for myself alone.
>
> (MD, 194)

The position has changed a little since June and is now more Mallarméan.[64] There is no sense in this entry that a monument is temporary, that 'tombs die too', and the reference more specifically to the dying of personal memory recalls Mallarmé's demand for writing, for a literary *tombeau*, in the 'so long as we ourselves live' of *feuillet* 48.

An entry dated 29 March 1979 covers similar ground when Barthes declares that he has 'no desire to be read later on (except financially, for M.)', that he accepts 'vanishing utterly', and that he does not wish 'for a "monument"' (MD, 234). He must mean a monument *to himself* at this point, for he adds immediately, again recalling Mallarmé's anxiety about personal memory: 'but I cannot endure that this should be the case for *maman* (perhaps because she has not written and her memory depends entirely on me)' (MD, 234).

After this entry, this meditation on the monument, the diary breaks off completely until 1 May 1979 while Barthes writes *Camera Lucida* – the text which has been called the '*Photo-Maman* book' earlier in the journal (MD, 136), just four days after the first discussion of monuments and tombs.[65] Does this achievement bring peace? Has a fitting, faithful monument at last been raised? Clearly not, for just a few entries later comes the weary sigh that 'All the "rescues" of the Project have failed', to which Barthes adds a remark about 'the solemn impact of mourning on any possibility of creating a work of any kind' (MD, 237). 'I find myself with nothing to do,' he writes, 'without any work ahead of me.' This stalling, this inability to create the work, is, he concludes, 'mourning's central, decisive trial' (MD, 237).

* * *

The trial, of course, comes to no happy conclusion. Writing *Camera Lucida*, 'the *Photo-Maman* book', does not lay matters to rest: there is still a desire for the 'new life' with its 'grand project of writing'. But the plans for *Vita Nova* will never be anything more than brief, bare sketches; there is, in the language of Barthes's final lecture course on the preparation of the novel, no passage from projection to accomplishment (PN, 127). Like Anatole, Henriette receives no gift of a *tombeau* from the writer, from he who lives on. Each is recognized and remembered elsewhere, otherwise, in posthumously published fragments that reach for words and works which will not come. In that desperate reaching lies a textual connection – a connection which is captured perfectly when, in Boucourechliev's *Thrène*, Barthes voices the following as his final contribution to the piece: '*cette oeuvre – trop vaste pour moi ... non*' ('this work – too great for me ... no').[66] Who is speaking there, we might ask, remembering *S/Z* and the opening of 'The Death of the Author' (SZ, 41–2; RL, 49)? Clearly Mallarmé, in grief, reaching, but also Barthes. '*La vie comme texte*', writes Barthes in 1974 – life as text.[67] Yes, indeed. But also death and mourning as unwritten text with shades of Mallarmé.

For H.

Notes

1 Julian Barnes, *Levels of Life* (London: Jonathan Cape, 2013), 70.
2 As Éric Benoit has pointed out in his *Néant sonore: Mallarmé ou la traversée des paradoxes* (Geneva: Droz, 2007), 154 n. 6, there is some uncertainty over the precise date of Anatole's death, with Jean-Pierre Richard giving 6 October and other critics offering 8 October.
3 Biographical information about Anatole Mallarmé is drawn from Jean-Pierre Richard's editorial material at the beginning of Stéphane Mallarmé, *Pour un*

tombeau d'Anatole (Paris: Seuil, 1961). The classic biography in the field, Henri Mondor's huge *Vie de Mallarmé* (Paris: Gallimard, 1941), contains less information about Anatole than Richard's lengthy introduction, perhaps because the biography was published two decades before *Pour un tombeau d'Anatole* came to light.

4 Information about the dimensions of Mallarmé's slips is taken from Richard, *Pour un tombeau d'Anatole*, 131. Richard's edition of *Anatole* – the first – gives the total number of fragments as 202. The more recent two-volume Pléiade edition of Mallarmé's *Oeuvres complètes* edited by Bertrand Marchal (Paris: Gallimard, 1998/2003) identifies a total of 210 slips, but then adds (vol. 1, 1366) that only 205 of these relate to the plans for the work inspired by Anatole. Marchal also retranscribes and reorders some of the *feuillets*. Throughout the present chapter, bracketed numbers in references are to the pages, not the *feuillets*, of *For Anatole's Tomb*, trans. Patrick McGuinness (Manchester: Carcanet, 2003). When I do invoke the numbering of the *feuillets*, I use the notation given in McGuinness's translation, which in turn takes these details from Marchal.

5 Raymond Bach, 'The "Tombeau idéal": Mallarmé's *Tombeau d'Anatole*', *Dalhousie French Studies* 20 (1991): 4.

6 Jean-Pierre Richard notes (*Pour un tombeau d'Anatole*, 34) that Mallarmé and his wife were later buried in the same tomb as Anatole.

7 Richard, *Pour un tombeau d'Anatole*, 9–10.

8 Richard explains his decision to publish the fragments in the introduction to his edition of *Pour un tombeau d'Anatole* (11). Henri Mondor describes Mallarmé's request that his notes be burnt in his *Vie de Mallarmé*, 801.

9 The slips are not numbered in the published text. I take the figure of 330 from Éric Marty, *Roland Barthes, la littérature et le droit à la mort* (Paris: Seuil, 2010), 15.

10 François Wahl, quoted in Jean Birnbaum, 'La publication d'inédits de Barthes embrase le cercle de ses disciples', *Le Monde* 21 January 2009. Available online at http://www.lemonde.fr/culture/article/2009/01/21/la-publication-d-inedits-de-barthes-embrase-le-cercle-de-ses-disciples_1144698_3246.html. Accessed 19 February 2016.

11 Éric Marty, quoted in Éric Aeschimann, 'Désaccords autour des notes posthumes de Roland Barthes', *Libération* 21 January 2009. Available online at http://www.liberation.fr/culture/2009/01/21/desaccords-autour-des-notes-posthumes-de-roland-barthes_304293. Accessed 19 February 2016. Aeschimann's article gives a good overview of the controversy surrounding the publication of the text. For an English-language counterpart, published on the same day as the pieces in *Le Monde* and *Libération*, see Henry Samuel, 'Roland Barthes' brother publishes philosopher's personal notes, "violating his intimacy"', *Daily Telegraph* 21 January 2009. Available online at http://www.telegraph.co.uk/news/worldnews/europe/

france/4309295/Roland-Barthes-brother-publishes-philosophers-personal-notes-violating-his-intimacy.html. Accessed 19 February 2016.
12 Marty, *Roland Barthes, la littérature et le droit à la mort*, 18.
13 Wharton relates this anecdote in her autobiographical *A Backward Glance* (London: Century, 1987), 117.
14 Mallarmé refers to Anatole's lack of awareness of death on numerous occasions in his notes. For illuminating discussions of this, see Richard, *Pour un tombeau d'Anatole*, 34; Bach, 'The "Tombeau idéal": 10–11; and Jean-Pierre Richard, *L'Univers imaginaire de Mallarmé* (Paris: Seuil, 1961), 239. Although the *Mourning Diary* is the record of a son grieving for his mother, there is a moment in the diary where, as in *Camera Lucida* (CL, 72), Barthes casts Henriette as his child (MD, 56). As Tiphaine Samoyault concludes, in *Roland Barthes: Biographie* (Paris: Seuil, 2015), 'when Barthes evokes the death of this mother, he does so in terms and sorrow which are those of parents who have lost their child' (63).
15 The more recent Pléiade edition of Mallarmé's *Oeuvres complètes* uses the slightly different title of *Notes pour un tombeau d'Anatole*. For examples of Mallarmé's '*tombeau*' poems, see 'The Tomb of Edgar Poe', 'The Tomb of Charles Baudelaire' and 'Tomb', in *Collected Poems*, trans. Henry Weinfield (Berkeley and Los Angeles: University of California Press, 1994), 71, 72 and 73, respectively.
16 See the reproduction and transcription of the plans for *Vita Nova* included in PN, 389–406. The title '*Journal de Deuil*' appears in the final sketch, dated 12 December 1979 (by which time Barthes had stopped writing the diary itself).
17 Towards the end of 'Deliberation', in fact, Barthes even reminds his readers that Mallarmé never kept a diary (RL, 371). For Éric Marty, however, the fact that Barthes's reflection were written on separat(abl)e slips of paper, coupled with their modern acceptance of 'not saying everything', means that there is a sense in which Barthes was not actually keeping a diary in the conventional sense of the term (Marty, *Roland Barthes, la littérature et le droit à la mort*, 17; see also 12 for the discussion of 'not saying everything' and the paradoxical status of Barthes's diary).
18 Marty, *Roland Barthes, la littérature et le droit à la mort*, 28.
19 Adam Watt, 'Reading Proust in Barthes's *Journal de deuil*', *Nottingham French Studies* 53, no. 1 (2014): 102–12. See also Marty, *Roland Barthes, la littérature et le droit à la mort*, 45, and Antoine Compagnon, 'Writing Mourning', trans. Sam Ferguson *Textual Practice* 30, no. 2 (2016): 209–19. For a more general discussion of the place of Proust in Barthes's mourning, particularly the mourning of *Camera Lucida*, see Chapter 7 of Katja Haustein, *Regarding Lost Time: Photography, Identity, and Affect in Proust, Benjamin, and Barthes* (London: Legenda, 2012). Proust, notably, is the first writer to be identified by name in the diary, on 4 November 1977 (MD, 33); further references can be found on 156, 157, 160,

170–1, 177, 183, 184, 185, 187 and 188. However, the unattributed quotation in a very early entry dated October 29 1977 ('the dear inflection' / '*la chère inflexion*'; MD, 14 / JD, 24) could be a misquotation from Verlaine's 'Mon rêve familier', which concludes: 'L'inflexion des voix chères qui se sont tues.' Paul Verlaine, *Choix de poésies* (Paris: Larousse, 1973), 25.

20 Barthes gets the title of Mallarmé's text wrong in *A Lover's Discourse*, however (LD, 99), and Richard Howard's translation on the same page of 'fils-enfant' (OC V, 131) as 'baby son' is somewhat misleading, given the age of Anatole at the time of his death. Barthes studied piano with Boucourechliev in the 1970s, not long before the death of his mother; see Marie Gil, *Roland Barthes: Au lieu de la vie* (Paris: Flammarion, 2012), 97; Samoyault, *Roland Barthes: Biographie*, 535; and François Noudelmann, *The Philosopher's Touch: Sartre, Nietzsche, and Barthes at the Piano*, trans. Brian J. Reilly (New York: Columbia University Press, 2012), 113. Éric Marty (*Roland Barthes, la littérature et le droit à la mort*, 29) mentions *A Lover's Discourse* and *Thrène*, but not the other examples given here. Barthes's 'Journal-Moisson' from the 'Atelier sur la Voix', which is reproduced in *Le Lexique de l'auteur*, refers to the reading of the Mallarmé passages for *Thrène* in the entry dated 30 January 1974 (LA, 365); Éric Marty's editorial notes in Barthes's *Album* state that the actual recording took place on 19 January (AL, 19). I have been unable to determine precisely when Barthes became aware of Mallarmé's text, but, if I had to speculate, I would suggest that it would have been earlier than the 1970s, for Barthes's friendship with Jean-Pierre Richard (the original editor of *Anatole*) went back as far as the mid-1950s. See Samoyault, *Roland Barthes: Biographie*, 286.

21 Some of the language of the diary haunts this brief review, in fact. Barthes refers to being 'moved' (*ému*) by the music, for example, just as one of the journal's early entries concludes: 'But all my life haven't I been just that: moved?' (MD, 43; translation modified). Meanwhile, the term 'lacerating' (*déchirant* or *déchirante*) cuts into both the review (OC V, 484) and the diary (MD, 185; translation modified). Barthes cannot have been present at the original staging of the opera on 26 July 1978, however, as this took place in Avignon, and the *Mourning Diary* has him returning from Casablanca and having dinner with friends in Paris on the day in question (MD, 169).

22 I call the diary's entries 'sighs' because this is the term used by Jean-Pierre Richard to describe Mallarmé's fragments (*Pour un tombeau d'Anatole*, 11).

23 In his *Roland Barthes, la littérature et le droit à la mort*, Éric Marty unearths less obvious echoes of Bataille (31) and even Saint Augustine (35) in Barthes's diary. Antoine Compagnon, meanwhile, finds a trace of Stendhal ('Writing Mourning': 210).

24 With this proposition in mind, I am struck by the way in which Barthes's handwriting in the entry of 1 May 1978 makes it impossible to know if he refers to his previous experience of death as '*borrowed* knowledge (clumsy, had from others, from philosophy, etc.)' or as '*borrowed* knowledge (clumsy, had from the arts, from philosophy, etc.)' (MD, 119 and editorial footnote). Léger, as editor of the diary, chooses 'others [*autres*]', but does not rule out 'arts' [*arts*].
25 Samoyault, *Roland Barthes: Biographie*, 633.
26 Samoyault, *Roland Barthes: Biographie*, 639.
27 My phrase 'the (house)work of mourning' is not an idle play on words. As my colleague Carrie Smith has reminded me, there is a moment in *The Second Sex* at which Simone de Beauvoir proposes that women whose lives are condemned to housework are like Sisyphus: 'day after day, one must wash dishes, dust furniture, mend clothes that will be dirty, dusty, and torn again. The housewife wears herself out running on the spot; she does nothing; she only perpetuates the present; she never gains the sense that she is conquering a positive Good, but struggles indefinitely against Evil. It is a struggle that begins again every day.' Simone de Beauvoir, *The Second Sex*, trans. Constance Borde and Sheila Malovany-Chevallier (New York: Vintage, 2011), 539. The sense of being unable to move forward in time colours much of the *Mourning Diary*. Barthes, in fact, even invokes the figure of Sisyphus when describing the sorting of his mother's belongings and the study of her photographs, and writes that '[a] cruel mourning begins again (but had never ended)' (MD, 139).
28 The separate diary fragments which were written in the summer of 1977 (when Barthes's mother was still alive), and which would later appear in 'Deliberation', also contain a reference to Barthes's mother's housework, albeit in Urt, not Paris: '*Mother feeling better today. She is sitting in the garden, wearing a big straw hat. As soon as she feels a little better, she is drawn by the house, filled with the desire to participate; she puts things away, turns off the furnace during the day (which I never do)*' (RL, 364). Richard Howard's translation perhaps gives the impression that Barthes enlisted the verb 'ranger' here as well, but the original French reads: 'elle fait rentrer les choses dans l'ordre' (OC V, 672).
29 McGuinness, 'Afterword: Mallarmé and the *Tombeau d'Anatole*', 82.
30 It should perhaps be noted, however, that the diary does eventually, nearly two years after the burial, refer to the cemetery and the grave (MD, 241).
31 See JD, 35, 45 (twice) and 160. For the translations (which do not make clear the common use of 'ranger' in the original French), see MD, 25, 35 and 148.
32 A further hint that the projected work would be a poem can be found in *feuillet* 82: 'or: ordinary Poem' (29). Meanwhile, *feuillet* 181 contains an untranslatable play on the French term 'vers' (which can mean either 'verse' or 'towards'): 'O mon fils

comme vers un ciel instinct spiritualiste.' Patrick McGuinness translates this line as 'O my son as towards a heaven spiritualist instinct' (67), but another possibility would be 'O my son as verse a heaven spiritualist instinct'. Although the notes appear to imagine a work in three principal sections, *feuillet* 158 refers to a fourth part (61). In his notes for the *Oeuvres complètes*, Marchal (1367) reads the 'perhaps in verse' of *feuillet* 23 as Mallarmé's wavering between poetry and prose for the *tombeau*, and also suggests that *feuillet* 37 might be proposing 'true return into the ideal' as a title only for the third section of the work.

33 Mallarmé, *Anatole*, 11. This reference to the son's being 'in us' ('en nous') is resurrected in several of the other *feuillets*, often in the wake of a defiant 'no'. See, for example, 19, 37, 43, 47, 63 (twice) and 69. For a discussion of the 'en nous' and the related 'en moi' in *Anatole* in terms of 'transfusion' (Mallarmé's term), see Benoit, *Néant sonore*, 159.

34 Further acknowledgement of death's power and Mallarmé's defiance can be found in *Anatole*, 45, 57.

35 Benoit, *Néant sonore*, 155. Benoit attends wonderfully to the different grammatical tenses – above all the conditional – in Mallarmé's notes, and concludes that 'the slips of *Tombeau d'Anatole* are thus founded on a vertiginous temporal tourniquet' (155).

36 McGuinness, 'Afterword', 85.

37 André Vial has, however, argued that there are signs of the projected *tombeau* for Anatole in some of Mallarmé's completed poems. See his *Mallarmé: Tétralogie pour un enfant mort* (Paris: Corti, 1976). For more on this possibility, see Benoit, *Néant sonore*, 161–2. This has been described as a 'highly debatable thesis' by Roger Pearson in his '«Une inaptitude délicieuse à finir»: Mallarmé and the Orthography of Incompletion', in *Esquisses/Ébauches: Projects and Pre-texts in Ninenteenth-century French Culture*, ed. Sonya Stephens (New York: Peter Lang, 2007), 220 n. 19.

38 The version of the *Oeuvres complètes* to which I am referring here is the original three-volume edition (Paris: Seuil, 1993–5); this was superseded by the five-volume revised version of 2002.

39 These facsimiles appear at the end of *Album* in a section which, rather confusingly, uses a different form of pagination (XXXIII-LXIV).

40 For a discussion how 'the possibility of failure was built into the basic conception' of *Vita Nova*, see Diana Knight, 'Idle Thoughts: Barthes's *Vita Nova*', *Nottingham French Studies* 36, no. 1 (1997): 88–98. (The quotation in the previous sentence is taken from page 91 of Knight's essay.) See also Chapter 5 of O'Meara, *Roland Barthes at the Collège de France* (Liverpool: Liverpool University Press, 2012).

41 Gil, *Roland Barthes: Au lieu de la vie*, 473, 487. In the actual title of the relevant section of the book, Gil uses a capital letter: 'journal de la Vie nouvelle' (468).
42 Nathalie Léger, Editor's preface to PN, xix. The actual writing of the book took place, according to the dates at the end of the original French text, between 15 April and 3 June 1979. These dates do not appear in Richard Howard's English translation.
43 As Diana Knight puts it in 'Idle Thoughts', the October lecture 'paved the way for the 1978–80 lecture course' (89).
44 For more on what apparently happened on 15 April 1978, see Samoyault, *Roland Barthes: Biographie*, 649; for Barthes's own account of the incident in his plans for *Vita Nova*, see the double-sided *fiche* dated 30 September 1979 which is reproduced in AL, LXI. *Satori* was evidently on Barthes's mind soon after 15 April 1978, for he devoted a section of the course on the Neutral to the term the following month (N, 172–5).
45 Mourning (or 'bereavement', to use the term enlisted by Kate Briggs to translate Barthes's original 'deuil') is mentioned explicitly in plans 1, 2, 3, 4 and 7; the 'decision' appears in plans 1, 2, 3, 5 and 8. The figure of the mother, meanwhile, is present in plans 3, 4, 5, 7 and 8.
46 Marie Gil has proposed, in fact, that *Vita Nova* is 'another name for mourning' (*Roland Barthes: Au lieu de la vie*, 472).
47 PN, 396 (facsimile) and 406 (transcription). The first and second plans for the project refer in the abstract to a diary, but they do not have the precision of the final sketch, so it is not quite clear *which* diary is intended in the earlier sketches. Kate Briggs has translated Barthes's 'Journal de Deuil' (the capital 'D' is Barthes's) literally and accurately as '*Journal of Mourning*' in her rendering of the plans (PN, 406), but I have opted for *Mourning Diary* here in order to strengthen the link to the text published under that name.
48 Éric Marty (*Roland Barthes, la littérature et le droit à la mort*, 34) notes that 'Evenings in Paris' and the *Mourning Diary* are linked to each other through the character identified as 'Marco'.
49 Marty, *Roland Barthes, la littérature et le droit à la mort*, 18.
50 My phrasing in this sentence – 'the longing for a *vita nova* in the wake of loss' – is deliberate, for there are references to the beginning of a '*vita nuova*' (the alternative spelling is Barthes's) in a letter to Michel Butor dated 19 February 1964 (AL, 189), in the seminar notes of 1973–4 (LA, 51), and, more significantly, in the inaugural lecture at the Collège de France on 7 January 1977, when Henriette Barthes, crucially, was still alive (and present in the audience, in fact). Towards the end of the lecture, having just invoked Thomas Mann's *Magic Mountain* and his own ageing body, Barthes announces (echoing his earlier letter to Butor): 'I must

make myself younger than I am. At fifty-one, Michelet began his *vita nuova*, a new work, a new love. Older than he . . . I too am entering a *vita nuova*, marked today by this new place, this new hospitality' (L, 43; cf. LA, 51, where Barthes has Michelet's new life beginning at fifty-*two*). (The recording of Barthes's inaugural lecture reveals that he sounds the '*u*' of '*vita nuova*' clearly on both occasions.) If all of Barthes's late references to a *vita nova* or *vita nuova* are taken to be somehow connected, this moment in the inaugural lecture (like the letter to Butor in 1964) cannot be fitted into a reading of the desire for a *vita nova* (or a *Vita Nova*) which emphasizes mourning: Barthes has not yet entered his period of grief in January 1977. It seems to me, however, that there is another possibility: a possibility that the reference to a '*vita nuova*' in the inaugural lecture is a reference to something else altogether – a possibility, in other words, that there is more than one *vita n(u)ova* in the late Barthes. I want to propose, then, that the '*vita nuova*' announced on 7 January 1977 is a more straightforward naming of the new stage of Barthes's professional life which is beginning, performatively, with the giving of the inaugural lecture at the Collège. I see evidence for this in the fact that Barthes introduces the phrase in question immediately before naming 'this new place' and 'this new hospitality'. (The linguistic echoes work far better in the original French: 'j'entre moi aussi dans une *vita nuova*, marquée aujourd'hui par ce lieu nouveau, cette hospitalité nouvelle'; OC V, 446.) The new life is beginning, too, not imagined or projected, for Barthes uses the present tense to describe his relation to the *vita nuova*. Finally, this long endnote cannot conclude without mentioning yet another reference to the desire for a *vita nuova*, this time in the session of *The Neutral* dated 13 May 1978 (N, 147–51). Barthes is now in his period of mourning, and he is still writing his diary of grief, but there is no sense in this particular discussion of the *vita nuova* that mourning figures.

51 Dante Alighieri, *La Vita Nuova (Poems of Youth)*, trans. Barbara Reynolds (London: Penguin, 1969). Barthes makes it clear on two occasions in *The Preparation of the Novel* that his use of the phrase '*vita n(u)ova*' is indebted to both Dante and Michelet (PN, 5, 212). However, the much earlier letter to Michel Butor dated 19 February 1964 introduces the term solely with reference to Michelet (AL, 189).

52 I should perhaps stress here that I am not proposing to investigate the Mallarméan quality of *Vita Nova* with reference to the poet's grand, unrealized, mythical project known as *Le Livre*; my more precise interest, rather, is in the spectres of *Anatole* in the *Mourning Diary*. Indeed, it seems to me that invoking *Le Livre* in discussions of *Vita Nova* is, however tempting, something of a dead end. The temptation is there in part because Barthes actually refers to Mallarmé's Grand Project in *The Preparation of the Novel*, notably in a session (PN, 182–3) which

comes just two weeks before an extended return to the concept of the *vita nova* (PN, 212–24); a related, yet different, discussion of *Le Livre* informs 'Deliberation' at roughly the same time (RL, 359–73). However, Barthes also points out that 'we don't know very much about the content' of Mallarmé's *Livre* because 'twenty-five years [were] spent on just the Form, pure fantasy' (PN, 183). I can see no persuasive evidence, then, that *Le Livre* was to have been a work of mourning for Anatole; Barthes's sketches for his *Vita Nova*, meanwhile, stress repeatedly the writing of grief. For the notes relating to *Le Livre*, see Mallarmé, '[Notes en vue du «Livre»]', in *Oeuvres complètes*, vol. 1, 547–626.

53 Until the publication of Barthes's *Album* in mid-2015, it seemed strange that the *Mourning Diary* should announce the failure of 'the Project' *before* the eight plans for *Vita Nova* were written. (The diary entry is dated 22 July 1979; the first of the eight sketches was written on 21 August 1979.) However, the *fiches* gathered by Éric Marty in the section of *Album* devoted to *Vita Nova* suggest that Barthes's note-taking began some time before August 1979. As the full *Vita Nova* archive has not yet been made public, the complete story of Barthes's project remains unknown and untold.

54 Although this problem appears here for the first time in the *Mourning Diary*, there is a sense in which it is not entirely new to Barthes, for an entry made a little over three months earlier in a separate diary touches upon similar ground: '*Depression, fear, anxiety: I see the death of a loved one, I panic, etc. Such an imagination is the very opposite of faith. For constantly to imagine the inevitability of disaster is constantly to accept it: to utter it is to assert it (again, the fascism of language)*' (RL, 362). When Barthes writes these words, his mother is still alive, which lends his lines some of the anxiety articulated by Mallarmé in his thinking of the *tombeau* for Anatole before the child has died. The problem of language itself, meanwhile, informs the *Mourning Diary*'s entry of 3 April 1978, where Barthes writes: '*Despair*: the word is too theatrical, a part of the language' (MD, 111). Having read Saussure and Jakobson, Barthes knows that language is trans-personal, non-unique and riddled with 'shifters'.

55 Compagnon, 'Writing Mourning': 216.

56 Diana Knight, 'What Turns the Writer into a Great Writer? The Conversion Narrative of Barthes's "Vita Nova"', *L'Esprit créateur* 55, vol. 4 (2015): 165–80.

57 Compagnon writes in his memoir *L'Âge des lettres* (Paris: Gallimard, 2015) that Barthes would habitually refer to him in writing by his initials (44). Later in the text, he discusses his unease at how he is presented in the *Mourning Diary* as 'the mouthpiece of reason, the champion of common sense, the defender of the norm' (146).

58 See also the entry of 14 November 1977, which simply reads: 'In a sense I resist the Invocation to the Status of the Mother in order to explain my distress' (MD, 48). Turning *maman* into the Mother would be precisely a case of generalising, of abstraction. There is, furthermore, a related moment near the beginning of *The Preparation of the Novel* at which Barthes discusses the difference between the general and the particular, noting that the haiku undoes the Western 'resistance to the Particular': 'No haiku deals in generalities and, as a result, the haiku genre is absolutely pure of all processes of reduction' (PN, 50). The remark occurs in the session of 27 January 1979 – a date which falls within the period covered by the *Mourning Diary*.

59 The lecture in question took place on 25 March 1978 – once again within the period covered by the *Mourning Diary*, in other words. Given this chronological overlap, it is not surprising that *The Neutral* should refer in its opening session to the death of Barthes's mother (N, 13) and also echo the diary's discussion of how long, according to the *Mémento Larousse*, mourning should last (N, 17; MD, 19).

60 The tension to which I am referring here is not quite the same as the tension described by Antoine Compagnon in 'Writing Mourning', his brilliant essay on Barthes's diary. For Compagnon, the contradiction in the journal is ultimately between mourning and *narrative* (where narrative is understood, in the wake of Ricoeur, as being on the side of life). Because narrative involves imagining a future, a living future in time, it is at odds with mourning's desperate dwelling on that which can have no place in the future, in time to come. As Compagnon writes: 'For recounting it, "[t]alking about it" (about his mourning), would involve ordering it, accepting the passage of time, accomplishing the work of mourning, explaining, rationalising. By a negative formulation, mourning is the perfect illustration of the connection between narrative and time. In mourning, to reject narrative means to reject time – time for living' (211). I find Compagnon's analysis compelling and astute, but I wish to approach matters in a different way in the present chapter. For me, the tension is between mourning and *language*, or mourning and *writing*, where the signifier has yet to be enlisted in the work of narrative. What interests me, that is to say, are the pressures exerted upon the writer who mourns when that writer knows all too well, having read Saussure, that language is an impersonal, external, general system.

61 MD, 133; translation modified. A little over a week before writing these lines in his diary, Barthes had discussed the theme of the monument in his course on the Neutral at the Collège de France (N, 175). Neither his mother nor mourning is mentioned there, but the reference to the monument occurs when he is discussing the 'fragility', 'contingency' and 'perishability' of the course itself, even though a trace of it exists in notes and recordings.

62 On the difference between 'tombe' and *'tombeau'*, I am struck by the manner in which *Le Grand Robert* handles the two terms. Although the dictionary notes overlaps in meaning, it begins the entry for *'tombeau'* with the words 'Monument ... funéraire servant de sépulture pour un ou plusieurs morts', before noting the specifically poetic or musical use of *'tombeau'* dating back to around 1700. The description of 'tombe', meanwhile, opens with the far more prosaic 'Lieu où l'on ensevelit un mort, fosse généralement recouverte d'une dalle de marbre, de pierre'. *Le Grand Robert de la langue française: Dictionnaire alphabetique et analogique de la langue française*, 2nd edn (Paris: Dictionnaires Le Robert, 1992), 9 vols, vol. 9, 339.

63 Barthes had linked writing and recognition some years earlier, in a short text entitled 'Ten Reasons to Write (VFG, 86).

64 It also recalls one of the diary entries which was written in the summer of 1977, when Barthes's mother was still alive, and which later appeared in 'Deliberation': *'Death, real death, is when the witness himself dies. Chateaubriand says of his grandmother and his great-aunt: "I may be the only man in the world who knows that such persons have existed": yes, but since he has written this, and written it well, we know it too, insofar, at least, as we still read Chateaubriand'* (RL, 362–3). In *L'Âge des lettres*, Antoine Compagnon calls these months 'that sombre summer' (116).

65 Although the *Mourning Diary* stops between 29 March and 1 May 1979, the diary entry headed 'Futile evening' in 'Deliberation' comes from this 'silent' period (RL, 367–9).

66 The phrase 'this work – too great for me' occurs in fragment 14 of *Anatole* (7) – a fragment which also contains the phrase 'truly son of father whose heart beat for projects too great'. The 'non' at the end of the line spoken by Barthes is repeated from earlier in *Thrène*, which often cuts up and manipulates sounds.

67 'La vie comme texte' is the title of a fragment written for, but never actually used in, *Roland Barthes by Roland Barthes*. Dated 11 July 1974, it was published posthumously in LA, 324–5. Marie Gil makes much of the phrase in her *Roland Barthes: Au lieu de la vie*. As Calum Gardner has reminded me, the chapter of *Sollers Writer* entitled 'Over Your Shoulder' (1973) contains a related moment in its final paragraph: 'For some people, *life is textual*' (SW, 92).

3

Punctum Saliens: Mourning, Film, Photography

'Maybe he wouldn't use photographs.'

E.L. Doctorow, *Homer and Langley*.[1]

Punctum saliens. The phrase identifies a starting point, an origin, a source, the heart of the matter. 'Linnæus, like a naturalist,' wrote Emerson in *The Natural History of Intellect*, 'esteeming the globe a big egg, called London the *punctum saliens* in the yolk of the world.'[2] Less figuratively, in biology the term names the earliest trace of an embryo's heartbeat in the form of a tiny pulsating point. As the physician William Harvey wrote in *On the Generation of Animals* in 1651:

> The ovum at this time is full of a colliquate matter, transparent, crystalline, similar to that fluid which in the hen's egg we have called the colliquament or eye, of far greater purity than that fluid in which the embryo by and by floats, and contained within a proper tunic of extreme tenuity, and orbicular in form. In the middle of the ovum, vascular ramifications and the punctum saliens – the first or rudimentary particle of the foetus – and nothing else, are clearly to be perceived.[3]

Where lies the *punctum saliens* of Roland Barthes's *punctum*? Where does life begin for his concept of the photographic detail that 'rises from the scene, shoots out of it like an arrow, and pierces' perception (CL, 26)? When can its heart first be seen to beat? For nearly three decades, the answer to these questions tended to go without saying: in the photographic analyses of *Camera Lucida*, in which Barthes articulated his influential distinction between the *studium* and the *punctum* of an image. However, the publication in 2009 of the *Mourning Diary* complicates matters by casting new light on the development of the *punctum* and, more generally, what has become, in Geoffrey Batchen's words, 'surely the most quoted book in the photographic canon'.[4]

Batchen goes on to relate the familiarity of *Camera Lucida* to what he calls 'a certain fatigue':

> Terms established by Barthes, such as *studium* and *punctum*, have become part of the standard lexicon of photographic debate, along with a particular understanding of photographic time and of photography's relationship to death and a certain narcissistic way of speaking. All these aspects of *Camera Lucida*, and more, have come to be so frequently repeated in the works of others that they have congealed into what Barthes himself would call a *doxa*.
>
> (3)

There is a degree of truth in these lines – it has become rather tedious to begin reading a new text on Barthes and photography and to encounter yet another summary of the difference between the *studium* and the *punctum* – but Batchen's book would have been in production before Barthes's *Mourning Diary* appeared.[5] I think that the *doxa* identified by Batchen is unsettled to some extent by the publication of the diary, and I want in what follows to examine how the *punctum* develops, sharpens and comes leaping forward (*saliens*) long before the writing of *Camera Lucida* has begun. I want, in other words, to develop details which had remained in the dark, in the *camera obscura*, until the posthumous exposure of the *Mourning Diary* – details which have not received extensive evaluation elsewhere.

My aim in this chapter is not simply and passively to list textual ancestors, to present a dead inventory of spectral correspondences. At the same time, I am not qualified to offer the kind of genetic analysis found in Jean-Louis Lebrave's remarkable 'La Genèse de *La Chambre claire*', which traces the delicate evolution of *Camera Lucida* through Barthes's layered manuscripts.[6] I wish, rather, to examine in careful detail how an artistic form comes to fade or fade out: while the photographic *punctum* of *Camera Lucida* has inescapably cinematic roots in the *Mourning Diary*'s 'fragments d'un discours douloureux' of 1977–9, this filmic conception, this *punctum saliens*, is left out of the frame when Barthes eventually publishes the book on photography in 1980.[7] It has already been pointed out, of course, that *Camera Lucida*'s account of the photographic *punctum* is indebted in notable ways to the analysis of film stills that Barthes developed in 'The Third Meaning' in 1970 (RF, 41–62). As Éric Marty, for example, puts it:

The 'obtuse meaning' of the photograph, in spite of major differences, has certain similarities with the *punctum*: it troubles and sterilises metalanguage (criticism), it is indifferent to any scenario, it is not filled, and 'it maintains itself in a state of perpetual erethism; in it desire does not attain that spasm of the signified which usually causes the subject to sink voluptuously into the peace of nomination. Ultimately the obtuse meaning can be seen as an *accent*, the very form of an emergence, of a fold (even a crease) marking the heavy layer of information and signification.' ... The insistent themes of the final years are there.[8]

Many others have made related observations; I have no desire to revisit that familiar ground at length in this chapter.[9] My investigation of spectral filmic foundations, rather, will have a new and different focus: instead of repeating well-known propositions about 'The Third Meaning', I will dwell more specifically upon the *Mourning Diary* as a closer, more exact precursor that has been visible only since 2009 in order to examine how that particular text, in the words of its editor, 'contributes to the elaboration of [Barthes's] oeuvre and, as such, illuminates it'.[10]

Preparation

While it is reductive to see the *Mourning Diary* as merely a set of notes towards *Camera Lucida*, it is above all for the latter that the journal reaches.[11] The entries, it might be said, cover a difficult period in which the book on photography undergoes *preparation*. This is also the period in which the grieving Barthes is, as I discussed in the previous chapter, trying to imagine his *Vita Nova*. One work is completed, then, but the other fails to form. My concern in Chapter 2 was with what never crystallized; my interest here is in a completed book.

The preparation of *Camera Lucida* is lengthy and turbulent; there were, Antoine Compagnon notes in his narrative of his friendship with Barthes during this period, 'blockages' and 'dissatisfactions'.[12] The first explicit reference in the diary to what would become the text can be found on 23 March 1978, when Barthes writes of 'getting to work on the book about Photography' (MD, 105). While this sounds promising, by early May the diary is less confident and appears to record Barthes's inability to begin the project: '(Readying for the day when I can finally write)' (MD, 121). By June, however, things look a little better when Barthes glimpses a solution to the troubles: he will, he vows, 'write this book around *maman*' (MD, 133).[13] A direction has now been established, but a few days later comes a scene of desperation:

> This morning, walking through Saint-Sulpice, whose simple architectural vastness delights me; to be *in* architecture – I sit down for a moment; a sort of instinctive 'prayer': that I bring off the *Photo-Maman* book.[14]

Those words were evidently slow to reach God's ears: *Camera Lucida* would not be written for around another ten months.

Before the publication of the *Mourning Diary*, the dates of composition given at the end of *La Chambre claire* (15 April–3 June 1979) suggested a book produced with speed and ease (OC V, 885).[15] What the journal reveals, however, is that the grieving Barthes was struggling to create the work for more than a year before April 1979. In the vocabulary of *The Preparation of the Novel*, *Camera Lucida* was rather slow to 'take'.[16] The room is darker than it once appeared. What the diary also brings to light is that this period of preparation was punctuated by poignant responses to a number of films – responses that show the theory of the *punctum* coming gently into focus. The room may be dark, but it is lit by moving pictures. And in this new light flickers a *punctum saliens*.

Details

A little over two weeks after referring for the first time in his diary to 'the book about Photography', Barthes records a viewing of a film while in the south of France:

> Urt. William Wyler's film *The Little Foxes*, with Bette Davis.
> – At one point the daughter mentions 'rice powder.'
> – All my early childhood comes back to me. *Maman*. The rice-powder box. Everything is there, present. *I am there*.
> → *The self never ages*.
> – (I am as 'fresh' as in the 'rice-powder' days)[17]

The moment has echoes of *In Search of Lost Time*'s famous early scene of involuntary memory, of course, and Proust, as I noted in Chapter 2, haunts the pages of the journal more than any other literary figure.[18] The Proustian quality of the incident is not my concern here, however. Even though the writing of *Camera Lucida* is still more than a year away, it seems to me that there are glimpses of the *punctum* in the account of the event: while Barthes looks at the screen, he is struck, overwhelmed, pierced without warning by a marginal element of the *mise en scène*. (The powder plays no significant part in *The Little Foxes*; it is not present at all in the play upon which Wyler's film is based.[19]) In the later language of *Camera Lucida*, this 'off-center' (CL, 51) element is an unexpected 'sensitive poin[t]' (CL, 27) in an otherwise serene *studium*, a bruising 'accident' (CL, 27) neither sought nor expected by the viewer.

Around five weeks later, the diary records another cinematic moment with hints of the *punctum*:

> Last night, a stupid, gross film, *One Two Two*. It was set in the period of the Stavisky scandal, which I lived through. On the whole, it brought nothing back. But all of a sudden, one detail of the décor overwhelmed me: nothing but a lamp with a pleated shade and a dangling switch. *Maman* made such things – in the same way that she made batik. All of her leaped before my eyes.[20]

The incident recalls the response to *The Little Foxes*. Once again, Barthes's viewing is initially in the realm of 'general and, so to speak, *polite* interest', to invoke *Camera Lucida*'s description of the *studium* (CL, 27). Nothing unsettles – 'On the whole, it brought nothing back…' – and there is no needling 'special acuity' (CL, 26). But then, 'all of a sudden', Barthes is 'overwhelmed' by an incidental object. (That this object is marginal is conveyed by the subsequent turn of phrase: '*nothing but* a lamp'.) And in describing this moment, the journal leaps closer to the account of the *punctum* that will appear eventually in *Camera Lucida* by introducing a noun that was not present in the response to *The Little Foxes*: 'detail'.

I cannot read these lines in the diary about *One Two Two* without thinking of how the *punctum* is described in the twenty-first section of *Camera Lucida*:

> A detail overwhelms the entirety of my reading; it is an intense mutation of my interest, a fulguration. By the mark of *something*, the photograph is no longer *anything whatever*. This *something* has triggered me, has provoked a tiny shock, a *satori*, the passage of a void (it is of no importance that its referent is insignificant).
>
> (CL, p, 49; typography modified)[21]

In short, *One Two Two* 'is no longer *anything whatever*' as soon as the lamp represented upon the screen – the leaping *detail* – has caught Barthes's eye. It does not matter 'that its referent is insignificant': it has a memorial might.

These responses to *The Little Foxes* and *One Two Two* occur long before Barthes has begun to write *Camera Lucida*, and it seems to me that the diary's accounts of the 'resurrections of the mother' in films leave their mark firmly and precisely upon the descriptions of the *punctum* that appear in the 'Photo-Maman book' – the book with which Barthes is struggling while he is moved by what he sees upon the screen.[22] What is revealed, then, by the publication of the *Mourning Diary* in 2009 – and in a manner more textually, linguistically exact than in 'The Third Meaning' – is that the *punctum saliens* of the *punctum* lies in film, not in photography. Its heart first flickers upon a screen, in images that move.

And yet, the opening paragraph of *Camera Lucida* contains a clear declaration:

> I decided I liked Photography *against* cinema, from which I nonetheless failed to separate it. This question grew insistent. I was overcome by an 'ontological' desire: I wanted to learn at all costs what Photography was 'in itself', by what essential feature it was to be distinguished from the community of images.[23]

When the *punctum* is enlisted in the pages that follow to pin down photography, to pierce it and isolate it from the wider 'community of images', it is in no way cinematic; its roots in film are obscured. *Camera Lucida*, moreover, especially in its second part, repeatedly privileges photography over cinema: the photograph's *noeme* 'deteriorates' in film (CL, 78), where its referent 'shifts [and] does not make a claim in favor of its reality' (CL, 89); cinema, at least in its endoxal fictional form, 'participates in [a] domestication of Photography', a taming of 'the madness which keeps threatening to explode in the face of whoever looks at it' (CL, 117). (I will return in detail to Barthes's so-called 'resistance to cinema' in the final chapter of this book.) All in all, and regardless of what took place when Barthes watched *The Little Foxes* and *One Two Two*, *Camera Lucida* is very much a meditation on *photography*, as its subtitle makes clear.

I want to investigate this shift, this silence, this silencing. Why does *Camera Lucida* leave the filmic origins of the *punctum* out of the picture? Why does cinema slip to a secondary status? Why is the *punctum saliens* not permitted to pulse in the '*Photo-Maman* book'?

Fade

It might be tempting to answer these questions with biography, with what is known of Barthes's 'person, his history, his tastes, his passions' (RL, 50), particularly because the *Mourning Diary* is so obviously an intimate, 'personal' text. (So much so, in fact, that François Wahl, as I noted in the previous chapter, saw its publication as a betrayal of its author.) Five years before *Camera Lucida* came to light, *Roland Barthes by Roland Barthes* articulated a '[r]esistance to cinema' on the grounds that the form relies upon 'a continuum of images' and a 'smooth [*lisse*]' signifier which lead to a 'statutory impossibility of the fragment, of the haiku' (RB, 54, 55; translation modified). In film, Barthes continued, 'everything is given to me', and the enigmatic reserve of writing is lost (RB, 55).[24] This 'resistance to cinema' returned in 'On Photography', an interview with Barthes which appeared one month after the publication of *Camera Lucida*.[25] The interviewer asks for a description of the new volume, and receives the following reply:

> To be more specific, it's a modest book, done at the request of *Cahiers du cinéma*, which is opening with this book a series in principle on film, but they left me free to choose my subject, and I chose photography.[26]

Later in the interview, Barthes discusses photography and film in a way that recalls the opening page of *Camera Lucida*:

> I should also say that if I chose photography as the subject of my book, I did so, in a way, *against* cinema. I realized that I had a positive relation to photographs, I love to look at them, whereas I have a difficult and resistant relation to cinema. I'm not saying that I don't go to the cinema, but in the end, paradoxically, I put photography above cinema in my little personal pantheon.[27]

I do not wish, however, to found an analysis upon a 'personal pantheon'. It would not be enough, I think, to claim that the filmic roots of the *punctum* are masked in *Camera Lucida* simply because Barthes was more fond of photography than of cinema. Instead, I want to approach the book's silence textually, genetically, by turning to a dramatic discovery described in the pages of the *Mourning Diary*.

On 11 June 1978, some time after he has seen *The Little Foxes* and *One Two Two*, Barthes writes in his journal:

> Afternoon with Michel, sorted *maman*'s belongings.
> Began the day by looking at her photographs.
> A cruel mourning begins again (but had never ended).
> To begin again without resting. Sisyphus.
>
> (MD, 139; translation modified)

Nothing more is said about the pictures at this point, but two days later an entry reads:

> This morning, painfully returning to the photographs, overwhelmed by one in which *maman*, a gentle, discreet little girl beside Philippe Binger (the Winter Garden of Chennevières, 1898).
>
> (MD, 143)

What Barthes has found, of course, is the image around which the second part of *Camera Lucida* will in time revolve – the image which will, in Éric Marty's account, inaugurate a new sequence of mourning and, in some ways, the end of the *Mourning Diary* itself.[28]

The publication of the diary raises a major question about the discovery of the Winter Garden photograph. While the journal locates the event in June 1978, *Camera Lucida* refers to the finding of the image 'one November evening shortly after' the death of Henriette Barthes (CL, 63). There is, I think, little reason to doubt the accuracy of the journal's entry, which was written at the time of the discovery and never intended for publication; as Nathalie Léger, Valérie Stiénon and Laurent Demoulin have pointed out, moreover, the diary's fragments are very precisely *dated*.[29] Suddenly, 'one November evening' seems vague when read alongside 'June 11, 1978'.

The *Mourning Diary* reveals, then, that Barthes altered the date when writing *Camera Lucida*, thus adding further weight to the familiar claim that the book on photography can be read, at least in part, as a work of fiction.[30] In simple terms, the decision could be seen as an aesthetic one: it is more conventionally, fittingly poetic to have the death-tinged photograph found in the dark depths of winter (*Camera Lucida* specifies 'evening') than in the bright warmth of summer (the journal speaks of 'morning').[31] Perhaps, though, there is another motivation. In describing the discovery of the image as taking place 'one November evening shortly after' the death of Barthes's mother, *Camera Lucida* closes the gap between her passing and the finding of the picture. (I take the 'shortly after' to refer to the November immediately following the fatal October.) In closing that gap, Barthes erases around seven months of mourning, and these, crucially, are the months in which, the diary reveals, he saw *The Little Foxes* and *One Two Two* – films whose details pave the way for the photographic *punctum*. When this period of time disappears, the cinematic roots of the *punctum* are further repressed. Film fades.

While *Camera Lucida* has a great deal to say about the Winter Garden image – the second half of the book is essentially a discussion of its implications – the diary is at first rather unforthcoming. The entry dated 16 June 1978 reads:

> Speaking to Cl. M. about my anguish at seeing the photos of *maman*, envisaging a labor starting from these photos: she tells me: that may be premature.[32]
>
> (MD, 148; translation modified)

Perhaps 'Cl. M.' (almost certainly Claude Maupomé[33]) was right, because when the diary next touches upon the picture, on 24 July, Barthes writes: 'Photo of the Winter Garden: I search desperately to find the obvious meaning' (MD, 168). It would appear that this search was difficult, for the journal then falls silent about the image until 29 December, when Barthes reports that he has had a reproduction made and is trying to keep it in front of him on his desk while he works (MD, 220).[34]

There is just one further reference in the journal to the picture (MD, 226), a little under three months before Barthes begins finally to write 'the *Photo-Maman* book', but the image continued to resonate, of course, for *Camera Lucida* would soon come to grant it a special, revelatory, emblematic status:

> Something like an essence of the Photograph floated in this particular picture. I therefore decided to 'derive' all Photography (its 'nature') from the only photograph which assuredly existed for me, and to take it somehow as a guide for my last investigation.
>
> (CL, 73)

It is 'this particular picture' which leads Barthes to what he calls 'the truth of the image' (CL, 76): 'The name of Photography's *noeme* will therefore be: "That-has-been", or again: the Intractable' (CL, 77). The full force of this truth, he insists, is not apparent in other images (CL, 77).

At the start of the thirty-ninth section of *Camera Lucida*, Barthes accordingly reconsiders the position concerning photography that the book has established over many pages:

> At the time (at the beginning of this book: already far away) when I was inquiring into my attachment to certain photographs, I thought I could distinguish a field of cultural interest (the *studium*) from that unexpected flash which sometimes crosses this field and which I called the *punctum*. I now know that there exists another *punctum* (another 'stigmatum') than the 'detail'. This new *punctum*, which is no longer of form but of intensity, is Time, the lacerating emphasis of the *noeme* ('that-has-been'), its pure representation. . . . In front of the photograph of my mother as a child, I tell myself: she is going to die: I shudder, like Winnicott's psychotic patient, *over a catastrophe which has already occurred*. Whether or not the subject is already dead, every photograph is this catastrophe.[35]

The Winter Garden photograph, in other words, brings about a radical refocussing. The first part of *Camera Lucida*, in which the *punctum* is described in terms of the detail, concludes with Barthes's admission that he has 'not yet discovered the nature (the *eidos*) of Photography' and that a palinode – a recantation, a retraction of an earlier statement – is therefore required (CL, 60).[36] In the palinodic second part of the book, therefore, one of the two key theoretical terms is recast, for the power of the image of Barthes's mother has revealed 'another *punctum* (another "stigmatum") than the "detail"'. Now it is not the marginal element of a picture which 'overwhelms the entirety of [a] reading'; it is something not found within form – Time itself (CL, 49).[37]

Camera Lucida builds to this proposition, this revelation, this faith in a photograph's extra-textual 'evidential power' (CL, 106) and status as a 'certificate of presence' (CL, 87). As it steps with time past the detail that wounds, it is able to drift away from the cinematic encounters with *The Little Foxes* and *One Two Two* described in the *Mourning Diary*, where the minutiae of the *mise en scène* are what matter and move. While viewing these films evidently unsettled Barthes, and while the *punctum* flickers precisely in those pages of the diary, the book on photography can distance itself ultimately from film and say nothing about the cinematic origins of the first *punctum* because the *punctum* of the detail comes in time, comes with Time, to fade. Invisible intensity intervenes.

Moving, touching

I have remained silent until now about a third cinematic encounter described in the pages of the diary. It is dated 29 July 1978, a little over two months after Barthes has watched *One Two Two*:

> (Saw a Hitchcock film, *Under Capricorn*)
> Ingrid Bergman (around 1946): I don't know why, I don't know how to say it: this actress, this actress's body moves me, touches something in me which reminds me of *maman*: her complexion, her lovely, simple hands, an impression of freshness, a non-narcissistic femininity . . .
> (MD, 172. Ellipsis in original; translation modified)

There is a stumbling here; language is at its limits. 'I don't know why, I don't know how to say it,' Barthes begins, searching and repeating himself, before turning to resigned generality – '*something* in me' – and stuttering after the colon: 'this actress, this actress's body'.

I hear an echo of this faltering moment in the passage on the *punctum* in *Camera Lucida* that is also touched by 'the detail': 'By the mark of *something*,' Barthes writes there, 'the photograph is no longer *anything whatever*. This *something* has triggered me . . .' (CL, 49; typography modified). These later words are connected to the viewing of *Under Capricorn* by the '*something*', by the inability of language to capture what leaps forth and shatters the serenity of the *studium*.[38] The term in question is profoundly ordinary, of course, but I think that its repetition here points to Barthes's inability to be specific, to name firmly, when unsettled by a detail of the text. As *Camera Lucida* later puts it: 'What I can name cannot really prick me. The incapacity to name is a good symptom of disturbance.'[39]

There is a further echo. When Barthes refers to Hitchcock's film, he declares that Ingrid Bergman's body *moves* him: 'le corps de cette actrice m'émeut', reads the original French (JD, 184). This is precisely the verb enlisted in *Camera*

Lucida's discussion of the *punctum* in James Van Der Zee's *Family Portrait*: 'Reading Van der Zee's photograph, I thought I had discerned what moved me [*je croyais avoir repéré ce qui m'émouvait*]: the strapped pumps of the black woman in her Sunday best' (CL, 53; OC V, 830). Being moved moves across texts and, more significantly, across forms of representation.

While the diary's account of watching Hitchcock's film has something in common with the earlier responses to *The Little Foxes* and *One Two Two*, it differs from them in a crucial way: it comes *after* the discovery of the Winter Garden photograph, *after* the reference to 'a labor starting from these photos', and *after* the identification of a search for 'the obvious meaning' of the image of Barthes's mother as a child. This may explain in part why the account of *Under Capricorn* does not focus on an inanimate, marginal detail of the *mise en scène*: Barthes's gaze falls now upon the living body of Ingrid Bergman, whose place in Hitchcock's film is central. (I will return to *Under Capricorn* from a different perspective in my final chapter.) What recalls the absent individual on this occasion is not a single element – rice powder, a lamp – but Bergman's form, her embodiment: 'her complexion, her lovely, simple hands, an impression of freshness, a non-narcissistic femininity...'

The peripheral, isolated detail – the heart of *Camera Lucida*'s first *punctum* – has faded from view, and this has occurred after Barthes has discovered the Winter Garden photograph, from which emerges, in *Camera Lucida*, the second *punctum* of Time. There is, in other words, a sense in which the *Mourning Diary* foreshadows the palinodic structure of the book on photography, albeit with a less explicit emphasis upon the recantation. Just as *Camera Lucida* offers a theory of the detail which it then withdraws, the journal responds to its first two films in April and May 1978 with accounts of lacerating details, but then records something significantly different when it reaches *Under Capricorn* in July. In each book, moreover, the palinode is prompted not by a film, but by a photograph: the image of the young Henriette in the Winter Garden at Chennevières.

In its dying moments, however, *Camera Lucida* allows the arresting textual detail to return to the stage that has been seized by Time. It does so, moreover, in an anecdote about watching a film:

[T]he same evening of a day I had again been looking at photographs of my mother, I went to see Fellini's *Casanova* with some friends; I was sad, the film bored me; but when Casanova began dancing with the young automaton, my eyes were touched with a kind of painful and delicious intensity, as if I were suddenly experiencing the effects of a strange drug; each detail (*détail*), which I was seeing with precision, savoring it, so to speak, down to its last evidence, overwhelmed me (*me bouleversait*).[40]

The language of the journal is here – *details* of the film *overwhelm* Barthes while he watches – and, in the light of the publication of the *Mourning Diary*, it is possible to read this passage as a late return from repression of the journal's cinematic encounters, albeit in the displaced form of a reference to a film that is mentioned nowhere in the *Mourning Diary*.[41] The silence is broken, pierced. However, after discussing briefly the details of the dancing figure, *Camera Lucida* halts the discussion of *Casanova* and cuts back to its real concern: 'At which moment I could not help thinking about Photography: for I could say all this about the photographs which touched me (out of which I had methodically constituted Photography itself).'[42] Silence has been restored, and the ensuing discussion of how Pity lies within 'the love stirred by Photography' (CL, 116) has at its heart not the poignant detail, but the force of 'what is dead, what is going to die' (CL, 117) – or, what is always in Time.

The burial of origins

Roland Barthes's *Journal de deuil* was published in February 2009.[43] The following month, Antoine Compagnon devoted part of a course at the Collège de France to his former teacher's diary. At one point, he identified a crucial textual nuance:

> Cinematic images play a completely different role in *Journal de deuil* than in *La Chambre claire*, which opposes the '*punctum*' of photography [*la photographie*] to the little interest aroused by cinema: images from films provoke full reminiscences in the mourning subject, whose past self [*le moi passé*], in contact with the deceased, is ready to rise [*ressusciter*] completely at the slightest stimulus.[44]

This observation underscores the impossibility of describing in the singular the relationship between photography and cinema in the *Mourning Diary* and *Camera Lucida*: values and vistas vary from text to text. In the absence of neat genetic synthesis, however, the posthumous publication of the journal makes it possible to read in a new light the tension between film and the photographic image which underlies the articulation of the *punctum* in *Camera Lucida* both before and after the announcement of the palinode. To turn again (*palin*) in conclusion towards *The Preparation of the Novel*, the *Mourning Diary* reveals that it is the Winter Garden photograph, not any of the films watched by Barthes during his period of grief, which allows *Camera Lucida* finally to leap from a preparatory 'state of *unconnectedness* [in which] the possible materials, the fragments, the bits of work are all there' to one of '*active crystallization*' (PN, 255, 256). What the diary records on 11 June 1978 is one of those miraculous, enabling '*discoveries* ("finds")' so crucial to a reluctant work's 'taking' (PN, 256).

My return to *The Preparation of the Novel* at this point is not coincidental: the *Mourning Diary* is, among other things, the preparation of *Camera Lucida*. When the journal records responses to *The Little Foxes* and *One Two Two*, it is 'like an engine trying to get going' (PN, 255); when it narrates the discovery of the Winter Garden image and the subsequent viewing of *Under Capricorn*, the diary shows *Camera Lucida* beginning to 'take', to feel beyond form for intensity, for Time, for what it sees as 'the nature – the genius – of Photography'. With the finding of the photograph comes a final finding of direction – or a finding of final direction.

There is sense, then, in the silence, in the burial of origins. The cinematic roots of the first *punctum* need not puncture the surface of the 'Photo-Maman book' extensively because the filmic incidents recorded in the diary are a form of preparation only for the *punctum* of the detail, which soon surrenders to 'another *punctum*': Time. In the language of the military, *The Little Foxes* and *One Two Two* have as their *detail* the preparing of the theory of the detail; it is this for which they are *cut out*.[45] When their work is done, these moving pictures fade and winter before the moving picture. Here lies the *punctum saliens*.

Notes

1 E.L. Doctorow, *Homer and Langley* (London: Little, Brown, 2010), 49.
2 Ralph Waldo Emerson, *The Natural History of Intellect* in *Emerson's Complete Works* (London: Waverley, 1883–93), 12 vols, vol. 12, 90.

3 William Harvey, *The Works of William Harvey, M.D.*, trans. Robert Willis (London: The Sydenham Society, 1847), 484.
4 Geoffrey Batchen, 'Palinode: An Introduction to *Photography Degree Zero*', in *Photography Degree Zero: Reflections on Roland Barthes's* Camera Lucida, ed. Geoffrey Batchen (Cambridge, MA and London: MIT Press, 2009), 3.
5 *Photography Degree Zero* appeared in October 2009; Barthes's *Journal de deuil* was published by Seuil in February of that year.
6 Jean-Louis Lebrave, 'La Genèse de *La Chambre claire*', *Genesis* 19 (2002): 79–107.
7 I take the phrase 'fragments d'un discours douloureux' from Jérôme Garcin, 'Barthes: Le mal de mère', *Le Nouvel observateur*, 29 January–4 February 2009: 48. Sophie Aouillé also makes a connection between the fragmentary *Journal de deuil* and Barthes's *Fragments d'un discours amoureux* in 'Roland Barthes: Journal de deuil', *Essaim* 23, vol. 2 (2009): 173.
8 Éric Marty, *Roland Barthes, le métier d'écrire* (Paris: Seuil, 2006), 153. The quotation within Marty's lines is from Barthes's 'The Third Meaning' (RF, 56). As Marty's own phrasing mirrors that of Barthes when he describes metalanguage (criticism), I have also enlisted Richard Howard's translation of 'The Third Meaning' (RF, 55) earlier in this passage.
9 See, among others: Derek Attridge, 'Roland Barthes's Obtuse, Sharp Meaning and the Responsibilities of Commentary' in *Writing the Image After Roland Barthes*, ed. Jean-Michel Rabaté (Philadelphia: University of Pennsylvania Press, 1997), 77–89; Steven Ungar, 'Persistence of the Image: Barthes, Photography, and the Resistance to Film' in *Critical Essays on Roland Barthes*, ed. Diana Knight (New York: G.K. Hall & Co., 2000), 236–49; Michael North, 'Authorship and Autography', *PMLA* 116, vol. 5 (2001): 1379; Adam Lowenstein, 'The Surrealism of the Photographic Image: Bazin, Barthes, and the Digital *Sweet Hereafter*', *Cinema Journal* 46, vol. 3 (2007): 64; Anselm Haverkamp, 'The Memory of Pictures: Roland Barthes and Augustine on Photography', *Comparative Literature* 45, vol. 3 (1993): 264; André Aciman, 'Deliberating Barthes' in *Roland Barthes: Critical Evaluations in Cultural Theory*, ed. Neil Badmington (Abingdon and New York: Routledge, 2010), 4 vols, vol. 3, 30; Raymond Bellour, '". . . Rait": Sign of Utopia', trans. Jeffrey Boyd, in *Roland Barthes*, ed. Badmington, vol. 4, 359; Andrew Brown, *Roland Barthes: The Figures of Writing* (Oxford: Clarendon Press, 1992), 233; Michael Fried, 'Barthes's Punctum', *Critical Inquiry* 31, vol. 3 (2005): 574; Georges Didi-Huberman, 'La Chambre claire-obscure', *Le Magazine littéraire* 482 (January 2009): 88; Kathrin Yacavone, *Benjamin, Barthes and the Singularity of Photography* (London: Continuum, 2012), 142; Jean Narboni, *La Nuit sera noire et blanche: Barthes,* La Chambre claire, *le cinéma* (Paris: Les Prairies Ordinaires / Capricci, 2015), 31.

10 Nathalie Léger, Foreword to MD, x. Léger discusses her editorial work on the diary in more detail in an interview with Valérie Marin La Meslée published as '«Chaque fiche est une figure du chagrin»', *Le Magazine littéraire* 482 (January 2009): 84–6. At one point, Léger remarks that the archive file from which the *Journal de deuil* was assembled is 'the almost "documentary" side' of *La Chambre claire* (86). This is true up to a point, of course, but I want in this chapter of *The Afterlives of Roland Barthes* to examine how the journal documents elements of the *punctum* that are not apparent in *La Chambre claire* itself – the pages of which appear accordingly in a new light.

11 I have discussed this point elsewhere. See Neil Badmington, 'Sighs and Citations', *Times Literary Supplement*, 15 July 2011: 25.

12 Antoine Compagnon, *L'Âge des lettres* (Paris: Gallimard, 2015), 134.

13 Richard Howard's translation does not quite capture a linguistic echo in the French here of the diary's very first reference (on 23 March 1978) to the troublesome project. At that earlier point, Howard gives 'getting work on the book' (MD, 105) for the original 'me mettre au livre' (JD, 114); when the English version of the June entry subsequently offers 'my present efforts of resignation' for 'mes efforts actuels de démission', it misses the etymological connection between 'mettre' and 'démission' which links the comments. The diary regularly uses the term 'maman' (usually abbreviated in the original French text to 'mam.'), but *La Chambre claire* prefers the more formal 'mère'. A touching handwritten note from the period, reproduced in Lebrave's 'La Genèse de *La Chambre claire*' perhaps explains the shift: 'Maman? Vous dites Maman? à votre age? et pour le public?' ('*Maman?* You say *Maman?* at your age? and for the public?') (97). Meanwhile, Barthes explains in a letter to Philippe Sollers on 1 August 1978 that rereading Proust has given him the courage to say 'maman' and not 'mère'. Philippe Sollers, *L'Amitié de Roland Barthes* (Paris: Seuil, 2015), 142–3.

14 MD, 136. Translation modified. There was a brief moment at which, thanks to Severo Sarduy, one of the possible titles for the book about photography was simply *Foto*. See Marty, *Roland Barthes, le métier d'écrire*, 93. For a poignant letter, dated 25 March 1979 and to his long-time friend Philippe Rebeyrol, in which Barthes explains how he imagines the book's being 'linked profoundly to images of *maman*', see AL, 253.

15 The English translation – even the revised Hill and Wang edition of 2010 – omits these dates of composition. It is worth recalling, however, that Lebrave's 'La Genèse de *La Chambre claire*' complicated the book's dates of composition seven years before the *Mourning Diary* came to light. Having consulted the Barthes archives, Lebrave concludes that the author drew upon notes written long before April 1979 when drafting the book. He also reveals a detail that the dates at the end of the

published French text conceal: Barthes was in Urt at the beginning of the writing period, and back in Paris by its end. Meanwhile, Jean Narboni refers in *La Nuit sera noire et blanche* to *Camera Lucida*'s two-year period of 'latency' (9).

16 See the section of *The Preparation of the Novel* entitled '"It Takes"' (PN, 255–7) and the related 'Ça prend' in OC V, 654–6.

17 MD, 112. Translation modified. Curiously, there is no reference specifically to *rice* powder in Wyler's film, although there is a moment at which Alexandra says disapprovingly, of Miss Jordan, 'She's got powder on her nose!' I presume, then, that the French subtitles or dubbing embellished the original English line; alternatively, perhaps Barthes's memory was not entirely accurate. As if remembering *The Little Foxes*, *Camera Lucida* returns near the beginning of its second part to the 'ivory powder box' (64) and 'rice powder' (65) once owned by the author's mother.

18 See Marcel Proust, *The Way by Swann's*, trans. Lydia Davis (Harmondsworth: Penguin, 2002), 47–50.

19 Lillian Hellman, *The Little Foxes* in *Six Plays by Lillian Hellman* (New York: Vintage, 1979), 147–225.

20 MD, 125. Translation modified. For Éric Marty's account of going to see *One Two Two* with Barthes, see *Roland Barthes, le métier d'écrire*, 97–8. Tiphaine Samoyault discusses the Stavisky affair and its notable place in Barthes's youth in her *Roland Barthes: Biographie* (Paris: Seuil, 2015), 108–9.

21 Richard Howard's translation makes the echo of the diary in *Camera Lucida* more exact than it is in the French. While the English uses 'to overwhelm' in each case – 'one detail of the décor overwhelmed me'; 'A detail overwhelms the entirety of my reading' – the French features different verbs: 'un détail de décor me bouleverse' (JD, 136) and 'Un détail emporte toute ma lecture' (OC V, 828).

22 The phrase 'resurrections of the mother' is taken from Antoine Compagnon, 'Writing Mourning', trans. Sam Ferguson, *Textual Practice* 30, vol. 2 (2016): 218. Compagnon's rich essay touches briefly upon Barthes's movement from film to photography as the writing of the diary gives way to *Camera Lucida*, but he does not dwell upon the phenomenon.

23 CL, 3. Translation modified. A handwritten draft of this passage shows the word 'ontologique' crossed out and replaced with 'idiotique'. For a facsimile, see Lebrave, 'La Genèse de *La Chambre claire*', 83.

24 For a related point, made in an essay published in the same year as *Roland Barthes by Roland Barthes*, see 'Leaving the Movie Theater', where the cinematic image is described as 'coalescent (its signified and signifier well melted together), analogical, total, pregnant' (RL, 348; translation modified). Because the signifier and signified coalesce in this manner in the cinema, there can be no gliding, no drifting, no 'magic of the signifier' (SZ, 4).

25 For discussions of Barthes's 'resistance to cinema', see, among others: Ungar, 'Persistence of the Image', 236–49; Dominique Païni, 'La Résistance au cinéma' in *R/B: Roland Barthes*, ed. Marianne Alphant and Nathalie Léger (Paris: Seuil/Centre Pompidou/IMEC, 2002), 116–18; Rachel Gabara, *From Split to Screened Selves: French and Francophone Autobiography in the Third Person* (Stanford, CA: Stanford University Press, 2006), 65–7.

26 GV, 357. Translation modified. For an overview of the commissioning and editing of *La Chambre claire*, see Narboni, *La nuit sera noire et blanche*. Narboni, who edited Barthes's book, notes at one point that *Cahiers du cinéma* first approached Barthes about the project early in the autumn of 1977 (37).

27 GV, 359. Translation modified. In *The Preparation of the Novel*, Barthes states that the way in which 'film artificially distorts the noeme of photography' leads him to 'attach more importance to photography' than to cinema (PN, 71).

28 Éric Marty, *Roland Barthes, la littérature et le droit à la mort* (Paris: Seuil, 2010), 41. Marty's point about the picture's bringing the journal to an end emerges from the fact that the diary breaks off, suspends itself, for a while not long after Barthes finds the photograph. *L'Âge des lettres*, Antoine Compagnon's memoir of his friendship with Barthes, describes the discovery of the Winter Garden photograph as the turning point in the writing of *Camera Lucida*. Until that moment, he recalls, Barthes had been struggling to find anything original to say about photography (134).

29 Léger, '«Chaque fiche est une figure du chagrin»': 85; Valérie Stiénon and Laurent Demoulin, 'Roland Barthes, ethnographe de lui-même: fiches, carnets et notes inédits', *Culture: le magazine culturel de l'Université de Liège*, June 2009: 2.

30 See, for example: Jean-Michel Rabaté, 'Le Roman de Roland Barthes' in *Barthes après Barthes: une actualité en questions*, ed. Catherine Coquio and Régis Salado (Pau: Publications de l'Université de Pau, 1993), 7–14; Chapter 5 of Nancy M. Shawcross, *Roland Barthes on Photography: The Critical Tradition in Perspective* (Gainesville, FL: University Press of Florida, 1997); Victor Burgin, 'Re-reading *Camera Lucida*' in *Roland Barthes*, ed. Badmington, vol. 3, 160; Batchen, 'Palinode', 10; Margaret Iversen, 'What is a Photograph?', in *Photography Degree Zero*, ed. Batchen, 57; Carol Mavor, 'Black and Blue: The Shadows of *Camera Lucida*', in *Photography Degree Zero*, ed. Batchen, 214; Marianne Alphant, 'Presque un roman' in *R/B*, ed. Alphant and Léger, 125; Michael Moriarty, *Roland Barthes* (Cambridge: Polity, 1991), 198; Brown, *Roland Barthes: The Figures of Writing*, 279; Bernard Comment, 'De la pensée comme autofiction', *Le Magazine littéraire* 482 (January 2009): 60; Laurent Nunez, 'Vie nouvelle, roman virtuel', *Le Magazine littéraire* 482 (January 2009): 75; Éric Marty, *Roland Barthes, le métier d'écrire*, 68; Marie Gil, *Roland Barthes: Au lieu de la vie* (Paris: Flammarion, 2012), 477; Claude Coste, *Bêtise de Barthes* (Paris: Klincksieck, 2011), 154; Compagnon, *L'Âge des lettres*, 135.

31 Antoine Compagnon suggests in 'Writing Mourning' that the discovery is moved from June to November 'for All Saints' Day' (215). While the day in question does indeed fall in November, and while it is one associated with death, it is not clear to me how Barthes's 'one November evening' can be read specifically as a reference to All Saints' Day. In his more recent memoir, *L'Âge des lettres*, Compagnon is even more specific, proposing that Barthes gives a date of 1 November in *Camera Lucida* for the discovery of the photo (135), but I can see no textual evidence to support this claim.

32 MD, 148. Translation modified. For a selection of fiches about photography and Barthes's mother from the period which were not included in the *Mourning Diary*, see Lebrave, 'La Genèse de *La Chambre claire*', especially 101–4.

33 For discussions of Barthes's friendship with Maupomé, who was a radio producer, see Marty, *Roland Barthes, le métier d'écrire*, 75 and Samoyault, *Roland Barthes: Biographie*, 666.

34 The Hill and Wang translation contains a central photographic section in which an image of Barthes at his desk on 25 April 1979 (when he is writing *Camera Lucida*) shows the Winter Garden photograph upon the wall. Although it is impossible to see the details of the picture, I think that its presence and the record of its examination in the *Mourning Diary* put an end to the speculation, offered by both Diana Knight and Margaret Olin before the journal was published, that the Winter Garden photograph never actually existed. See Diana Knight, 'Roland Barthes, or the Woman Without a Shadow', in *Writing the Image After Roland Barthes*, ed. Rabaté, 138; Margaret Olin, 'Touching Photographs: Roland Barthes's "Mistaken" Identification', *Representations* 80 (2002): 108. The photographic section found in the Hill and Wang translation is in neither the original French edition nor the British translation published (without a subtitle) as *Mourning Diary* (London: Notting Hill Books, 2011). Kathrin Yacavone adds a fascinating twist to the tale of the Winter Garden photograph when she points out (*Benjamin, Barthes and the Singularity of Photography*, 164–6) that the image was actually visible in two pictures of Barthes which were taken during his lifetime, one of which even appeared on the cover of *Le Grain de la voix* in 1981.

35 CL, 94–6. Winnicott's discussion of a fear of that which has already occurred – linked in *Camera Lucida* to the death of Henriette Barthes entombed in the photograph of her as a child – is first mentioned in the *Mourning Diary* some time *before* the discovery of the Winter Garden photograph (MD, 122). What the publication of the diary makes apparent, then, is that the *actual* death of Barthes's mother – not her passing as anticipated by the photograph – prompted him to consider the significance of Winnicott's account. To put matters differently, Winnicott had marked mourning before the finding of the picture led to the *punctum* of Time;

this *punctum* therefore has roots beyond cinema and the photographic image – in Barthes's reading of Winnicott. Pursuing this point further would require another chapter (one not focussed on mourning, film and photography).

36 CL, 60. For a fine discussion of *Camera Lucida*'s palinodic structure, see Jean-Claude Milner, *Le Pas philosophique de Roland Barthes* (Lagrasse: Éditions Verdier, 2003), 69–70. The publication in 2007 of the teaching notes from the 'discours amoureux' seminar of 1974–6 revealed that Barthes had been aware of the phenomenon of the palinode some years before the writing of *Camera Lucida*; see the session dated 8 January 1976 (DA, 319–44), where the roots in Plato are explored.

37 Jean Narboni calls Time 'the principal character' in *Camera Lucida* (*La Nuit sera noire et blanche*, 58).

38 Barthes's French (JD, 184; OC V, 828) features 'quelque chose' in each case.

39 CL, 51. Derek Attridge points out ('Obtuse, Sharp Meaning', 79) that this moment echoes a phrase in the earlier essay on the Eisenstein stills: 'we cannot describe the obtuse meaning' (RF, 55).

40 CL, 115–16. Translation modified. I have inserted Barthes's French (OC V, 882) to show that the linguistic echoes of the journal mark his original phrasing.

41 He did, however, mention the same strange scene from *Casanova* during the session of *The Preparation of the Novel* which took place on 10 March 1979 (PN, 106) – a date which was towards the end of the period covered by the *Mourning Diary*, but just before the beginning of the writing of *Camera Lucida* on 15 April. This latter fact makes Barthes's introduction of the Fellini reference in *The Preparation of the Novel* somewhat puzzling: 'I've said this elsewhere,' he begins, even though, by the dating provided by Barthes himself at the end of *La Chambre claire*, he has yet to start the book on photography.

42 CL, 116. Richard Howard makes the shift from film to photography more dramatic than it is in the French by inserting an ellipsis immediately before 'At which moment'.

43 Details of the text's controversial publication history can be found in the previous chapter of this book.

44 Antoine Compagnon, *Écrire la vie: Montaigne, Stendhal, Proust*, course at the Collège de France, 2009. Text taken from the summary of the lectures of 10 and 17 March 2009 given in the online *annuaire* of the Collège available at http://annuaire-cdf.revues.org/200 (consulted 22 February 2016).

45 Etymologically, a 'detail', as Jacques Derrida has noted, is something that is cut out. The link between the cut (*la taille*), size (also *la taille*) and the detail (*le détail*) cuts regularly into Derrida's *The Truth in Painting*, trans. Geoff Bennington and Ian McLeod (Chicago and London: University of Chicago Press, 1987). See, for instance, 120–1.

4

The 'Inkredible' Roland Barthes

'Frequently he exclaimed:
– "Charming! . . . Very pretty!"
Then he would begin writing again, dipping his pen in the ink-horn he was holding in his left hand.'

Gustave Flaubert, *Madame Bovary*.[1]

'Inkidents'

History repeats itself, but not quite as Marx imagined.

It is well known that, on 25 February 1980, just two days after delivering the final lecture of his course about the preparation of the novel at the Collège de France, Roland Barthes was involved in the accident in Paris that would bring his life to an end. Returning from a lunch organized by Jack Lang on a day that he described in his daily planner as 'cold' and 'golden yellow', Barthes stopped to cross the road at 44 rue des Écoles.[2] He was on his way, according to Tiphaine Samoyault, to the Collège, 'not to give a lecture there, but to sort out the technical details of his next seminar, which he intend[ed] to devote to Proust and photography, and for which he need[ed] a projector'.[3] Stepping into the street, Barthes was hit by a truck. He was taken to the Salpêtrière hospital, where he died on 26 March.

This has become a somewhat familiar tale – even if Samoyault's wonderful recent biography has added nuance to the narrative, and Laurent Binet's irreverent counterfactual novel *La Septième fonction du langage* has reimagined the event as an assassination attempt prompted by Barthes's involvement in a conspiracy aimed at world domination.[4] What has received much less attention, however, is an accident in which Barthes was caught up almost two years earlier. Quite unlike the tragedy of February 1980, the earlier incident had a decidedly farcical quality, and thus inverted Karl Marx's famous remark about the tendency of history to repeat itself, first as tragedy, and only later as farce.[5] Barthes described the accident to the audience of his course on the Neutral on 11 March 1978, but his account was not actually published until 2002, when *The Neutral* became the first volume of his lecture notes from the Collège de France to appear in print.

> Thursday, March 9 [1978], fine afternoon, I go out to buy some colours (Sennelier inks) → bottles of pigment: following my taste for the names (golden yellow, sky blue, brilliant green, purple, sun yellow, cartham pink – a rather intense pink), I buy sixteen bottles. In putting them away, I knock one over: in sponging up, I make a new mess: little domestic complications . . . And now, I am going to give you the official name of the spilled colour, a name printed on the small bottle (as on the others vermilion, turquoise, etc.): it was the colour called Neutral (obviously I had opened this bottle first to see what kind of colour was this Neutral about which I am going to be speaking for thirteen weeks). Well, I was both punished and disappointed: punished because Neutral spatters and stains (it's a type of dull gray-black); disappointed because Neutral is a color like the others, and for sale (therefore, Neutral is not unmarketable): the unclassifiable is classified → all the more reason for us to go back to discourse, which, at least, cannot say what the Neutral is.
>
> (N, 48; translation modified)[6]

Barthes's second course at the Collège de France is, in other words, coloured early in its unfolding by an incident involving ink – an 'inkident', if you will. Although the spillage comes out of the blue in *The Neutral*, I want to suggest in this chapter that it is by no means an isolated moment, for it seems to me that Barthes's vast, diverse *oeuvre* is covered with what might be called 'ink blots', by which I mean points at which an obsession with the materials and materiality of writing pools and marks the page.[7] If Barthes is a scribbler, as Andrew Brown has argued so persuasively, then, as is so often the case with scribblers, he has ink on his hands – or maybe his cuffs, as in Charles's Bovary's vision of his daughter.[8] (Indeed, when Éric Marty, Antoine Compagnon and Philippe Sollers remember their friendship with Barthes, they all find themselves specifically recalling his blue ink.)[9] I cannot possibly hope to soak up all of Barthes's ink blots with the pages of this book, so I will call forth just a few notable spillages in order to open my ink quest.

In 1970, a section of the euphoric *Empire of Signs* celebrated the delights of a Japanese stationery shop, the 'site and catalogue of things necessary to writing' (ES, 85). *The Neutral* would later record Barthes's unflagging 'drive to purchase' (N, 150), and this compulsion clearly figures in *Empire of Signs*, where he details with great love and care how pens, brushes, inkstones, paper and techniques of inscription change with the movement from West to East:

> Everything, in the instrumentation, is directed toward the paradox of an irreversible and fragile writing, which is simultaneously, contradictorily, incision and glissade; papers of a thousand kinds, many of which hint, in their texture powdered with pale straws, with crushed stems, at their fibrous origin; notebooks whose pages are folded double, like those of a book which has not been cut so that writing moves across a luxury of surfaces and never runs, ignorant of the metonymic impregnation of the right and wrong side of the page (it is traced above a void): palimpsest, the erased stroke which thereby becomes a secret, is impossible. As for the brush (passed across a faintly moistened inkstone), it has its gestures, as if it were the finger; but whereas our old pens knew only clogging or loosening and could only, moreover, scratch the paper always in the same direction, the brush can slide, twist, lift off, the stroke being made, so to speak, in the volume of the air; it has the carnal, lubrified flexibility of the hand.
>
> (ES, 86)

'The felt-tipped pen, of Japanese origin,' he concludes, 'has taken up where the brush leaves off: this stylo is not an improvement of the point, itself a product of the pen (of steel or of cartilage), its immediate ancestry is that of the ideogram' (ES, 87).

Three years later, far from Japan, two much larger ink blots emerged. In September 1973, Barthes was interviewed for *Le Monde* by Jean-Louis de Rambures. During the course of their conversation, Barthes revealed his fondness for a specific type of shopping:

> I would say . . . that I have an almost obsessive relation to writing instruments. I often switch from one pen to another just for the pleasure of it. I try out new ones. Besides, I have far too many pens – I don't know what to do with all of them. And yet, as soon as I see them, I start craving them. I cannot keep myself from buying them.
>
> When felt-tipped pens first appeared in the stores, I loved them a lot. (The fact that they were originally from Japan was not, I admit, displeasing to me.)

> Since then I've become tired of them, because the point flattens out too quickly. I've also used nibs – not the 'Sergeant-Major', which is too dry, but softer nibs, like the 'J'. In short, I've tried everything ... except Bics, with which I feel absolutely no affinity. I would even say, a bit nastily, that there is a 'Bic style', which is really just for churning out cheap copy, writing that merely transcribes thoughts.
>
> In the end, I always return to fine ink pens. The essential thing is that they can produce that soft, smooth writing I absolutely hold dear.[10]

Somewhat strangely, perhaps, the interview made no reference whatever to a text entitled 'Variations sur l'écriture' which Barthes had written earlier that same year. Like *The Neutral*, 'Variations' would not reveal its ink blot until some years after Barthes's death, for it remained unpublished until the posthumous appearance of the *Oeuvres complètes*.[11] This charming piece, which Marie Gil is right to call 'little known', approached a term familiar to readers of Barthes in a strikingly different way:[12]

> The first object that I encountered in my past work was writing, but back then I understood the word in a metaphorical sense: it was for me a variety of literary style, as part of the collective in a way, the totality of linguistic features through which a writer assumes the historical responsibility of his or her form and relates through his or her work to a certain ideology of language. Today, twenty years on, by a sort of return towards the body, it's the manual meaning of the word that I want to approach, it is 'scription' (the muscular act of writing, of tracing letters) which interests me.
>
> (OC IV, 267).

'Variations' accordingly turns its gaze to the histories and implications of the human hand leaving a signifying trace upon a surface set aside for inscription. Five years before chromophilia would lead him to splash out on sixteen bottles of Sennelier ink in one afternoon, Barthes devoted a section of his text to colour:

> To be examined: coloured writings – the few of them that exist. Colour is impulse; we are afraid to sign our messages with it; that is why we write black [*nous écrivons noir*]; we only allow ourselves well-ordered, flatly emblematic exceptions: blue for distinction, red for correction. Any change of colour [*saute de couleur*] is particularly incongruous: can you imagine yellow, pink, or even grey missives? Books in red-brown, in forest green, in Indian blue? And yet, who knows if the meaning of the words would not be changed?
>
> (OC IV, 302)

In its narration of the history of writing, 'Variations' has much in common with a far shorter text by Barthes entitled 'Writing' which first appeared in 1976 as the preface to Roger Druet and Herman Grégoire's *La Civilisation de l'écriture*. The piece, which runs to fewer than three pages, opens with the following remarkable sentence:

> I have often wondered why I liked to write (manually, I mean), to such a degree that the often thankless effort of intellectual work has on many occasions been redeemed in my eyes by the pleasure of having before me (like the handyman's bench) a fine sheet of paper and a good pen: at the same time as I am thinking about what I am to write (this is what is happening at this very moment), I feel my hand acting, turning, connecting, going down, lifting up and very often, as corrections are made, striking something out or breaking up a line, expanding the space into the margin and in this way, with slender, apparently functional strokes (letters), constructing a space that is quite simply the space of art: I am an artist not through crafting an object but more fundamentally because, in writing, my body thrills to tracing something out, to rhythmically incising a blank surface (blankness offering infinite possibility).
>
> (VFG, 168)[13]

Although 'Variations sur l'écriture' remained unpublished in Barthes's lifetime, it made a brief, ghostly appearance on 9 February 1980 in the course on the preparation of the novel, when, prompted by a marginal mnemonic that read 'My text on writing', Barthes discussed the relationship between a writer's style, 'obsessive care (or so it appears to others) taken over which pen, what kind of paper, etc. to use', and the way in which he or she formed letters upon the page (PN, 265). Those who deride such things as 'only an absurd extravagance', he adds, are 'foolish' (PN, 265). As so often in his later years, Barthes turned to Proust as an example:

> [T]he whole of Proust's oeuvre, its wordiness, the almost infinite character of his sentences, the abundant correspondence, the appearance of his handwriting suggests that Proust wrote very quickly by hand, and the whole of his oeuvre owes much to that muscular facility. Proust was aware (letter to Robert Dreyfus, 1888) that he wrote *at a gallop*.[14]

'We could risk defining the work in general terms,' Barthes concluded, '*as a kinetic relationship between the head and the hand*' (PN, 265).

One final ink blot. *Roland Barthes by Roland Barthes*, book-ended in its original form by elegant handwritten statements which recalled those of the earlier *Empire of Signs* (ES, 13, 17, 23 and 37, for example), reveals the obsessive care with which the narrator constructed his working environments:

> Another *Argo*: I have two work spaces, one in Paris, the other in the country. Between them there is no common object, for nothing is ever carried back and forth. Yet these sites are identical. Why? Because the arrangement of tools (paper, pens, desks, clocks, ashtrays) is the same: it is the structure of the space which constitutes its identity. This private phenomenon would suffice to shed some light on structuralism: the system prevails over the very being of objects.[15]

Elsewhere the text incorporates photographs of Barthes surrounded by the materials of writing and painting, and a list of passions that includes 'pens, writing nibs' (RB, 116; translation modified). The elusive narrator even manages to reel in a form of ink that had left a smudge upon *Mythologies* almost twenty years earlier: 'I am writing this day after day; it takes, it sets: the cuttlefish produces its ink.'[16]

Ink: Well?

Why should these 'inkidents' matter? Why have I allowed them to blot my copybook? Why does it matter if, as Chantal Thomas puts it, 'Barthes makes visible the pleasure of writing'?[17] It seems to me that the interview given to *Le Monde* in 1973 secretes an answer to these questions. At first glance, Jean-Louis de Rambures's incipit appears to be a little bland: 'Do you,' he asks, 'have a method of working?' (GV, 177). After giving three brisk sentences in response, however, Barthes turns his attention to the implications of the question itself. There is, he notes, 'a kind of censorship which considers this topic taboo, under the pretext that it would be futile for a writer or an intellectual to talk about his writing, his daily schedule, or his desk' (GV, 177). And then, recalling the work of *Mythologies*, he adds:

> When a great many people agree that a problem is insignificant, that usually means it is not. Insignificance is the true locus of significance. This should

never be forgotten. That is why it seems so important to me to ask a writer about his writing habits, putting things on the most material level, I would even say the most minimal level possible. This is an anti-mythological action: it contributes to the overturning of that old myth which continues to present language as the instrument of thought, inwardness, passion, or whatever, and consequently presents writing as a simple instrumental practice.

(GV, 177)

I want to argue in this chapter that Barthes's many blots are the marks of this 'anti-mythological action' at work. Those who take the time to gaze into the pools of ink found in his work will see *doxa* dissolving.

Resistance to the myth which makes language the expressive instrument of thought runs through Barthes's texts – or, to be more precise, in texts written by Barthes after his discovery of Ferdinand de Saussure's *Course in General Linguistics*. *Sade, Fourier, Loyola*, for instance, denounces 'the old modern myth according to which language is merely the docile and *insignificant* instrument for the serious things that occur in the spirit, the heart or the soul' (SFL, 39). *A Lover's Discourse*, meanwhile, spurns the advances of what it calls 'the illusion of expressivity' (LD, 98), and *Sollers Writer* shines light upon the way in which a text like *H* halts the notion that language is merely 'used to transmit ideas or information' (SW, 84). In 'Variations sur l'écriture' lie the playful words, 'Writing, expression of personality? Really? I myself have three writings, according to which I write texts, take notes, or correspond' (OC IV, 280), while a letter to Michel Butor dated 2 March 1962 denounces Robert Kanters as an 'idiot' who 'believes that literature serves to *express* something' (AL, 188).

But it is in the posthumously published course on the Neutral, I think, that the connection between ink blots and 'anti-mythological action' becomes particularly clear, particularly caustic. This amounts to saying that *The Neutral* is the inkiest of Barthes's inky texts – a fact illustrated beautifully by the design of the cover of the English translation published by Columbia University Press, which features against a plain white background a large bottle of Sennelier 'Neutre' ink.

On a very simple level, the course of 1977–8 refers repeatedly to the materials and materiality of inscription; so much so, in fact, that certain of its passages appear to have seeped back through time from the second part of *The Preparation of the Novel*. Almost two months after the tale of the spilt Sennelier ink, for instance, in a short subsection entitled 'Private Rites', Barthes returned to the interview of 1973 in which he had discussed his 'almost obsessive relation to writing instruments' with Jean-Louis de Rambures, and which had been reprinted in the latter's *Comment travaillent les écrivains*:[18]

> One specific example of private rite: the secret ritual the writer has to follow in order to write, recent book by Rambures → amused irony of the *petite presse* (Pivot) in front of the manias of the writer (fountain pens, places, etc.): the idea that it's crazy and that it's not worth the trouble: futile, derisory, together with affectionate and superior recognition: these writers, what do you expect from them?
>
> (N, 123)

In response to such a question, Barthes turns to an anecdote recounted by Gustav Janouch:

> My friend Ernst Lederer wrote poems with especially bright blue ink on engraved sheets of hand-made paper. I told Kafka about it. He said, 'That's quite right. Every magician has his own rites. Haydn for example only composed in a ceremonially powdered wig. Writing is, after all, a kind of invocation of spirits.
>
> (N, 124)

Elsewhere in the course, shortly after discussing the writing habits of Proust and Swedenborg, Barthes once again records his commitment to his fountain pen when describing the 'slight obsessionality' involved in 'attachment to minor belongings' (N, 144); this, I presume, is the same pen that later in the same session he places at the top of a list of objects that he would be unable to surrender if performing 'an act of self-destitution' intended to leave him with 'only a minimum number of objects: nothing in double' (N, 150).[19]

Beyond these basic niblets, however, I want to propose that *The Neutral* more generally sees the link between ink blots and 'anti-mythological action' taking on a particularly caustic, vivid form. The moment at which things suddenly became clear to me – the moment at which the ink of the cuttlefish began to disperse and leave clear water – occurs within minutes of *The Neutral* setting off on its way. At the very beginning of the first session, Barthes works through the routine practicalities of the teaching, distributes 'a list of the texts whose reading, in various ways, has punctuated the preparation of this course' (N, 1), recites four epigraphs (from Joseph de Maistre, Tolstoy, Rousseau and

Lao-tzu), and then at last, in sentences which recall the 'Exemption from Meaning' section of *Empire of Signs* (ES, 73), outlines what he calls 'the object of this course, its argument':

> I define the Neutral as that which outplays [*déjoue*] the paradigm, or rather I call Neutral everything that baffles the paradigm. For I am not trying to define a word; I am trying to name a thing: I gather under a name, which here is the Neutral.
>
> The paradigm, what is that? It's the opposition of two virtual terms from which, in speaking, I actualize one to produce meaning.
>
> (N, 6–7)

That, at least, is how matters are presented in the printed version of *The Neutral*. In the original oral context of the lecture theatre, however, something rather strange occurred during the reciting of the four epigraphs. Barthes begins with the long passage by Joseph de Maistre, which he calls 'le premier' (the first), and then moves on to Tolstoy, which he calls 'un second' quotation. When Barthes finishes the account of Prince Andrei's fall on the battlefield, the recording of the lecture reveals that he introduces the next epigraph, by Jean-Jacques Rousseau, as the 'quatrième' (fourth) quotation. A long pause some moments later perhaps marks Barthes's recognition of his error, but he proceeds to the passage from Rousseau's *The Reveries of the Solitary Walker* without correcting himself. He then moves on to his concluding epigraph, by Lao-tzu, which he introduces, without numbering, simply as 'le dernier texte' (the final text).

Keen listeners in the audience at the Collège de France on 18 February 1978 might have wondered, therefore, if Barthes had forgotten his third epigraph, overlooked a third name in his scene-setting list (first, second, fourth, final). Freud devoted many pages of his *Psychopathology of Everyday Life* to the ways in which slips of the tongue signify, and I think that the curious parapraxis in Barthes's introductory lecture points towards a name which might well have been used to set the discussion of the Neutral on its way.[20] That unspoken name surfaces moments after the reading of the lines by Lao-tzu, in fact, as if it were returning from repression. Expanding on his propositions about the paradigm, Barthes says: 'Put another way, according to the perspective of Saussure, to which, on this matter, I remain faithful, the paradigm is the wellspring of meaning; where there is meaning, there is paradigm, and where there is paradigm (opposition), there is meaning' (N, 7). Preliminaries aside, here lies the first proper name of *The Neutral*: Saussure.²¹ In addition, a certain fidelity towards this name is professed.

Although the *Course in General Linguistics* does not appear anywhere in the list of formative texts that Barthes has just distributed to his audience at the Collège de France, I think that it is penned there in invisible ink, sympathetically; one course courses through another, each of them posthumously published.²² Ink, in fact, is the key to understanding this, for minutes after recounting the tale of the spilled Sennelier 'Neutral' on 11 March 1978, Barthes makes an explicit pledge of allegiance: 'I am "Saussurian" = not a "faith" but a willingness to have recourse to Saussurian models in order "to understand" [to speak]' (N, 54; translation modified; interpolation in square brackets in original). What if this article of faith flowed freely from the spillage that has just been announced in the most linguistic of Barthes's courses at the Collège de France?²³ What if Roland Barthes were Saussurian in his repeated references to the materials and materiality of writing?

Course: Ink, general linguistics

'I had just read Saussure.' These words appear in the second preface to *Mythologies*, which Barthes added in 1970 to reflect upon the original time and tenor of the book:

> This book has a double theoretical framework: on the one hand, an ideological critique bearing on the language of so-called mass culture; on the other, a first attempt to analyse semiologically the mechanics of this language. I had just read Saussure and as a result acquired the conviction that by treating 'collective representations' as sign-systems, one might hope to go further than the pious show of unmasking them and account in detail for the mystification which transforms petit-bourgeois culture into a universal nature.
>
> (M, xvii)

Barthes's reading of Saussure – at the suggestion of Algirdas Greimas – makes *Mythologies* possible by clearing a space for the science of semiology that Saussure had only been able to imagine and, more specifically, by offering a way to theorize the dangers of naturalizing meaning by seeing the relationship between signifier and signified as eternal.²⁴

But that is by no means the end of the tale. As Tiphaine Samoyault puts it: 'This reading [of Saussure] ... is fundamental to structuring the years of writing which follow.'[25] I would go one step further, in fact, and propose that the discovery of Saussure – the 'revelation of the Sign', in Jean-Claude Milner's suggestive phrase – is an intellectual discovery more significant to Barthes's development than the formative encounters with Gide, Marx, Sartre, Brecht and the various other figures of influence described so vividly by Samoyault in her account of Barthes's life.[26] For me, it is Saussure who makes Barthes 'Barthes'; without that encounter, without that revelation, there would be no sign, no semiology, and, crucially, no signifier in the *oeuvre*.[27]

The relationship to Saussure's work changes over time, of course, particularly as the mood moves from structuralism to poststructuralism. *Elements of Semiology* (1964), for instance, with its sombre and scientific exposition of the sign, is a world away from *S/Z* (1970), with its 'magic of the signifier' (SZ, 4); Barthes had, as several of the texts gathered posthumously in *The Semiotic Challenge* confirm, evidently read Derrida and come to recognize that the signifier defers the signified.[28] And even in the immediate wake of the discovery of Saussure, Barthes seemed unsure when writing the theoretical 'Myth Today' essay which concludes *Mythologies* how extensive and explicit he should be about the debt: as Tiphaine Samoyault reveals, 'five notes on Saussure are deleted between the second manuscript version (which still carries the title "Esquisse d'une mythologie") and the published text'.[29]

But even though Barthes's work developed from the obedient Saussurean sign to the wild signifier, and even though a rejected fragment written in 1974 for *Roland Barthes by Roland Barthes* noted with mocking despair that delegates at the Congrès internationale de sémiologie in Milan 'seemed to believe that to each signifier there corresponds a signified' (LA, 299), evidently he remained persuaded in his later years by *something* in Saussure's work. Why else would he continue to use the vocabulary of the *Course in General Linguistics*, particularly the term 'signifier', in later works such as *S/Z*, *Roland Barthes by Roland Barthes* and *Empire of Signs*? Why else would he, as I have already noted, describe himself as a 'Saussurian' in March 1978? An answer to these questions is easier to discern in the light of the posthumous publications, and above all in the inkiness of *The Neutral*. Scrying is sometimes associated with visions of death – Borges's 'The Mirror of Ink' comes to mind – but occulted in the ink of *The Neutral* I glimpse the living sign of Saussure drifting towards me.[30]

In the section of the *Course in General Linguistics* entitled 'Linguistic Value', Saussure makes the ground-breaking proposition upon which so much poststructuralist theory has depended:

> Psychologically our thought – apart from its expression in words – is only a shapeless and indistinct mass. Philosophers and linguists have always agreed in recognizing that without the help of signs we would be unable to make a clear-cut, consistent distinction between two ideas. Without language, thought is a vague, uncharted nebula. There are no pre-existing ideas, and nothing is distinct before the appearance of language.[31]

The sign, in other words, is the condition of genuine thought, not its instrument, medium, expression or echo. Language is not a nomenclature which follows humbly behind thought, adding labels to what was already in mind; language, rather, forms thoughts and determines what it is possible to think. 'Whether we take the signified or the signifier,' Saussure writes, 'language has neither ideas nor sounds that existed before the linguistic system, but only conceptual and phonic differences that have issued from the system' (120).

That, as I see it, is Saussure's great discovery, the move which makes a world of difference. In this respect, I do not quite agree with Jonathan Culler when he makes the distinction between *langue* and *parole* the starting point for understanding Barthes and the study of signs.[32] *Langue* and *parole* certainly matter, of course, but only up to a point, I think: they become less relevant as Barthes moves away from what he would go on to call his 'structuralist phase' (RB, 103). The propositions in the chapter of the *Course in General Linguistics* entitled 'Linguistic Value' are far more resonant, far more significant, in Barthes's work. They are also, I want to suggest, the theoretical principles to which Barthes is faithful ('I am "Saussurian"') when he sets his interest in the materials and materiality of writing in an 'anti-mythological' struggle against the endoxal, idealist, expressive model of language.

In the vocabulary of *The Neutral*, I read Barthes's 'ink blots' as marks of a desire for a *non-arrogant* theory of language. Arrogance is one of the themes that arises regularly in the course of 1977–8.[33] It appears as early as the opening lecture, in fact, just moments after Barthes has affirmed his fidelity to Saussure.

Continuing his discussion of the paradigm, of opposition, Barthes notes: 'temptation to suspend, to thwart, to elude the paradigm, its menacing pressure, its arrogance → to exempt meaning → this polymorphous field of paradigm, of conflict avoidance = the Neutral' (N, 7). The reference here is brief and relatively undeveloped, but Barthes returned to the theme a little over three months later, when he named a whole section of the course 'Arrogance'. Detail and definition are now provided:

> Under the word 'arrogance', I gather all the (linguistic) 'gestures' that work as discourses of intimidation, of subjection, of domination, of assertion, of haughtiness: that claim the authority, the guarantee of a dogmatic truth or of a demand that doesn't think, that doesn't conceive of the other's desire.
>
> One is assaulted by the arrogance of discourse everywhere there is faith, certitude, will-to-possess, to dominate, be it by means of an insistent demand: the inventory of arrogant discourses would be endless, from the political discourse to the advertising discourse, from the discourse of science to that of the 'scene'. We will not draw up this inventory, this typology; it would be more useful to ask under what difficult conditions a discourse manages not to be arrogant (cf. *in fine*, on writing).
>
> (N, 152)

I am struck by how the contemplation of non-arrogance brings close to itself a consideration of writing. When the course imagines an alternative to 'discourses of intimidation, of subjection, of domination, of assertion, of haughtiness', it pictures *writing*. Later in the same session of *The Neutral*, in fact, Barthes explicitly pursues the connection. 'Can writing be arrogant?' he asks in the opening line of a subsection entitled, quite simply, 'Writing' (N, 162). 'My immediate (partial) answer,' he continues, 'is: Writing is the very discourse that unfailingly baffles the arrogance of discourse → I have not (or not yet) the conceptual means to theorize this position (that would suppose a "what is writing?")' (N, 162). In the light of 'Variations sur l'écriture', which five years earlier began, as I noted earlier, by approaching the term 'écriture' in a rather different manner, I find the term 'writing' undecidable at this point in *The Neutral*. Which shade of the signifier does Barthes intend here? Is he referring to what 'Variations sur l'écriture' calls 'the metaphorical meaning', or is it 'the manual sense of the word' that raises its hand here? Might it even, in keeping with the non-dualistic spirit of *The Neutral*, be appropriate to hear both possibilities at the same time, to suspend the demand to choose and to come down confidently on one side or the other?

I have no desire to settle these questions with a spilled, spurred solution, but I should like to consider how and why 'the manual sense of the word' matters, both at this specific moment and elsewhere in *The Neutral*. How might an attention to 'the muscular act of writing, of tracing letters' baffle arrogance? How do Roland Barthes's ink blots smudge or suspend 'discourses of intimidation, of subjection, of domination, of haughtiness'?

An answer lies in the work of Saussure, whose theories, I think, are once again penned sympathetically in invisible ink at the point in *The Neutral* where Barthes asks if writing can be arrogant. The brief discussion that follows the question concludes with an account of the activity of inscription:

> The writer: a *Draufgänger* ... someone carried away, a breakneck, but not arrogant → a drive that generate a stubbornness in practice, not in conviction, in idea: to believe in the importance of what one writes, not of what one thinks → therefore: not loyalty to the idea, but persistence of a practice = what the writer calls 'working' (in his intransitive use of the verb): word of every writer = the last word of Michelet at Hyères before dying: *Laboremus* (no mystique of work ≠ lucid submission to the persistence of language).
>
> (N, 162–3)

In the emphasis upon 'the importance of what one writes, not of what one thinks', and in the subsequent outlawing of 'loyalty to the idea', I glimpse an inkling of Saussure's challenge to the idealism of the traditional, referential model of meaning. And I read that very challenge – in which the sign is neither expressive nor in the service of the individual – as a glancing blow to a remarkably *arrogant* account of language. If the linguistic sign, as common sense would have it, is merely a secondary expression of a preceding idea, then the human being dominates language, calls it close and directs it according to his or her prior intentions. Thought precedes and proceeds as the great dictator. It is precisely this arrogance, this 'will-to-possess', that Saussure's theory of language calls into question. What the *Course in General Linguistics* describes, particularly in the piercing chapter on value, is a human subject whose thoughts are shaped by language, not labelled later by it. Language, that 'social fact' which baffles possession, is where meaning resides.[34]

In his description of the linguistic sign, Saussure, it seems to me, touches upon the desire for the Neutral articulated by Barthes, with its pursuit of 'that which outplays [*déjoue*] the paradigm'. Barthes's many ink blots, meanwhile, accomplish a similar unsettling. Their 'anti-mythological action' involves their suspension of an anthropocentric account, an *arrogant* account, of meaning. Ink reveals, to those who stare long enough into its pools, that writing is not the expression of a pre-existing meaning; sense, rather, takes shape in inscription. By writing repeatedly about the sheer materiality of writing, by 'putting things on the most material level', Barthes signs a commitment to Saussure that works against *doxa*. The 'almost obsessive relation to writing instruments', that is to say, sedates the arrogance of idealism: ink, as matter, matters; there is significance in its shades, its smudges, its spillages. This, for me, is why Barthes's ink blots deserve detailed attention, especially now that the blots have grown and become more noticeable with the posthumous publication of texts such as *The Neutral* and 'Variations sur l'écriture'. To ignore Barthes's ink, to make it invisible or wipe it away with a sweeping hand, is to miss a movement against myth.

Plumes

There are, of course, risks.

My commitment in this chapter to what I have called 'ink blots' could be misread as an effete re-inscription of a memorable moment in Heidegger's *Parmenides*. Having proposed that 'the hand is, together with the word, the essential distinction of man', Heidegger immediately insists that '[n]o animal has a hand, and a hand never originates from a paw or a claw or talon'.[35] Several lines later, after stressing that 'the word as script is handwriting', the text points an accusing finger at the way in which 'modern man writes "with" the typewriter' (80):

> This 'history' of the kinds of writing is one of the main reasons for the increasing destruction of the word. The latter no longer comes and goes by means of the writing hand, the properly acting hand, but by means of the mechanical forces it releases. The typewriter tears writing from the essential realm of the hand, i.e., the realm of the word. The word itself turns into something 'typed'.
>
> (81)

When this key shift takes place, Heidegger adds, 'a transformation occur[s] in the relation of Being to man' (85), and the latter is 'plunged into an eminent oblivion of Being' (86).

My interest in Barthes's 'ink blots' is not rooted in a Heideggerian nostalgia for 'the essential realm of the hand', for an authentically and elegantly human antidote to contemporary Western patterns of writing, where pen and paper are often seen as arcane.[36] As Jacques Derrida pointed out in one of his late texts, 'when we write "by hand" we are not in the time before technology; there is already instrumentality, regular reproduction, mechanical iterability. So it is not legitimate to contrast writing by hand and "mechanical" writing, like a pretechnological craft as opposed to technology.'[37] I do, however, have an anxiety about the ways in which the act – common today – of writing directly onto a computer screen could go hand in hand with what Barthes called 'the illusion of expressivity' (LD, 98), for, as Derrida remarks, '[t]he figure of the text "processed" on a computer is like a phantom to the extent that it is less bodily, more "spiritual", more ethereal. There is something like a disincarnation of the text in this.'[38] Word-processing without a handwritten script can make writing feel effortless, natural, intimate, instant. The myth of expression may be more manipulative than ever when the unmistakably material moments – the old 'rhythm' and 'timing' to which Derrida points – are masked by the dust that now tends to cloak pen and ink.[39]

Meanwhile, an obsessive interest in the habits of writing could be drawn easily into a fixing fascination with the private lives of Authors that would honour and reify the individuals who stand behind and before the words on the page.[40] I can think of few things more tedious, but I am also aware that I am writing and walking the finest of lines. Biography is a magnet for mediocrity. Its presence in literary studies is a curse that curdles the discipline into vacuous self-satisfaction. Donna Haraway once remarked that 'teaching modern Christian creationism should be fought as a form of child abuse', and I feel much the same about the fostering of biography-based literary criticism.[41] In writing lives, biographers write the obituary of textuality. The signifier has no magic, no future, if it has a signified which is guaranteed by an individual. I am not interested in ink blots if they are taken to honour an Author who has nourished a work. For me, rather, they underscore how inscription cannot be reduced to expression, the transmission of an aching emotion, the sacred sharing of an inner self. Myth drowns in ink, which burns at its root *(encaustum)*, making Barthes's ink blots into spills for a work of fire that glows with the desire for the Neutral.

Notes

1 Gustave Flaubert, *Madame Bovary: Provincial Lives*, trans. Geoffrey Wall (Harmondsworth: Penguin, 1992), 240. Ellipsis in original.
2 Information about Barthes's entry in his planner is taken from Tiphaine Samoyault, *Roland Barthes: Biographie* (Paris: Seuil, 2015), which includes a sombre facsimile of the page dated 25 February 1980 at the end of its final chapter (685).
3 Samoyault, *Roland Barthes: Biographie*, 13. While the seminar on Proust and photography was, for obvious reasons, never actually given, Barthes's preparatory notes were published posthumously with illustrations as 'Proust and Photography: Examination of a Little-known Photographic Archive', in PN, 305–75.
4 Laurent Binet, *La Septième fonction du langage* (Paris: Grasset, 2015). I discussed my responses to the novel in 'Follow that Vaporetto!', *Times Literary Supplement*, 11 December 2015: 22.
5 Karl Marx, 'The Eighteenth Brumaire of Louis Bonaparte', in *Surveys from Exile: Political Writings, Volume 2*, ed. David Fernbach (Harmondsworth: Penguin, 1973), 46. Barthes admits to having an obsession with Marx's proposition in N, 80–1 and RB, 88; for a further reference, see SPC, 18–19. Meanwhile, his book on Sollers adds a twist: 'History repeats itself, without doubt, but it must be repeated: *as a spiral*' (SW, 93; translation modified).
6 The printed version of the course does not record two things that can be heard at this point in the audio recording of the session of 11 March 1978: the laughter that greets Barthes's revelation about the number of bottles purchased, and an aside in which Barthes explains further his fascination with the names given to inks.
7 Does this account at least in part for the way in which Barthes's body of work is tattooed with numerous references to Gustave Flaubert's *Bouvard and Pécuchet*, trans. Mark Polizzotti (Normal, IL: Dalkey Archive Press, 2005)? (*Bouvard and Pécuchet* must surely be the fictional text to which Barthes refers more than any other.) Flaubert's tale, after all, incorporates its own spillage of ink (246) and revolves around two copyists with excellent handwriting (8–9), one of whom has a name that recalls *un buvard*, the French term for a blotter; so much so, in fact, that the English translation of Barthes's *Fragments d'un discours amoureux* is actually

blotted at one point by a reference to 'Buvard and Pécuchet' (LD, 199). For fine discussions of the place of Flaubert's novel in Barthes's work, see Chapter 2 of Claude Coste, *Bêtise de Barthes* (Paris: Klinksieck, 2011) and Anne Herschberg Pierrot, 'Présence de *Bouvard et Pécuchet* chez Roland Barthes', *Oeuvres & Critiques* 34, vol. 1 (2009): 33–42. Pierrot notes on her opening page that *Bouvard and Pécuchet* 'is constantly present in the writings of Roland Barthes, from *Writing Degree Zero* to *Camera Lucida*' (33). While most of Barthes's references to Flaubert's text are brief and scattered, the publication of *Album* in 2015 finally made available in print an extended discussion of the novel under the title 'Sur sept phrases de *Bouvard et Pécuchet*' (AL, 257–81).

8 See Chapter 4 ('The Scribbler') of Andrew Brown, *Roland Barthes: The Figures of Writing* (Oxford: Clarendon Press, 1992). Charles Bovary pictures his daughter with inky cuffs when he imagines her growing up and 'coming home from school at the end of the day, all laughter, her cuffs stained with ink' (Flaubert, *Madame Bovary*, 157). Although associated here with joy, ink will go on to be tinted with death: the poison swallowed by Emma leaves 'an awful taste of ink' in her mouth (258).

9 Éric Marty, *Roland Barthes, le métier d'écrire: essai* (Paris: Seuil, 2006), 27; Antoine Compagnon, 'Roland Barthes's Novel', trans. Rosalind Krauss, *October* 112 (2005): 25 and *L'Âge des lettres* (Paris: Gallimard, 2015), 17; Philippe Sollers, *L'Amitié de Roland Barthes* (Paris: Seuil, 2015), 10, 42. I have been unable to determine the precise type of blue ink used by Barthes in his manuscripts, but I suspect it to have been Waterman (a French company, after all), as one of Barthes's acquaintances from the sanatorium years has reported that Barthes used the brand at the time. See Samoyault, *Roland Barthes: Biographie*, 193. The Sennelier ink described in *The Neutral* would, I should perhaps add, have been unsuitable for use in a fountain pen.

10 GV, 178. Translation modified; second ellipsis in original. Andrew Brown notes (*Roland Barthes: The Figures of Writing*, 193) that this interview is singled out for particular ridicule in Michel-Antoine Burnier and Patrick Rambaud's *Le Roland-Barthes sans peine* (Paris: Balland, 1978). For a collection of essays which, as examples of genetic criticism, address Barthes's practices of writing in the context of specific published works and their preparatory materials, see the special issue of *Genesis* 19 (2002) entitled 'Roland Barthes'. Particularly instructive is Jean-Louis Lebrave's 'La Genèse de *La Chambre claire*' (79–107).

11 For a detailed account of the complicated (non-)publishing history of the text, see Carlo Ossola's foreword to PDT ('L'instrument subtil'), 7–22.

12 Marie Gil, *Roland Barthes: Au lieu de la vie* (Paris: Flammarion, 2012), 405. For 'Variations sur l'écriture' itself, see OC IV, 267–316. For reasons of internal textual

consistency, all page references here will be to the version contained in the *Oeuvres complètes*, but a more informative, complete and elegantly illustrated incarnation can be found in PDT, 23–81, along with an excellent foreword by Carlo Ossola and textual variations which are not included in the *Oeuvres complètes*.

13 Chris Turner's careful translation makes Barthes's opening paragraph into several sentences, but the punctuation in the original French (OC IV, 983) is such that the lines form a single flowing sentence; I have amended the material accordingly here.

14 PN, 265. Proust cannot have been aware when writing to Dreyfus in 1888 that Stendhal's autobiography, which was written in 1835–6 but not actually published until 1890, would contain a note in which the author complained: 'Handwriting: my thoughts go at a gallop, if I don't record them quickly I lose them.' Stendhal, *The Life of Henry Brulard*, trans. John Sturrock (Harmondsworth: Penguin, 1995), 217. (The text contains many examples of Stendhal's script – some of which gallop merrily into the realm of illegibility.) For the letter to Robert Dreyfus, which is tentatively dated 28 August 1888, see Marcel Proust, *Selected Letters: 1880–1903*, ed. Philip Kolb, trans. Ralph Manheim (London: Collins, 1983), 14, although it should be noted that Proust's original 'au galop' is translated there as 'at a breakneck speed'. Barthes, incidentally, appeared to have the opposite problem: in a letter to Georges Perros dated 7 February 1960, he writes that his pen 'goes so much slower' than his head (AL, 297).

15 RB, 46. Translation modified. (Richard Howard for some reason renders Barthes's 'cendriers' as 'calendars'.) For more by Barthes on the composition of his workspaces, see N, 141 and GV, 180. While the original *Roland Barthes par Roland Barthes* (Paris, Seuil, 1975) features handwritten notices on the inside of the front and back covers, the Papermac English translation places the first handwritten image *after* the title page and, more strangely, the first photograph of Barthes's mother. The second example duly comes at the very end of the text, but is not actually printed on the inner face of the back cover.

16 RB, 162; M, 183. Barthes was evidently fond of the inky cuttlefish, for he allowed it to swim across his pages on five notable occasions. In addition to the two examples already provided, see: RB, 112 (although Richard Howard misleadingly translates 'seiche' as 'squid' on this occasion); OC IV, 777; LA, 75.

17 Chantal Thomas, *Pour Roland Barthes* (Paris: Seuil, 2015), 123.

18 Jean-Louis de Rambures, *Comment travaillent les écrivains* (Paris: Flammarion, 1978).

19 Barthes does not specify which type of pen he means here – the original French text simply refers to 'un stylo' (LN, 193), as does the audio recording – but I find it hard, given what he says about ballpoints in the interview with *Le Monde*, to believe that it could be anything but a 'stylo plume'. It would seem, moreover, that Barthes's audience on 13 May 1978 (the day on which he spoke of self-destitution

and fountain pens) was well aware of his contempt for Bics, for when he announced, near the beginning of the session, that he had just received an anonymous note urging him to retire, there is laughter as soon as he mentions that the letter was written '*with a green ballpoint pen*' (N, 136). This response is not mentioned in the printed text, but it can be heard on the audio recording.

20 Sigmund Freud, *The Psychopathology of Everyday Life*, trans. Anthea Bell (London: Penguin, 2002).

21 In its published form, the first session of *The Neutral* contains many proper names before this reference to Saussure, but the long bibliography which occupies around two pages in the book (1–3) was not actually read out by Barthes on 18 February 1978. In other words, the audience at the Collège encountered far fewer proper names in the introductory session before hearing 'Saussure' than those reading the printed version of the course.

22 Barthes discusses the way in which the term 'course' is rooted etymologically in that which flows, courses, at the beginning of the session of 11 March 1978 (N, 47).

23 Linguistics matters in *How to Live Together* and *The Preparation of the Novel*, of course, but not, it seems to me, with the same force and frequency as in *The Neutral*, where 'what's at stake', Barthes announces at one point, is 'an ethics of language' (N, 60). As he notes in the opening sentence of the summary of the whole course, moreover, 'It is natural that in its research literary semiology should take its guidance from the categories developed by linguistics' (N, 211); there is no statement of this kind in the summaries of *How to Live Together* or the first part of *The Preparation of the Novel*. (A summary for the second part of the latter appears not to exist, presumably because of the timing of Barthes's road accident.)

24 Samoyault explains how Greimas introduced Barthes to Saussure's work in her *Roland Barthes: Biographie*, 235. See also Gil, *Roland Barthes: Au lieu de la vie*, 175 and Louis-Jean Calvet, *Roland Barthes: A Biography*, trans. Sarah Wykes (Bloomington and Indianapolis: Indiana University Press, 1995), 94. Calvet points out that 'there is some contradiction in the accounts of when Barthes first discovered Saussure: Greimas and [Charles] Singevin are both certain that it was while he was in Alexandria, between 1949 and 1950, whereas Barthes himself says he first came across the Swiss linguist in 1951' (94–5). However, the second part of Calvet's claim is unreliable: an endnote directs the reader to 'The Semiological Adventure' (SC, 3–8), where Barthes actually locates his first encounter with Saussure in 1956 (SC, 5).

25 Samoyault, *Roland Barthes: Biographie*, 235.

26 Jean-Claude Milner writes repeatedly of 'la révélation du Signe' ('the revelation of the Sign') in *Le Pas philosophique de Roland Barthes* (Lagrasse: Éditions Verdier, 2003). See above all Part 3.

27 This is not to ignore the possibility that there are Saussurean or vaguely Saussurean moments in Barthes's work before 1956, but it is to insist on the radical difference or shift brought about by the discovery. For discussions of those earlier flickers, see, for example: Diana Knight, *Barthes and Utopia: Space, Travel, Writing* (Oxford: Clarendon Press, 1997), 55; Annette Lavers, *Roland Barthes: Structuralism and After* (London: Methuen, 1982), 51–2; and Patrizia Lombardo, *The Three Paradoxes of Roland Barthes* (Athens, GA and London: University of Georgia Press, 1989), 2, 7. Lombardo argues that Barthes absorbed Saussure 'secondhand' through Viggo Brøndal (2), while Lavers writes that: 'precisely because of Saussure's position as the founding father of modern linguistics his name did not actually have to be pronounced for his ideas to be assimilated' (51). Barthes actually acknowledged reading Brøndal 'as early as 1947', calling him 'a "Minor" structuralist' (SPC, 22).

28 See, for instance, SC, 6 ('Derrida vigorously displaced the very notion of sign, postulating the retreat of signifieds, the decentring of structures'), 210 ('The signified becomes a signifier in its turn, and ... we can never halt a sign at a final signified'), and 241–2 ('Jacques Derrida's philosophical investigation has taken up in a revolutionary fashion this problem of the final signified, postulating that there is never ultimately, in the world, anything but the writing of a writing: a writing always finally refers to another writing, and the prospect of the signs is in a sense infinite. Consequently to describe systems of meaning by postulating a final signified is to side against the very nature of meaning'). Barthes does not name specific works by Derrida on any of these occasions, but I suspect that his allusions are to 1967's *Of Grammatology*, trans. Gayatri Chakravorty Spivak (Baltimore: Johns Hopkins University Press, 1976), which contains, among other things, the long, brilliant rereading of Saussure, and to 1968's essay 'Differance', in *'Speech and Phenomena' and Other Essays on Husserl's Theory of Signs*, trans. David B. Allison (Evanston, IL: Northwestern University Press), 129–60; Barthes alludes to these texts, I think, when he mentions Derrida's analysis of Saussure in the session of *The Neutral* dated 4 March 1978 (N, 41). I was not surprised to discover, therefore, in the letters published as part of *Album* in 2015 that Barthes wrote to Derrida on 20 November 1967 to thank him for *Of Grammatology*, while Derrida wrote to Barthes on 22 March 1970 to articulate his admiration for *S/Z* (AL, 336–7).

29 Samoyault, *Roland Barthes: Biographie*, 329. Samoyault adds that there were 69 notes in the second manuscript version of *Mythologies*, but only thirty in the finished book.

30 Jorge Luis Borges, 'The Mirror of Ink', in *Collected Fictions*, trans. Andrew Hurley (New York: Penguin, 1998), 60–2. I learnt much about the use of ink in scrying ceremonies from a decidedly Borgesian essay by William H. Worrell entitled 'Ink,

Oil and Mirror Gazing Ceremonies in Modern Egypt', *Journal of the American Oriental Society* 36 (1916): 37–53.

31 Ferdinand de Saussure, *Course in General Linguistics*, ed. Charles Bally, Albert Sechehaye and Albert Reidlinger, trans. Wade Baskin (London, Fontana, 1974), 111–12.

32 Jonathan Culler, *Barthes* (London: Fontana, 1983), 72: 'Most important is Saussure's distinction between *langue* and *parole*.' A similar position can be found in Culler's earlier *Structuralist Poetics: Structuralism, Linguistics and the Study of Literature* (London: Routledge and Kegan Paul, 1975), 8.

33 It features in related ways elsewhere in Barthes's work, too. See, for instance: RB, 46–7; GV, 212 and 219–20; and RL, 110 and 240. These last two occurrences have much in common with the discussion of arrogance in *The Neutral*.

34 Saussure, *Course*, 6.

35 Martin Heidegger, *Parmenides*, trans. André Schuwer and Richard Rojcewicz (Bloomington and Indianapolis: Indiana University Press, 1992), 80.

36 For a pointed critique of Heidegger's anthropocentrism in this respect, see Jacques Derrida, '*Geschlecht* II: Heidegger's Hand', trans. John P. Leavey, Jr., in *Deconstruction and Philosophy: The Texts of Jacques Derrida*, ed. John Sallis (Chicago and London: University of Chicago Press, 1987), 161–96. See also Chapter 2 of Cary Wolfe, *Animal Rites: American Culture, the Discourse of Species, and Posthumanist Theory* (Chicago and London: University of Chicago Press, 2003).

37 Jacques Derrida, 'The Word Processor', in *Paper Machine*, trans. Rachel Bowlby (Stanford: Stanford University Press, 2005), 20.

38 Derrida, 'The Word Processor', 30.

39 Derrida, 'The Word Processor', 24. Barthes also refers to the rhythm of writing in 'Variations sur l'écriture' (OC IV, 310).

40 Jonathan Culler reported in 2008 that he found Barthes's discussions of 'the habits of writers' in the course on the preparation of the novel at the Collège de France in 1979–80 so irritating that he attended irregularly, 'preferring other Parisian intellectual activities of greater substance or theoretical interest'. This, he adds immediately, was a decision that he came to regret. Jonathan Culler, 'Preparing the Novel: Spiraling Back', *Paragraph* 31, vol. 1 (2008): 109.

41 Donna J. Haraway, 'A Cyborg Manifesto: Science, Technology, and Socialist-Feminism in the Late Twentieth Century' in *Simians, Cyborgs, and Women: The Reinvention of Nature* (London, Free Association Books, 1991), 152.

5

Bored with Barthes: Ennui in China

'In the desert of the Orient, how my ennui grew!'

Jean Racine, *Bérénice*.[1]

In the beginning was boredom. So believes the troubled narrator of Alberto Moravia's *La Noia*, who tells us that he planned as a boy to write a 'universal history according to boredom'.[2] He outlines his masterpiece in the following way:

> In the beginning was boredom, commonly called chaos. God, bored with boredom, created the earth, the sky, the waters, the animals, the plants, Adam and Eve; and the latter, bored in their turn in paradise, ate the forbidden fruit. God became bored with them and drove them out of Eden; Cain, bored with Abel, killed him; Noah, bored to tears, invented wine; God, once again bored with mankind, destroyed the world by means of the Flood; but this in turn bored Him to such an extent that He brought back fine weather again. And so on. The great empires – Egyptian, Babylonian, Persian, Greek and Roman – rose out of boredom and fell again in boredom; the boredom of paganism gave rise to Christianity; that of Catholicism, to Protestantism; the boredom of Europe caused the discovery of America; the boredom of feudalism kindled the French Revolution; and that of capitalism, the revolution in Russia.
>
> (8–9)

The preparation of this epic history begins well: the narrator relates how he sketched out a summary and started to write 'with great enthusiasm' (9). But things soon go wrong: 'I grew bored with the whole project and abandoned it,' he recalls (9).[3]

I was not surprised to discover that Roland Barthes was familiar with Moravia's tale.[4] He mentioned it in passing at the Collège de France on 9 February 1980, a little over two weeks before the traffic accident which would lead to his death. The lecture was part of the course on 'the preparation of the novel', and Barthes ended the week's discussion by turning to the relationship between writing and boredom. The meaning of the term 'ennui', he observed, referring back to the discussion of acedia in the first of his courses at the Collège, has changed over time: while in the seventeenth century it had a 'much stronger' sense of 'unbearable pain, intolerable torment, violent despair', in the modern era 'it means the complete opposite: a state without hate and without love, a loss of drive' (PN, 271).[5] Boredom, he concluded, is 'actually a very subtle word: it refers to the strength, as it were, of a weakness, to the intensity of a lack of intensity' (PN, 271).

It is equally unsurprising to find this explicit engagement with ennui towards the end of Barthes's life, for it seems to me that his body of work becomes increasingly beset by boredom as time goes on. This is something that has not received extensive attention to date, perhaps because Barthes's ennui is, as I will explain in what follows, at its most apparent and acute in the posthumous body of work. One of Barthes's afterlives is a life of boredom. The condition certainly figures in the texts that appeared during Barthes's lifetime and established his reputation, but not with quite the same force, the same visibility, the same intensity. When it does come to bloom, moreover, its incarnation is elusive and resistant to incorporation into a grand narrative, a sweeping story about 'the human condition'. Before I turn at length to the posthumously published journal in which ennui reaches its excruciating peak, I want to set the scene by surveying boredom in Barthes.[6] If this prelude becomes unbearably, well, boring, the reader is advised to leap ahead to the section entitled 'The Writing of Boredom', which is where things become *really* boring – for Roland Barthes, that is.

Barthes, bored

Ennui is there early in Barthes. (*In the beginning was boredom . . .*) In a letter to Philippe Rebeyrol dated 13 August 1932, the young Roland begins by apologizing for not having been in touch sooner with his friend. 'I was afraid of boring you,' he writes, before reporting that his current ascetic practices of erudite reading, education and meditation are turning him into a 'positively boring boy' (AL, 27–8). Barthes was just sixteen years old when he wrote those words, and he would go on, many of the letters published for the first time in the *Album* of 2015 reveal, often to raise the prospect of boredom in his correspondence with acquaintances.[7] Ennui surfaces early in the chronologically presented *Oeuvres complètes*, too. The fourth text in the first volume is a short piece of just three paragraphs published in *Existences* in 1943. Its focus is a huge recent issue of the journal *Confluences* devoted to 'Problems of the Novel'. Barthes is not persuaded by much of what the 57 authors have to say, and he writes of 'an impression of confusion, of boredom, of uselessness' likely to beset a reader (OC I, 52).

Existences was the journal of the sanatorium of Saint-Hilaire-du-Touvet, where Barthes was a patient in the 1940s while he was suffering from tuberculosis.[8] It was during this confinement that he undertook the early work for what would become his second book, *Michelet* (1954), in which the mapping of the historian's 'organized network of obsessions' (MI, 3) included two sections in which Michelet discusses boredom and, more specifically, '*the literature of boredom*' which made its mark as a genre in the time of Bonaparte (MI, 68–70). One year after the publication of *Michelet*, a short piece for *Les Lettres nouvelles* entitled 'La Vaccine de l'avant-garde' addressed the place of ennui in the reception and staging of Jean-Louis Barrault's adaptation of Christopher Fry's *A Sleep of Prisoners*, in which 'boredom ... has become an intolerable physical pain' (OC I, 563–4).

But these are early examples with swift and somewhat slight resonance. It is not until the 1970s, I think, that the theme becomes much more noticeable, more frequent and forceful, in Barthes's work. If this is the decade in which Barthes, as Éric Marty puts it, 'profoundly reorient[ed] his journey through the notion of pleasure, through first-person writing, through the use of the novelistic or of autobiographical elements', it is also, I would argue, the period in which there is a more marked turn to ennui.[9] With pleasure comes a blooming of boredom. (Were these the years of *ennuisance*?) In the opening pages of *The Pleasure of the Text* (1973), for example, ennui arises from writing which 'might be said to *prattle*' (PT, 4), while a later section announces famously that '[b]oredom is not far from *jouissance*: it is *jouissance* seen from the shores of pleasure' (PT, 26; translation modified). (I will return in time to the unmoored, drifting fame of this line.) Two years later, in the pages of *Les*

Nouvelles littéraires, Barthes told Jean-Louis Ézine that books can easily bore him, which leads to their being cast aside (GV, 199). Meanwhile, speaking to Jacques Chancel on 17 February 1975, he recalled that he had been bored often as a child, but added that this was much less common in his adult life (SPC, 73–4).

When Barthes invoked these bouts of childhood boredom, he had recently finished *Roland Barthes by Roland Barthes,* the text which contains what is probably the most significant discussion of boredom in the work published during his lifetime.[10] In the photographic section which opens the book, beneath a picture of Barthes taken in 1923, when he would have been around eight years of age, sits the following paragraph:

> As a child, I was bored often and greatly. This evidently began very early, it has continued my whole life, in gusts (increasingly rare, it is true, thanks to work and to friends), and it has always been obvious. It is a panic boredom, to the point of distress: like the kind I feel in colloquia, lectures, parties among strangers, group amusements: wherever boredom *can happen*. Might boredom therefore be my hysteria?
>
> (RB, 24; translation modified)[11]

The opposite page of the text continues the diagnosis. A photograph taken in Tokyo in 1966 shows Barthes at the podium, his left hand holding his spectacles and pressed to his face. '*Distress: lecturing*', reads the caption (RB, 25).[12] Beneath lies another image, this time captured in Milan in around 1968. Barthes is in front of a microphone, seated and surrounded by a number of other men. A rather weary expression darkens his face. He appears to be frowning and fidgeting with a pen. '*Boredom: a roundtable discussion*', runs the accompanying text (RB, 25; translation modified).[13]

Here the ennui is personalized, an attribute of the narrator of the text, which must, a handwritten notice at the beginning of the book stresses, 'all be considered as if spoken by a character in a novel' (1). But *Roland Barthes by Roland Barthes* is, as Sophie Létourneau has observed, a volume whose photographs establish subtle family connections in the depicted poses, notably in the 'pensive elbow' apparent in images of Barthes, his father and his father's father.[14] And boredom appears to have been inherited with pensiveness, for elsewhere in the book the reader encounters a photograph of Captain Binger, Barthes's maternal grandfather, with the following caption: '*In old age, he grew* bored. *Always seated early at the table (even though the dinner hour was constantly brought forward), he lived further and further ahead of time, more and more bored*' (RB, 12; translation modified). This, in fact, is the first appearance of ennui in *Roland Barthes by Roland Barthes* – and it is one that reaches back to the distant past. Between this inaugural textual flicker and the paragraphs about the narrator's childhood boredom lie two related references. First, beneath a photograph of Les Allées marines in Bayonne, a long sentence about evening strolls contains a reference to 'boredom's drift' (RB, 17). Then, several pages later, underneath a delightful image of a toddling Barthes on a beach in Ciboure circa 1918, in a paragraph about childhood there promenades a sentence in which the narrator sees in his younger form 'the dark underside of myself'. At the very beginning of the ensuing list of personal qualities sits boredom (RB, 22).

All of these references gather near the beginning of the text, in the section where the narrator announces that he will discuss a number of images as a 'treat to himself for finishing his book' (RB, 3). In the celebration, in the celebration of writing, in the celebration of having written, boredom's refrain resounds. And it resounds beyond this initial section of the book, for the reader later encounters statements about: boredom and avant-garde texts (RB, 54); boredom and Michelet (RB, 55); the way in which cruising arises from boredom (RB, 72); the boring nature of accounts of dreams (RB, 87); the possibility that the repressed boredom of childhood is responsible for migraines (RB, 124); the boredom of self-commentary (RB, 142); the boredom of 'foreseeable discourses' (RB, 149); boredom and scholarship, apropos of Bataille (RB, 159); the narrator's tendency to postpone until later what bores him (RB, 174); and even the boredom which has haunted the writing of *Roland Barthes by Roland Barthes* itself (RB, 71).[15]

But however striking the eruption of ennui in this late book might be, and however much the text foregrounds a theme which had circulated less forcefully in Barthes's work for decades, it is in one of the posthumously published texts that Barthes is at his most bored – and maybe even at his most boring. The volume in question is related closely to *Roland Barthes by Roland Barthes*, for, although it was not published in full until 2009, it was written in 1974 while Barthes was working on his self-commentary; perhaps its profound boredom tinted the developing pages of *Roland Barthes by Roland Barthes*.[16]

I am referring to the *Carnets du voyage en Chine*, known in English as *Travels in China*.

The writing of boredom

The text has its roots in a visit that Barthes paid to Mao's China between 11 April and 4 May 1974, following an invitation from the Chinese embassy in France, which was in turn initiated by Maria-Antonietta Macciocchi.[17] Accompanying Barthes on the trip were François Wahl (who was, among other things, Barthes's editor at Seuil) and, representing *Tel Quel*, Julia Kristeva, Marcelin Pleynet and Philippe Sollers. Jacques Lacan and Severo Sarduy had been due to travel as well, having been chosen by Sollers in his capacity as organizer for *Tel Quel*, but these plans fell through.[18] As Pleynet noted in the introduction to his account of the expedition, those three weeks produced 'a vast series of news reports, no fewer than five articles in *Le Monde*, two issues of the journal *Tel Quel* and, a little later, a book by Julia Kristeva, *Des Chinoises*, published by Editions des Femmes'.[19] He might also have mentioned in the list his own book, which appeared under the title *Le Voyage en Chine* in 1980, and it is now possible, of course, to add Barthes's *Travels in China*.[20]

On 8 May 1974, just a few days after returning from China, Barthes gave an account of the voyage to his students in Paris. The written version of this presentation, which runs to about fifteen pages, was published posthumously in 2010 as 'Compte rendu du voyage en Chine' (LA, 227–45), and it bears a close relation to one of the articles mentioned by Marcelin Pleynet as having appeared in *Le Monde*. The latter piece – which is in some respects a condensed version of what Barthes reported to his students – was entitled 'Alors, la Chine?' ('So, How Was China?') and was published in the paper on 24 May 1974.[21] Looking back on the recent trip, Barthes makes a startling statement: 'In a sense (apart from the political answer), we come home with – *nothing*' (SM, 97). The travellers arrived, he reports, armed 'with a thousand pressing and, it seems, natural questions' (SM, 97), but nothing fell from 'the tree of knowledge' when it was shaken:

> We want there to be impenetrable things so that we can penetrate them: by ideological atavism, we are creatures of decipherment, hermeneutic subjects;

we believe our intellectual task is always to uncover a meaning. China seems reluctant to deliver up this meaning, not because it hides it but, more subversively, because (in a way that is far from Confucian) it undoes the constitution of concepts, themes and names... It is the end of hermeneutics.

(SM, 97–8; see also LA, 230 and 235)

The disappointment continues when Barthes describes China as insipid, filled with repetition, clichés and what he calls 'bricks' [*briques*] – rigid, stubborn, predictable, pre-formed units of discourse.[22] All that China offers for reading, he concludes, is 'its political Text' (SM, 100).[23]

Ennui does not figure in an explicitly extensive manner in either 'So, How Was China?' or the 'Compte rendu'. For boredom, and for a great deal of it, we need to turn instead to *Travels in China*. The book, which was prepared for publication in 2009 by Anne Herschberg Pierrot, transcribes the journal that Barthes kept throughout the visit to China – the journal which preceded 'So, How Was China?' and the 'Compte rendu'.[24] It would be more accurate, in fact, to refer to journals, in the plural, for Barthes's observations were spread across several notebooks, as Pierrot explains:

Right from the start, Barthes had been thinking of bringing back a text from China. He filled three notebooks on this theme, in blue biro or felt-tip. The first two notebooks, 'Spiral Crown', with a blue hardback cover (Notebook 1), and a red one (Notebook 2), respectively, brought with him from France, are complemented, for the end of the journey, by a Chinese notebook, smaller, in black moleskin, bearing a quotation by Chairman Mao printed in red on the first page (the last, in the order used). These three notebooks are entirely paginated in red felt. Barthes reread them, set out a contents page for each of them, and drew up a thematic index in a fourth notebook.[25]

I dwell on these material details because it seems to me that the original form of the text that we now know as *Travels in China* – or, to be more precise, the original form of its inscription – is significant. About eight months before he published 'So, How Was China?' in *Le Monde*, Barthes confessed in the pages of the same newspaper that, as I discussed at length in Chapter 4, he suffered from what he called 'an almost obsessive relation to writing instruments' which led him to 'return to fine ink pens' repeatedly because only they could generate the desired 'soft, smooth writing' (GV, 178; translation modified).

This elegant, gentle, precise handwriting can be seen in many of the reproductions of Barthes's manuscripts which have been published since his death.[26] The notebooks from the Chinese trip, however, look completely different. As the facsimiles included in the *R/B* exhibition catalogue show (208–25), Barthes's observations were made in loose, untidy handwriting and, worse still, often with a ballpoint pen – that object which he had dismissed just seven months earlier as 'really just for churning out cheap copy, writing that merely transcribes thoughts'. Gone is the habitual elegance, the 'soft, smooth' script, the delicate care that Barthes admires in Chairman Mao's calligraphy; in its place is uneven, sprawling scrawl. I would, in fact, go so far as to call the pages of the original Chinese notebooks *ugly*: this is what Barthes dismissed as 'Bic style', in every sense of the phrase. If, as Claude Coste has argued, *Travels in China* contains little for lovers of fine writing (*beau style*), it also offers nothing for admirers of fine *hand*writing.[27]

There are, perhaps, straightforward practical explanations. First, the notebooks are sites of immediate observation 'in the field', so to speak: on the move, surrounded by information, Barthes needs to write quickly and easily, and a ballpoint pen can be more suitable for such jottings. Indeed, in her editor's introduction to *The Preparation of the Novel*, Nathalie Léger points out that Barthes 'did not like using [ballpoints] but, considering them useful for making the odd note, always carried one with him' (PN, xx); Antoine Compagnon's memoir about his friendship with Barthes, meanwhile, notes that the author would carry a grey Bic pen and a spiral notebook (as used during the trip to China) for jotting down ideas.[28] Second, air travel with a fountain pen – and Barthes appears even to be taking notes during the flights to and from Beijing (TC, 6, 193) – can be a risky, messy business, as the change in air pressure can cause ink to leak or even squirt out of the nib.[29] Perhaps Barthes wanted simply to arrive in Beijing fresh and clean, and ready to take rapid notes.[30]

Whatever the reason for the choice of writing instruments used in the Chinese notebooks, however, the presence of ballpoint inscription suggests to me, before I have begun to treat the words as anything more than patterns on a page, that this is writing without passion, writing without desire, writing without what Barthes called, in a short piece entitled 'Writing', 'the pleasure of having before me (like the handyman's bench) a fine sheet of paper and a good fountain pen' (VFG, 168; translation modified). 'For a week,' he observes while visiting Nanjing Normal University on 19 April, 'I haven't felt any opening up in my writing, any *jouissance* in it. Dry, sterile' (TC, 75).[31] A handwritten page, he proposes in 'Writing', can be 'a space that is quite simply the space of art' (VFG, 168), but not here, it seems to me, not in the ugly notebooks filled during the trip to China. This, rather, is the writing of boredom.

Indeed, it is not long before ennui bores its way into the journal. Although he wrote to Philippe Sollers in December 1973 to signal his 'joy and excitement' about the forthcoming trip, Barthes ends up being bored before the plane has even arrived in Beijing.[32] Immediately after commenting while airborne how disappointed he is to find the aircraft full of Europeans, Barthes refers for the second time in two pages to a mention of the trip in *Le Quotidien de Paris*, the newspaper which had just been launched by Philippe Tesson (TC, 6). 'Go back over the echo in the *Quotidien de Paris*,' he writes, 'show the lousy ethics it's based on. How boring! To have the downsides of fame (the echo of a private trip) and none of the (financial) advantages' (TC, 6).

But this minor irritation is nothing compared to the boredom experienced by Barthes when he reaches his destination. The main problem, he soon discovers, is that the French visitors' encounters with Mao's China are controlled strictly by the Luxingshe Agency responsible for overseeing their visit and for, in Barthes's phrase, 'mothering' the visitors unnecessarily.[33] The day after arriving, for instance, the guests are taken to see a puppet show in a suburban hall, where Barthes is dismayed to find that the French party is 'penned in with two rows of elderly European females' (TC, 14). It is, he writes, '[i]mpossible to mingle. The organizers don't want us to. Hands off bodies. Exclusions' (TC, 14).[34] (Barthes would expand upon this theme in the account of his trip given to his students back in Paris on 8 May, where he spoke in summary of 'ethnic segregation' and a 'separation of bodies; on one side a mass of millions of Chinese people, on the other side five granules, five European *petits pois*' [LA, 233].[35])

In the place of mingling, of spontaneity, of surprise, the visitors are made during their stay to sit through many presentations – in a printing works, a naval dockyard and a housing development, for example – about the glory of Mao's China and, regularly, about the failings of Confucius and Lin Biao.[36]

'Endlessly repeated Doxa,' writes Barthes two days into the trip, 'Lin Biao and Confucius had the same point of view' (TC, 15). Although the visitors are able to ask questions about what they have heard at these presentations, Barthes eventually gives up: 'I can't be bothered,' he scribbles, 'since the replies are always idyllic' (TC, 110).[37]

In short, Barthes is bored in China, bored by China. ('Boring', in fact, is the first word for which the fictionalized Philippe Sollers of Laurent Binet's *La Septième fonction du langage* reaches when he is asked how Barthes found the trip.[38]) 'This is bound to be really boring,' he remarks when the group arrives at a museum in Xi'an (TC, 142), before adding, on the following page of the journal, 'This museum is boring me to death' (TC, 143). Even Philippe Sollers bores him because he also 'proceeds by *campaigns* – and it's tiring: from one period to the next, he always bangs away at the same old theme, with variations of examples in support, jokes, etc.: at present it's: Lacan as a henchman of religion, idealist, etc.' (TC, 102).[39]

In addition to articulating the boredom as a lack of spontaneity and surprise, Barthes presents matters in terms of the signifier, and it is here, I think, that the place of *Travels in China* within his wider body of work becomes clear. "[S]ignifiers are rare,' he writes in his report for *Le Monde*, explaining that signifiers are 'the things that exceed meaning, cause it to overflow and to press on, towards desire' (SM, 99; translation modified). The Chinese journal both repeats (TC, 144) and rephrases this statement about rarity.[40] The entry for 25 April, for example, states the following, in brackets, in between accounts of visits to the Pagoda of the Great Goose and a pre-historic museum:

> My phenomenological level = the level of the signifier.
> In China, the only signifier = writing (Mao, *dazibao*.)
>
> (TC, 119)[41]

Although Barthes changes his mind in his notes about the nature of the signifier in China – he later adds gymnastics, food, children, clothing and hands to the list (TC, 127, 129), only then to remove clothing again (TC, 144) – the heart of the problem remains: in the midst of the 'bricks', of what he also calls 'a sort of monstrous ventriloquism' (TC, 184), Barthes feels trapped at the '[l]evel of the signified: in other words: what blocks the place, what bars the signifier. Total eviction of the signifier' (TC, 122).⁴² And the signifier, he notes on 26 April, is 'basically: everything I like and that alone' (TC, 127).

To understand the resonance and relevance of these remarks, this laying of the 'bricks' on the side of the signified, it is necessary to revisit the source, for Barthes, of the distinction between signifier and signified: Ferdinand de Saussure's *Course in General Linguistics*, in which it is proposed that the linguistic sign is made up of the components in question. Although the relationship between the two is arbitrary, unmotivated, the elements of the sign are, in Saussure's account, 'intimately united':[43]

> Language can also be compared with a sheet of paper: thought is the front and the sound the back; one cannot cut the front without cutting the back at the same time; likewise in language, one can neither divide sound from thought nor thought from sound; the division could be accomplished only abstractedly, and the result would be either pure psychology or pure phonology.[44]

This account of a unified sign was clearly influential in the early work of Roland Barthes, notably in texts such as *Mythologies* and *Elements of Semiology*, and I discussed the importance of Saussure from a different perspective in Chapter 4. But things change significantly in the later Barthes – the Barthes who is bored in China; the Barthes who looks back, in *Roland Barthes by Roland Barthes*, to 'his structuralist phase' (RB, 103); the Barthes who, in one of the unused fragments of that same book, reports on an international congress of semiology by saying that the discipline is no longer for him because it 'seems to believe that to each signifier there corresponds a signified' (LA, 299).[45] With the waning of structuralism, with the drift away from semiology in its conventional form (a development which was also discussed in Chapter 4 of this book), Barthes's texts become more interested in, more seduced by, the signifier. More specifically, there emerges a celebration of what, four years before the encounter with the reality of Maoism, *S/Z* named 'the magic of the signifier' (SZ, 4).[46]

This is precisely the magic that is missing in China. Because meaning is fixed, repeated, endoxal, predictable, leaden, there can be little plurality, play, drifting. As Barthes writes in his journal on 23 April, 'it's the continual presence, smooth as a tablecloth, of Agency officials that blocks, forbids, censors, rules out the possibility of the Surprise, the Incident, the Haiku' (TC, 102–3).⁴⁷ This is why *Travels in China* so often articulates boredom.

Barthes does his best to find something to break up the ennui, however. One of his strategies is best understood, I think, by remembering a moment in *Roland Barthes by Roland Barthes*. In the section entitled 'Movement of Objects into Discourse', Barthes writes:

> It is a good thing, he thought, that out of consideration for the reader, there should pass through the essay's discourse, from time to time, a sensual object (as in *Werther*, where suddenly there appear a dish of green peas cooked in butter and a peeled orange separated into sections). A double advantage: sumptuous appearance of a materiality and a distortion, a sudden gap wedged into the intellectual murmur.
>
> Michelet gave him his example: what relation between the anatomical discourse and the camellia blossom? – 'The brain of a child', Michelet says, 'is nothing but the milky blossom of a camellia.' Whence, no doubt, the habit of *diverting himself*, as he writes, by unusual enumerations. Is there not a kind of voluptuous pleasure in inserting, like a perfumed dream, into a sociological analysis, 'wild cherries, cinnamon, vanilla, and sherry, Canadian tea, lavender, bananas'? to relieve the burden of a semantic demonstration by the vision of 'wings, tails, crests, plumes, tufts of hair, scarves, smoke, balloons, belts, and veils' out of which Erté forms the letters of his alphabet – or again, to introduce into a sociological journal 'brocade trousers, capes, and the long white nightshirts' worn by hippies?
>
> (RB, 135)⁴⁸

Barthes is quoting his earlier published work here, but the technique of allowing a 'sensual object' to disrupt the flow, to create a gap in the murmur, also operates in *Travels in China*.⁴⁹ While the journal is profoundly listless, it is not list-less, simply because it contains many lists. Often while Barthes is listening to yet another dull and predictable presentation about the glory of Mao's China, he copies into his notebook, in the form of long lists, some of the information that is being presented. When, for instance, the visitors are taken to inspect a new residential district, they are required to sit through a talk by a member of the Revolutionary Committee. Barthes begins to make an inventory, a very boring inventory: '35 buildings, 1,800 homes, 7,000 men. Workers + teachers, doctors, employees. All the public services. Primary school. Crèche. Food. Workshop for spare parts. Hairdresser's, bookshop, bank' (TC, 27). But then, after describing what he is hearing as a 'deadly "speech"' (TC, 27), he interrupts his list, diverts himself, allows a sensual object to sparkle, in brackets, within the dull discourse: '[I look at my glass of tea: the green leaves have opened wide and form a thick layer at the bottom of the glass. But the tea is very light, tasteless, barely a herbal tea, it's just hot water]' (TC, 27).

Infusing listless lists with asides about tea becomes something of a habit, in fact. A bland transcription of what the visitors are being told about shipping at a naval dockyard, for instance, is disturbed by the following phrase: '[Shanghai tea is much less nice than Beijing tea, which was golden and perfumed]' (TC, 23).[50] The following day, meanwhile, an inventory relating to a presentation by the Revolutionary Committee in a hospital is fractured by another aside:

> Mao's principles: 1) first prophylaxis. 2) Service provided to the Peasants, Soldiers, Workers. 3) Mass movement in the hospital. 4) European medicine + Chinese medicine.
> 1) Prophylaxis, Common and epidemic illnesses. Peripatetic teams.
> [The tea is better: more golden, with jasmine]
> 2) Europe + China. 30% of operations under acupuncture.
> 3) Scientific research: especially into common illnesses. Examples: chronic bronchitis in the elderly, coronary arthrosis, cancer, cataracts.
> 4) Education (University level).
>
> (TC, 32)

Here the diversion about tea breaks into the steady, stupefying enumeration, the listless list.[51] For a brief moment, another possibility percolates. The numbering continues, of course, gets back on track and makes it as far as a fourth point, but the earlier interruption remains upon the page as an invention within the inventory. (An invention, Jacques Derrida reminds us, is that which comes or comes in from an elsewhere.[52]) What the notebook records is a utopian flicker, a fleeting difference and a fleeting *desire for difference* within monotony.

We might even read the interruption anachronistically by considering it in the language of *The Neutral*, Barthes's course of 1977–8 at the Collège de France, in which a great deal of time is devoted to that which baffles or outplays (the French term is *déjouer*) arrogant, paradigmatic discourse. 'Under the term "arrogance", Barthes explains, as I noted in Chapter 4:

I gather all the (linguistic) 'gestures' that work as discourses of intimidation, of subjection, of domination, of assertion, of haughtiness: that claim the authority, the guarantee of a dogmatic truth or of a demand that doesn't think, that doesn't conceive of the other's desire.

(N, 152)

Tea, in fact, is served up as a form of non-arrogant resistance in *The Neutral* when, on 25 February 1978, Barthes turns his attention to a Japanese tea ceremony as a ritual which, in its intricacy, 'verg[es] on the useless or enigmatically useful detail: minutia: at the edge of eccentricity. In short: art of the useless supplement' (N, 30). The cultural context of the disruptive '[The tea is better: more golden, with jasmine]' in 1974 is, of course, different – Barthes is writing there about China, not Japan – but it nonetheless seems to me that there is a foreshadowing of *The Neutral*'s celebration of the 'pleasure in the "futile"' (N, 30) and the delicate detail which unsettles its surroundings.

The turn to tea as a sensual object reaches something of pinnacle in *Travels in China* when, on 18 April, the visitors find themselves in the company of a group of philosophy teachers from Shanghai. There follows what Barthes calls a '[v]ery precise lecture, very historically detailed. A lecture in Marxist history' (TC, 51). So bored by this is Barthes that he cannot record things in the usual manner: '[Trying to take notes, this morning, but I give up]', he writes (TC, 51).⁵³ He attempts to get back on track by jotting down the time, '10.07am', but then can only manage, 'This history lecture on the Legalists is still going on' (TC, 51). There then follows the longest diversion about tea in the entire journal:

[Analyse the Tea system in depth: long session, tablecloth, glasses in wickerwork covers, big Thermos. From time to time they pour more warm water into every glass. It's insipid. But, this, existing on the table, then in gestures, a protocol, a *spectacle*, turns the spoken word into something indirect.]

(TC, 51)

Tea breaks up the boredom, provides an alternative to ennui, by offering something 'indirect' in the midst of the *doxa*, which is both direct and correct (in that it repeatedly confirms its own authorized account of life under Mao).

In *Le Pas philosophique de Roland Barthes*, Jean-Claude Milner observes that Barthes's use of 'italics, quotation marks, parentheses, quotation marks within parentheses, etc.' is 'knowing' and therefore deserving of critical attention.[54] As the preceding tea-related quotations from *Travels in China* reveal, Barthes often places his sensual digressions within square brackets. This gives many of the journal's attempts to break up the ennui a visual, typographical quality: the page repeatedly looks different when Barthes is struggling against boredom.[55] The specific use of square brackets, moreover, makes the diversions more marked, more striking than they would have been if Barthes had enlisted softer, curved parentheses. With the harsher '[ ]', Barthes squares up to ennui in what might be called a series of 'tea breaks'.

But the brackets ultimately fail: the various sensual diversions away from the overwhelming boredom are brief and slight. What the journal calls 'the subtlest, most futile things' (TC, 95) are no match for the endless bricks, the weight of the political signified. The magic of the signifier flickers, yes, and Barthes pursues its promise, but it fades all too quickly. Not for all the tea in China, therefore, is Barthes tempted to linger. As he writes on the day before returning home to France:

> [Personally, I won't be able to live in this radicalism, in this fanatical monologism, in this obsessive, monomaniac discourse]
> [in this *fabric*, this text without a gap]
>
> (TC, 192)

As the plane takes off from Peking, he writes a word of sheer relief in his notebook, emphasizing it with an exclamation mark and a surrounding rectangle: 'PHEW! [*OUF!*]' (TC, 193) 'So,' he concludes in one of the journal's final statements, 'it would be necessary to pay for the Revolution with everything I love: "free" discourse exempt from all repetition, and immorality' (TC, 195). Little wonder, then, that François Wahl, looking back on the trip some years later in an essay actually called 'Ouf!', described Barthes's position in the group of travellers as one of 'prisoner'.[56]

The literature of boredom

And yet, in spite of all of this boredom – not merely the boredom of the posthumously published Chinese journals, but also that which haunts many of the other writings – Barthes tends to be excluded from, or at best marginalized in, scholarly studies of boredom in Western culture. If Barthes was in fact a great professor of ennui, to modify Steven Ungar's description of him as a professor of desire, I am nonetheless struck by how detailed and persuasive accounts of boredom often implicitly profess an ignorance of Barthes.[57]

Peter Toohey's *Boredom: A Lively History*, for example, offers precisely what its title promises, and it takes in a wide range of cultural materials – Degas, Goncharov, Edward Hopper, Jean-Paul Sartre and so on – to tell an engaging story.[58] Roland Barthes, however, never appears. He does feature in Lars Svendsen's influential *A Philosophy of Boredom*, but in just one paragraph containing the quotation about boredom and *jouissance* from *The Pleasure of the Text*.[59] We find something very similar if we go back in time to the moment of a monument: Reinhard Kuhn's epic, magisterial survey of ennui in Western literature, *The Demon of Noontide*, which was first published in 1976. The book's introduction has as its epigraph twenty-four words from *The Pleasure of the Text* – 'There are no two ways about it: ennui is not simple. We cannot summarily dispose of ennui … with a gesture of annoyance or dismissal' – but Kuhn never actually engages with them.[60] Near the end of the study he returns again to *The Pleasure of the Text*, this time quoting the famous line about ennui and the shores of pleasure (372). Another sixteen words from Barthes, then, but, once again, there is no engagement with them. The only other reference to Barthes in the entire volume, which runs to nearly 400 pages and sweeps from Plato to Beckett, is in a footnote which directs readers to a short piece by Barthes on Chateaubriand's *Vie de Rancé* (214 n. 12).[61]

Elizabeth S. Goodstein begins her formidable *Experience Without Qualities: Boredom and Modernity* by taking Kuhn to task for his ahistorical approach and his 'elitist presuppositions'.[62] Her critique is brilliant and compelling. And yet, she inherits something from Kuhn (not to mention Svendsen). Barthes's sentence about boredom and the shores of pleasure stands, in French, as the epigraph to her introduction (1). Once again, however, the words are never actually discussed, and Barthes makes no further appearance in Goodstein's lengthy book. Boredom, it might be said, is Barthes glimpsed from the shores of epigraphs.

How might we begin to account for this repeated absence or passing presence in the form of a sentence or two from *The Pleasure of the Text*? Why does my professor of boredom find himself overlooked in otherwise diligent studies of the condition? Why is Barthes's boredom not, well, *interesting* to scholars of ennui?

I will address those questions and move towards concluding – move towards putting an end to your boredom, dear reader – by turning to one of the very few texts to discuss Roland Barthes and boredom in any significant way. In 'Public Parks and Private Gardens: Sartre's Nausea and Barthes's Ennui', Betty R. McGraw distinguishes delicately between the two authors in question. The difference, for McGraw, is that Sartre's discussion of ennui is metaphysical, in that it makes the condition part of 'his ongoing philosophical inquiry into the universal substance of bourgeois existence'.[63] The key term here, I think, is 'universal': with Sartre, McGraw proposes, we are in the realm of grand theory, metanarrative, a totalizing account of the way of the world. But Barthes, she continues, offers another possibility:

> Barthes's writing *about* ennui always overflows the boundaries of phenomenological and existential rhetoric, spilling over as figures of a bodily sort of language. . . . Distrusting the militant imperatives of *littérature engagée*, Barthes does not attempt to put the writing of ennui at the service of an existential anterior truth.
>
> (78; emphasis in original)

In short, he 'speaks of ennui differently' (83). Gone is the Sartrean insistence upon the 'Absolutely Universal' (84). For McGraw, rather, Barthes 'wrenches ennui from the totalizing moment of idealistic philosophy and sets it with a semiotic pursuit linked to the personal, the emotional involvement of an unknown praxis' (79).

To put things another way, there is no grand theory of boredom in the work of Barthes. Ennui occurs repeatedly, and it is tiresome, but the narrative is always specific, local, located; there is no sense that Barthes's ennui is part of 'the human condition', something metaphysical, something universal. This, I think, is perhaps one of the main reasons why my professor of boredom is often absent, or nearly absent, from critical studies of the condition. Barthes's ennui does not fit, does not fit neatly into an epic tale, a vast and general vista. It would escape the approval, the mighty gaze, of a critic like Reinhard Kuhn, for example, who announces in the introduction to *The Demon of Noontide* that ennui is 'a metaphysical malady' (9), 'a state that affects both the soul and the body. Though its origins are always to be found in the soul, its manifestations are both spiritual and physical' (12). It is, he continues:

> the state of emptiness that the soul feels when it is deprived of interest in action, life, and the world (be it this world or another), a condition that is the immediate consequence of the encounter with nothingness, and has as an immediate effect a disaffection with reality.
>
> (13)

Ennui in this account is special, and it is significantly different from routine, everyday boredom where the source of irritation is 'a temporary state dependent almost entirely on external circumstances' (6). That kind of boredom, Kuhn states, giving the loaded example of a housewife standing in a queue at the supermarket, is trivial, 'superficial' (181) and 'hardly worth serious study' (6).

Kuhn was writing over thirty years before *Travels in China* was published, and he died in the same year as Roland Barthes. It is impossible to know, therefore, precisely what he would have made of the Chinese notebooks, but I doubt very much that they would have been of interest, would have counted as an expression of ennui to be counted alongside the authentic existential howls of Pascal, Kierkegaard and Beckett. For Kuhn, I suspect, Barthes's journal would have been easy to ignore, 'hardly worth serious study', because the statements about ennui in China are not metaphysical, not matters of the soul, the spirit or the human condition. Barthes's boredom, rather, is temporary and has precise external causes: the 'bricks', the stifling of the signifier, the clichés, the working of the Agency. In Martin Doehlemann's typology, Barthes's is a 'situational boredom' – a minor, fleeting, non-existential boredom caused by a common situation such as waiting for a train or reading a long chapter in an academic monograph.[64]

There, I think, lies the heart of the problem. Scholarly accounts of boredom often seek to develop a grand theory, a metanarrative, a metaphysics of ennui. But the bored texts of Roland Barthes, of which the posthumous *Travels in China* is the most extreme and extensive example, resist such designs. The notebooks from the trip to China are filled with episodes of ennui, but these are never enlisted in a magisterial conclusion, a gathering overview. If critics want a mighty truth, an overarching essence of ennui, they will have to neglect Barthes, the subtle and specific professor of boredom.

Roland Barthes, I have been arguing, has a place in the literature of boredom – but it is an overlooked, undeveloped place. This chapter offers a correction and an invitation to scholars in the field. An invitation to visit the distant, foreign land of Barthes's writings. An invitation to rewrite the familiar (meta)narrative, to hear and tell another story. An invitation to read Barthes's boredom, to follow its fretting and share its sighs. An invitation to share Barthes's company, to face his ennui. An invitation not to be bored *by* Barthes. An invitation, rather, to be bored *with* Barthes.

Notes

1. Jean Racine, *Bérénice*, in *Andromache, Britannicus, Berenice*, trans. John Cairncross (London: Penguin, 1967), 1.4.234. Translation modified. Barthes actually quotes this line from *Bérénice* in 'Objective Literature' (CE, 14). He then returns to it around a quarter of a century later in the last of his courses at the Collège de France, noting the difficulty of translating Racine's seventeenth-century 'ennui' into modern French (PN, 271). As Claude Coste has pointed out in his *Bêtise de Barthes* (Paris: Klincksieck, 2011), 127, Barthes is echoing Valéry when he makes this point about translation.
2. Available in English as Alberto Moravia, *Boredom*, trans. Angus Davidson (New York: New York Review Books, 1999), 8. Some English editions carry the title *The Empty Canvas*.
3. This act of literary abandonment recalls an earlier and far more famous text about ennui, Jean-Paul Sartre's *Nausea*, trans. Robert Baldick (Harmondsworth: Penguin, 1965), in which Roquentin abandons his planned biography of the Marquis de Rollebon.
4. It is not clear if Barthes read the book in the original Italian or in French translation; the latter appeared soon after the Italian text was published, as *L'Ennui*, trans. unnamed (Paris: Flammarion, 1961). The biblical opening of the long passage quoted in English above ('In the beginning was boredom ...') has a counterpart in the French text – 'Au commencement donc était l'ennui ...' (9) – although the French, with its 'donc', is closer to the Moravia's original sentence: 'In principio, dunque, era la noia, volgarmente chiama caos.' Alberto Moravia, *La Noia* (Milan: Bompiani, 1964), 10.
5. For Barthes's earlier discussion of acedia, see HTLT, 21–3.
6. What follows in this section of the chapter is not intended to be a complete catalogue of references to boredom in works by Barthes – the boredom of such a

thing! – but is meant, rather, merely to identify some of the notable occurrences that surround the eruption of ennui in the text which sits at the heart this chapter.

7   See, for instance, AL, 30, 33, 46, 49, 65, 86, 94, 97, 122, 345, 353 and 357. See also the letter from Barthes to Philippe Sollers dated 25 October 1966 and included in the latter's *L'Amitié de Roland Barthes* (Paris: Seuil, 2015), 68–9.

8   For a remarkable online archive of scanned issues of *Existences*, see http://www.cme-u.fr/index.php?option=com_content&task=view&id=164&Itemid=33 (accessed 22 February 2016). Information about Barthes's sanatorium years can be found in: Chapter 3 of Louis-Jean Calvet, *Roland Barthes: A Biography*, trans. Sarah Wykes (Bloomington and Indianapolis: Indiana University Press, 1995); Chapter 2 of Marie Gil, *Roland Barthes: Au lieu de la vie* (Paris: Flammarion, 2012); Chapter 5 of Tiphaine Samoyault, *Roland Barthes: Biographie* (Paris: Seuil, 2015); Philippe Roger, *Roland Barthes, roman* (Paris: Grasset, 1986), 325–40; and Chapter 2 of Andy Stafford, *Roland Barthes* (London: Reaktion, 2015). For Barthes's own account of sanatorium life, see 1947's 'Esquisse d'une société sanatoriale' (AL, 87–9) and, more briefly, SPC, 7–9.

9   Éric Marty, *Roland Barthes, la littérature et le droit à la mort* (Paris: Seuil, 2010), 10.

10 According to the dates given at the end of the text, the book was composed between 6 August 1973 and 3 September 1974 (RB, 180).

11 The beginning of this passage recalls a letter by the young Flaubert which Barthes would go on to quote in the session of *The Preparation of the Novel* dated 9 February 1980, moments after invoking Alberto Moravia: 'I was,' writes Flaubert in 1846, 'born bored; it is the leprosy that eats away at me. I tire of life, of myself, of other people, of everything' (PN, 272).

12 The discontentment associated in this image with the conventional, masterful form of the lecture, where the one who knows speaks and transmits pre-existing knowledge, should be compared with another photograph in the same book. In it, Barthes is shown smiling and surrounded by members of his seminar at the École Pratique des hautes études. The text beneath the image celebrates the space of the seminar as having a phalansteric, novelistic quality and as being 'the space of the circulation of subtle desires, mobile desires' (RB, 171). I was prompted to think more about the relationship between the distressed image from Tokyo and this happy photograph of the seminarists by a passing reference to the latter in Lucy O'Meara, *Roland Barthes at the Collège de France* (Liverpool: Liverpool University Press, 2012), 33. The whole of Chapter 1 of O'Meara's book offers a brilliant account of Barthes's 'heretical teaching'.

13 François Wahl reports that Barthes often commented on the boredom generated by conference trips. See 'Ouf!', in *R/B: Roland Barthes*, ed. Marianne Alphant and Nathalie Léger (Paris: Seuil/Centre Pompidou/IMEC, 2002), 108.

14 Sophie Létourneau, 'Le Prince de la jeunesse: Roland Barthes, cet écrivain mineur', *Études françaises* 46, vol. 3 (2010): 149–50. Barthes uses the phrase 'pensive elbow' in RB, 19.
15 Some of the unused fragments from the book also feature references to Barthes's boredom. See LA, 256 and 285 n. 1, for instance.
16 I use the phrase 'not published in full' deliberately, for sixteen pages of the original notebooks appeared in facsimile in the exhibition catalogue *R/B: Roland Barthes*, ed. Alphant and Léger.
17 Marie Gil (*Roland Barthes: Au lieu de la vie*, 378) explains that Macciocchi had visited China some years earlier and, upon her return, had published a book which celebrated the 'socialist paradise' of Mao's China and which won an audience among Parisian intellectuals who had become interested in Maoism. For the English translation of Macciocchi's book, see *Daily Life in Revolutionary China* (New York: Monthly Review Press, 1972). In her *Roland Barthes: Biographie*, Tiphaine Samoyault speculates that Barthes had probably read, or was at least familiar with, Macciocci's text (499). For more on the background to the trip, see Philippe Forest, *Histoire de* Tel Quel *1960–1982* (Paris: Seuil, 1995), 475–6.
18 Gil, *Roland Barthes: Au lieu de la vie*, 378–9.
19 Marcelin Pleynet, *Le Voyage en Chine: Chroniques du journal ordinaire 11 avril – 3 mai 1974 – extraits* (Paris: Hachette, 1980), 16. For a letter dated 25 February 1979 from Barthes to Pleynet about the publication of this text, see AL, 247. For the English translation of Kristeva's book, which first appeared in French in 1974, see *About Chinese Women*, trans. Anita Barrows (New York and London: Marion Boyars, 1986). For overviews of *Tel Quel*'s engagement with Maoism, see: Chapter 4 of Patrick ffrench, *The Time of Theory: A History of* Tel Quel *(1960–1983)* (Oxford: Clarendon Press, 1995); Chapter 4 of Danielle Marx-Scouras, *The Cultural Politics of* Tel Quel*: Literature and the Left in the Wake of Engagement* (University Park, PA: Pennsylvania State University Press, 1996); and Chapters 11 and 13 of Forest, *Histoire de* Tel Quel. Forest's book also provides (481–3) more information about the various publications which emerged from the voyage to China.
20 For Philippe Sollers's brief discussion of the trip, see the penultimate chapter ('Supplice chinois') of his *L'Amitié de Roland Barthes*.
21 For excellent accounts of the differences between 'So, How Was China?', the 'Compte rendu' and Barthes's journals from the trip, see Chapter 6 of Coste, *Bêtise de Barthes*; Lucy O'Meara, 'Barthes and Antonioni in China: The Muffling of Criticism', *Textual Practice* 30, vol. 2 (2016): 267–86; and Andy Stafford, 'Roland Barthes's Travels in China: Writing a Diary of Dissidence within Dissidence?', *Textual Practice* 30, vol. 2 (2016): 287–304.

22 I have modified Chris Turner's translation here, giving 'bricks' instead of 'building blocks' for the original 'briques'. Barthes explains (SM, 100) that the term in question comes from cybernetics, where, as Andrew Brown notes in his English translation of Barthes's *Carnets du voyage en Chine*, 'it means something like "module"'. But, Brown continues, 'Barthes seems to draw on its more basic meaning as "brick", a heavy, mass-produced block out of which to construct a discourse' (TC, 199 n. 20). As Claude Coste has pointed out (*Bêtise de Barthes*, 208–9), Barthes had used the term in question in *The Fashion System* some years before travelling to China, although the English translation obscures this fact by translating the original 'briques' (OC II, 984) as 'building blocks' (FS, 85). Additionally, there are numerous further uses of 'brique' in the seminar on *Sarrasine* of 1967–9 (SDB, 255, 261 and 265, for example).

23 See also LA, 229 and 239. For a related point, see Pleynet, *Le Voyage en Chine*, 38–9.

24 In her fascinating 'Roland Barthes and Literary Minimalism', *Barthes Studies* 1 (2015): 100–22, Diana Leca calls *Travels in China* a 'generically promiscuous text (travelogue? personal diary? reportage?)' (103). While I do not disagree with her, I will call the text a journal or a diary here, mainly for the sake of simplicity, but also because it seems to me that the terms 'diary' and 'journal' are exceptionally elastic in English.

25 Anne Herschberg Pierrot, Foreword to Barthes, TC, viii. Tiphaine Samoyault points out in *Roland Barthes: Biographie* that, by way of contrast, the notes relating to Japan were made on the habitual *fiches* (471).

26 See, for instance, the images which accompany Armine Kotin Mortimer, 'Coïncidence: Reécriture et désécriture de *Roland Barthes*', *Genesis* 19 (2002): 169–89 and many of the manuscript facsimiles in *R/B: Roland Barthes*, ed. Alphant and Léger.

27 Coste, *Bêtise de Barthes*, 200. I am nonetheless drawn to one of the facsimiles in the *R/B* exhibition catalogue (216) because, thanks to a spelling error on Barthes's part, my surname actually appears in the text. Barthes means to refer to the sport badminton, but he adds a 'g' by mistake and writes 'Badmington'. The error was preserved in *Carnets du voyage en Chine* (CVC, 22), but Andrew Brown corrects it without comment in his English translation (TC, 7). I was a couple of weeks away from my third birthday when Barthes wrote my name in his notebook; I am grateful to him for spotting my potential so early.

28 Antoine Compagnon, *L'Âge des lettres* (Paris: Gallimard, 2015), 54, 165.

29 An episode from the beginning of the third series of *Mad Men* dramatizes this danger memorably, in a scene involving Salvatore, a character who has spent the last two series concealing his desire for other men behind his marriage and enduring rejection from gentlemen who have caught his eye. At the beginning of

the third series, however, while he is away from New York on a business trip, it seems that Sal is finally going to get what he wants. He checks into his hotel, and the bellhop comes to his room. Before Sal can hand over a tip, the man moves towards him. They kiss. The stranger undoes Sal's waistcoat ... and discovers a large, wet ink stain on his shirt. The fountain pen in his breast pocket has leaked. 'Airplane,' he gasps, and the seduction continues until a fire alarm brings things to a halt. I like to think that Roland Barthes would have enjoyed this inkily erotic – or erotically inky – scene. 'Out of Town', *Mad Men*, series 3, episode 1. First broadcast on 16 August 2009.

30 Except that he failed to arrive in Beijing fresh and clean, of course: the first page of the journal records his failure to wash his ears before leaving and then his dropping of some 'greyish, greasy rice' onto his new trousers before the plane has even taken off (TC, 5).

31 Barthes also refers to the poverty of his notes in 'Compte rendu du voyage en Chine' (LA, 238).

32 Sollers, *L'Amitié de Roland Barthes*, 112–13.

33 TC, 94: 'Odd the way we are completely mothered by the Agency.' See also LA, 231. Marcelin Pleynet makes precisely the same complaint about being 'mothered' in *Le Voyage en Chine*, 68.

34 The English translation might give the impression that boredom (*ennui*) figures specifically in Barthes's summary of the evening – Andrew Brown's rendering has Barthes commenting, 'A crashing bore' (TC, 14) – but there is no mention of ennui in the original text, where Barthes writes 'Assommant et inévitable' (CVC, 28).

35 Kristeva's *About Chinese Women* also notes in its opening pages a sense of distance between the visitors and the Chinese citizens – 'I don't feel like a foreigner, the way I do in Baghdad or New York. I feel like an ape, a martian, an *other*,' she writes when recalling a visit to Huxian (12) – but this distance is due to radical cultural difference, not the controlling interference of the Agency. Indeed, Kristeva's book exhibits none of the anxieties articulated by Barthes – and none of the boredom, either. It is often hard to believe, in fact, that Barthes and Kristeva are writing about the same trip to China.

36 The visit occurred when the 'Pi-Lin Pi-Kong' campaign to denounce these two figures was at its height. Returning to his visit to China several years later in the course at the Collège de France on the Neutral, Barthes would describe the Pi-Lin Pi-Kong campaign as a '[r]hythmic outburst (I prefer that to the word "orchestration")' (N, 122).

37 See also TC, 163. For a related point, see Pleynet, *Le Voyage en Chine*, 81, 86. It is worth at this point recalling how Barthes subsequently defined the idyllic in *How*

To Live Together: 'Let's call "idyllic" any space of human relations defined by an absence of conflict' (HTLT, 88).

38 Laurent Binet, *La Septième fonction du langage* (Paris: Grasset, 2015), 167.
39 In his *L'Amitié de Roland Barthes*, Sollers responds to Barthes's depiction of him (162).
40 A further repetition of the statement about the rarity of the signifier in China can be found in 'Compte rendu du voyage en Chine' (LA, 236).
41 Barthes does not name the museum, but Kristeva's *About Chinese Women* (58) mentions a trip made by the visitors to the Panpo Museum of pre-history; I presume that this is the institution to which Barthes refers.
42 The barring image recurs on page 155 of the text. Another entry in the journal refers to the surrounding 'repression of the signifier' (TC, 141) and then its 'silencing' (TC, 142). For a different list of signifiers discovered in China, see LA, 237.
43 Ferdinand de Saussure, *Course in General Linguistics*, ed. Charles Bally, Albert Sechehaye and Albert Reidlinger, trans. Wade Baskin (London, Fontana, 1974), 66.
44 Saussure, *Course*, 113.
45 This latter fragment is dated 15 July 1974. An editorial footnote states that Barthes participated in the conference in Milan between 2 June and 5 June 1974 (LA, 299 n. 7). Barthes's presentation at the conference was published as 'Introduction: The Semiological Adventure', in SC, 3–8, and he describes the event briefly in a letter to Renaud Camus dated 2 June 1974 (AL, 346).
46 Indeed, one of the unused fragments of *Roland Barthes by Roland Barthes* has the narrator claiming that, for him, 1970 (the year of *S/Z*) was a turning point. From that date, he writes, 'the signifier is no longer a semiological entity' (LA, 309).
47 See also TC, 75 and LA, 238. The image of the tablecloth also appears in TC, 64, while Pleynet has similar regrets about the lack of surprise (*Le Voyage en Chine*, 68). The haiku became an object of fascination in Barthes's later writings. The *Preparation of the Novel* course at the Collège de France in the late 1970s devoted a great deal of time to the form, for instance, but the interest went back further, notably to *Empire of Signs*, where the haiku is celebrated for its ability to be both readable *and* to suspend meaning, to provide an exemption from meaning, to baffle the traditional Western desire to decipher, to pierce, to master the text. '[I]t makes impossible,' Barthes proposes, 'the most ordinary exercise of our language, which is commentary' (ES, 81). The haiku enlists signifiers, then, but delivers no signified. The magic of the signifier, precisely. For a fine overview of the haiku and 'japonisme' in Barthes's later work, see Chapter 4 of O'Meara, *Roland Barthes at the Collège de France*.
48 For a related comment, made some years later, see the discussion of 'tangibilia' in PN, 56. Further discussion of the tendency to enumerate can be found in

one of the unused fragments of *Roland Barthes by Roland Barthes* included in LA, 277.

49 The invocation of wild cherries is from OC II, 38; the Erté material occurs in RF, 120; and the reference to clothing worn by hippies comes from LF, 111. Diana Leca offers a wonderful account of the Barthes's tendency to 'stockpile' tangibilia in her 'Roland Barthes and Literary Minimalism'.

50 The passages on tea in *Travels in China* sometimes recall the descriptions of Japanese food in *Empire of Signs*, particularly the discussion in the latter text of soup (ES, 14).

51 For another bracketed digression about golden tea, see TC, 105.

52 See, notably, 'Psyche: Invention of the Other', in *Psyche: Inventions of the Other: Volume I*, trans. Peggy Kamuf and Elizabeth Rottenberg (Stanford: Stanford University Press, 2007), 1–47.

53 See also TC, 30 and 64, where, during different events, Barthes records that he is unable to take notes on the 'set theme'.

54 Jean-Claude Milner, *Le Pas philosophique de Roland Barthes* (Lagrasse: Verdier, 2003), 11. For another discussion of Barthes's punctuation, see Chantal Thomas, *Pour Roland Barthes* (Paris: Seuil, 2015), 124–8.

55 For a different analysis of typography in *Travels in China*, see Leca, 'Roland Barthes and Literary Minimalism'.

56 Wahl, 'Ouf!', 107. Marcelin Pleynet's *Le Voyage en Chine* repeatedly records a certain distance between Barthes and the other visitors. See, for instance, 43 (Barthes looks at his colleagues 'as a fish would an apple' while they discuss politics), 51 (Barthes isolates himself on the train to read his beloved *Bouvard and Pécuchet*) and 59 (Barthes stays in the car while the others go exploring).

57 Steven Ungar, *Roland Barthes: The Professor of Desire* (Lincoln, NE: University of Nebraska Press, 1984). My use of the term 'professor of ennui' to describe Barthes should not be confused with the way in which Chantal Thomas uses the phrase 'professeurs d'Ennui' when referring to those against whom she sets Barthes in *Pour Roland Barthes* (Paris: Seuil, 2015), 12. Thomas is referring there to those conventional, endoxal figures within academia whose position was called into question by Barthes's anti-normative writings. This, for me, does not eclipse the fact that those same writings often professed boredom.

58 Peter Toohey, *Boredom: A Lively History* (New Haven and London: Yale University Press, 2011).

59 Well, almost. Svendsen writes incorrectly of 'desire', not 'jouissance', although this may simply be an error caused by layered translation: Svendsen's book is translated from Swedish and the relevant footnote points to a German edition of Barthes's text. This possibility does not change the fact that Svendsen has nothing more to

say about Barthes in his book. Lars Svendsen, *A Philosophy of Boredom*, trans. John Irons (London: Reaktion, 2005), 47. I thank Fred Botting for first bringing Svendsen's book to my attention during a taxi ride across Lancaster which was anything but boring.

60 Reinhard Kuhn, *The Demon of Noontide: Ennui in Western Literature* (Princeton, NJ: Princeton University Press, 1976), 3. Ellipsis in original. The complete quotation can be found in PT, 25, although it should be noted that Kuhn has provided his own translation of the original French words.

61 It is not clear if Kuhn's dismissal of the *Tel Quel* writers as 'Maoist terrorists' (4) is meant to include Roland Barthes.

62 Elizabeth S. Goodstein, *Experience without Qualities: Boredom and Modernity* (Stanford: Stanford University Press, 2005), 55. The detailed critique of Kuhn occupies the whole of the first chapter of Goodstein's book (33–64).

63 Betty R. McGraw, 'Public Parks and Private Gardens: Sartre's Nausea and Barthes's Ennui', in *Signs in Culture: Roland Barthes Today*, ed. Steven Ungar and Betty R. McGraw (Iowa City: University of Iowa Press, 1989), 78.

64 Doehlemann distinguishes between situative boredom, the boredom of satiety, creative boredom and existential boredom in his *Langeweile?: Deutung eines verbreiteten Phänomens* (Frankfurt: Suhrkamp, 1991). As no English translation exists, and as I am unable to read German, I have had to rely on the summary provided by Lars Svendsen in *A Philosophy of Boredom* (41–2). In his *Boredom: A Lively History*, Peter Toohey translates the first form of boredom in the typology as 'situational'.

6

Hitchcock *Hapax*: Realism Revisited

'Yes, she said, away in the opposite direction, and you walk along until you come to a cinema.'

Ali Smith, *Artful*[1]

Brief encounter

For a long time, I went to bed early, disappointed that Roland Barthes had nothing to say about Alfred Hitchcock.

When Barthes died in March 1980, a little over a month before Hitchcock, his published work contained references to many film directors and their work: Eisenstein, Fellini, Dreyer, Antonioni, Chaplin, Mankiewicz, Pasolini, Kazan, Buñuel, Bresson and Chabrol, for example.[2] But nowhere was there a word about Hitchcock. The posthumous appearance early in the new millennium of the notes from Barthes's courses at the Collège de France and the seminar on 'le discours amoureux' brought to light further cinematic references, as had the publication of *Incidents* seven years after Barthes's death, but Hitchcock remained absent.[3] (My heart fluttered when I spotted *The Birds* nesting in the index to *The Neutral*, but I realized quickly that this was a reference to the play by Aristophanes, not Hitchcock's film of the same name.)

The long silence was at last broken in 2009 with the publication of the *Mourning Diary*, which contains the following parenthetical statement at the beginning of an entry that I quoted in full in Chapter 3: '(Saw a Hitchcock film, *Under Capricorn*)' (MD, 172).

This remains, at the time of my writing, the only reference to Alfred Hitchcock in the published work of Roland Barthes. Brief and fleeting, it is also deeply uncharacteristic, in that Barthes looks through the fiction, through the signifier, for reality, for a lost referent. The silence had been broken, but not with textual analysis, not with anything more than a somewhat disappointing aside with no true taste for fiction. While Hitchcock now figured, he hardly mattered: he was merely a way to regain *maman*. The encounter of which I had dreamed turned out to a brief encounter, maybe even a non-encounter, a slight glance that went nowhere.

In Barthes, then, Hitchcock is a pale *hapax*, a *hapax legomenon*. I want in the present chapter to address this strange state of affairs, this near-silence which has been neglected by other critics. Why did Barthes refer to many other filmmakers but say next to nothing about Hitchcock? Why is Alfred the man who appears too little, even though he was the most famous director of all for much of Barthes's writing career?[4] And what might Barthes have been missing? More precisely, I wish to approach these questions from the perspective of realism, textual analysis and what Barthes called the 'readable'. There are several interwoven reasons for this. First, the publication in 2011 of Barthes's seminar notes of 1967–9 on Balzac's 'Sarrasine' invites us, just two years after the appearance of the reference to Hitchcock in the *Mourning Diary*, to revisit the remarkable way of reading realism announced in 1970 in *S/Z*. The afterlives of Roland Barthes, that is to say, call us back to realism soon after calling our attention to the author's brief encounter with Hitchcock.

Second, it seems to me that a book about the posthumous legacy of Roland Barthes which failed to put Barthes to work in textual analysis would be something of a failure. Barthes, to my mind, was first and foremost a *reader*, primarily of literature, of course, but also of other signifying practices: art, photography, film, music, fashion and so on. To proceed as if his body of work, posthumous or otherwise, were merely a set of ideas or theories to summarize and transmit would be to miss the point. Whether he is understood as a critic, a theorist, or an *écrivain*, Barthes wrote reading, and I see in that gesture an invitation to read with him and to write in this wake. If the preceding chapters in *The Afterlives of Roland Barthes* have been largely readings of Barthes, this final chapter opens out with reading, with a reading, with Barthes enlisted on the trail of a text.

Third, Hitchcock's films, at least in the Hollywood years (1940–76), are examples of popular realism which, as such, descend from the literary tradition to which Balzac's 'Sarrasine' belongs. If the afterlives of Roland Barthes beckon us back to realism, and if they also expose at last the name of Alfred Hitchcock, then it strikes me as a good moment to revisit Hitchcock's realism with Barthes. This will involve returning to *Under Capricorn* – the only one of Hitchcock's films known to have caught Barthes's eye – and leading Barthes, to some extent, where he chose not to wander for long.[5] This is not wilful perversity; it seems to me, rather, that the recently published seminar notes on 'Sarrasine' offer, like their offspring *S/Z*, timely strategies for rereading the realism of mainstream cinema. If the posthumous appearance of Sarrasine *de Balzac* puts realism back on the agenda, why can't this realism be the realism of the screen, and not merely that of page?

Cinephobia[6]

As I noted in Chapter 3 of this book, there is a marked 'resistance to cinema' in the work of Roland Barthes. Cinema flickers across Barthes's pages regularly, however, even if, as Rachel Gabara has observed, his most famous extended analysis of film treats Eisenstein's *Ivan the Terrible* (1944/1958) as a series of stills – photographs, effectively – and not as a flow of moving images.[7] Alongside the resistance to cinema, that is to say, there is a persistence of cinema.

This persistence, as the list of directors given in the opening paragraph of this chapter hints, tends to involve references to films produced outside the limits of mainstream commercial cinema – outside 'Hollywood', in a word. When Hollywood productions are discussed by Barthes, they are usually cast in a negative light.[8] Joseph L. Mankiewicz's *Julius Caesar* (1953), for example, partakes in 'degraded spectacle' (MY, 17) and is guilty of 'a duplicity which is peculiar to bourgeois art: between the intellectual and the visceral sign is hypocritically inserted a hybrid, at once elliptical and pretentious, which is pompously christened "*nature*"' (MY, 18).[9] Elia Kazan's *On the Waterfront* (1954), meanwhile, 'is a good example of mystification' (ET, 39), in which 'what is orchestrated for us, despite all the caricatures, is the *restoration of order*' in the face of a challenge to established social norms (ET, 40).[10] Hollywood, for Barthes, tends to lie on the side of myth.[11] If its works register, they are to be resisted, exposed by the mythologist as part of the business of '*semioclasm*' (MY, xviii).

One of Barthes's discussions of the films of Sergei Eisenstein contains a more precise explanation of this resistance to the form and workings of mainstream Western cinema. Towards the end of 'Diderot, Brecht, Eisenstein', the discussion specifically of *The General Line*, *Battleship Potemkin* and *Mother Courage* suddenly cuts away to consider representation itself:

> In theater, in cinema, in traditional literature, things are always seen *from somewhere*; this is the geometric basis of representation: there must be a fetishistic subject in order to project this tableau. This point of origin is always the Law: law of society, law of struggle, law of meaning. Every militant art, therefore, must be representative, legal. For representation to be really deprived of origin and for it to transcend its geometrical nature without ceasing to be a representation, the price to pay is enormous: it is nothing less than death. In Dreyer's *Vampyr*, a friend reminds me, the camera tracks from the house to the graveyard and takes in *what the dead man sees*: this is the limit-point where representation can be baffled: the spectator no longer need occupy any specific point, for he cannot identify his eye with the corpse's closed eyes; the tableau has no point of departure, no support, it is a gap.
>
> (RF, 96–7)[12]

In this digression, this drift into Dreyer, realism raises its head. Hollywood, of course, is a realm of realism – of stabilized referents, of consciousness which is protected from doubt, as Jean-François Lyotard would put it.[13] It is 'an excessively obvious cinema' in which vision tends to remain untroubled and the certainty of the viewer is sustained by form and technique.[14] In the language of Barthes's *S/Z*, which had appeared three years before 'Diderot, Brecht, Eisenstein', classical Hollywood cinema is *readable*: its voices and its visions usually have unchallenged origins and aims.[15] It believes in the referent, as Barthes would later say when speaking about the realism of the haiku (PN, 85).

What catches Barthes's eye in Dreyer's *Vampyr* is a wonderfully un-Hollywood moment – a moment at which consciousness is opened to doubt by the baffling of representation itself. Appearing upon the screen in the film's remarkable dream sequence is an impossible sight, a sight which cannot be contained by realism: the viewer sees at length what a dead man sees – the ceilings and scenery pass overhead as, en route to the grave, he stares through the window in the lid of the coffin – and yet, of course, a dead man sees nothing at all in the safe realm of reality. *Vampyr* touches a troubling limit-point in its dream sequence. Who is looking? From where? How? Under what conditions can dead eyes see? What am I, the viewer, witnessing upon the screen? How can I possibly believe in the referent?

Classical Hollywood cinema usually avoids moments of such strangeness, such piercing impossibility, simply because it is a cinema of realism. This, it seems to me, accounts in part for Barthes's acute resistance to mainstream narrative film. 'I'm not a partisan of realism in art,' he stated in an interview published in 1980 (GV, 356) – a year in which he also used his affectionate speech about Michelangelo Antonioni's films to call realism a 'terrorist operation' (DAN, 65). Antonioni's 'great subtlety', Barthes claimed, consists in his 'always leaving the road of meaning open and as if undecided', so that the viewer is left 'to doubt the meaning of the message. This leakage of meaning, which is not the same as its abolition, enables [Antonioni] to disturb the psychological certitudes of realism' (DAN, 65).[16] These, I think, are the certitudes which prevent Barthes's work from embracing Hollywood cinema.

While the writings of Roland Barthes are my great professional love, I nonetheless find it disappointing that his engagements with Hollywood cinema effectively take the films at face value and never subject them to the kind of patient, close analysis bestowed upon the literary text in *S/Z* and *Sarrasine de Balzac*.[17] Barthes might have gone further with Hollywood, I think, and I want in this chapter to lead him against his will in that direction. If he resists cinema, especially Hollywood cinema, I want, with Hélène Cixous's *Manhattan* in mind, to resist fiercely his resistance.[18]

Parsimonious plurality

The incipit of *S/Z* crafts a certain calmness: 'There are said to be certain Buddhists whose ascetic practices enable them to see a whole landscape in a bean' (SZ, 3). The preparatory notes of 1967–9 on 'Sarrasine', however, begin with a sense of urgency. Barthes opens the first session by recalling the title of the projected seminar: 'Recherches sémiologiques: analyse d'ouvrages récents, compte rendu et discussion de travaux en cours' ('Semiological research: analysis of recent publications, account and discussion of works in progress'). He then adds immediately that this title had been chosen 'some months ago' and that his research has since shifted direction (SDB, 55). A new task, he announces, now strikes him as 'more urgent' (SDB, 55): the seminar will work instead on a single text, Honoré de Balzac's 'Sarrasine', in order, it eventually transpires, both to overthrow structuralism and to offer a new way of reading classical realism which involves an attention to 'parsimonious' plurality (SDB, 490; SZ, 6, 14, 260). Balzac's nineteenth-century tale of a young man who falls in love with a beautiful opera singer named La Zambinella, only to discover that the object of his desire is in fact a castrato, will be studied extremely closely in order to establish its wild resistance to closure, to unity, to systems and to resolution. Realism will be read so that it reads otherwise.

When *S/Z* appeared in 1970, a preliminary note acknowledged that the book was 'a trace of work done during a two-year seminar (1968–9) at the École pratique des Hautes Études'.[19] What only became clear with the publication of Sarrasine *de Balzac* in 2011, however, was that Barthes, in spite of his initial articulation of urgency, had moved remarkably slowly through Balzac's tale in the classroom: while *S/Z* would make it to lexia 561 of 561, the seminar had reached no further than the end of the tale's prologue (lexia 152) after two years. (Little wonder, then, that Barthes spoke in the second teaching session of a 'drugged reading', of hyperaesthesia and of the 'right to digression' [SDB, 79, 75]). I want to reactivate the urgency of the opening of the seminar on 'Sarrasine' by returning to realism, to Hitchcock's *Under Capricorn*, in the afterlife of Roland Barthes. This will involve rereading *S/Z* – a text which argues for the importance of rereading, after all (SZ, 15–16) – alongside the more recently published Sarrasine *de Balzac*. This is not a simple revisiting of *S/Z* nearly half a century on from its appearance; it is, rather, a reopening of realism prompted by the sometimes different propositions found in the preparatory seminar of 1967–9.

Barthes's analysis of Balzac's tale distinguishes famously between the 'readable' (*lisible*) and the 'writable' (*scriptible*) text.[20] Readable texts, he explains, 'are products (and not productions), they make up the enormous mass of our literature' (SZ, 5). They are 'classic' cases which 'can be read but not written' (SZ, 4; see also SDB, 488). They are 'committed to the closure system of the West, produced according to the goals of this system, devoted to the law of the Signified' (SZ, 7–8). They are institutional, too, the seminar adds, in that social 'institutions refuse *en bloc* the *non-readable* [*le non lisible*]; for them, the non-readable is outside the system [*hors système*]' (SDB, 85). The readable text is one in which 'everything holds together' (SZ, 156) and comes together: enigmas established early in the narrative will be resolved by the end. A piece of readable fiction leads its audience comfortably to knowledge, to 'symbolic plenitude' (SZ, 201), to the 'plenitude of meaning' (SZ, 79; SDB, 86). Although its unfolding is often punctuated by 'snares' – 'deliberate evasion[s] of the truth' (SZ, 75) which keep the narrative alive by delaying closure – the readable text travels essentially from trembling expectation to truth (SZ, 76).

As a readable text, 'Sarrasine' appears to tie up its loose ends – to reveal at last its mobilizing truth – by its final page: the identity of the enigmatic little old man, the history of La Zambinella, and the secret source of the Lantys' wealth all come to light, having begun in shadowy intrigue. 'All the enigmas are now unveiled, the vast hermeneutic sentence is closed', writes Barthes towards the end of *S/Z* (209; translation modified). What was once unknown is now known; with the turning of each new page, the reader moves gradually but surely from wondering to knowledge. If the readable is a 'known' form, as the seminar puts it (SDB, 488), it is at once a form committed to making things known.

The writable text, however, is less easy to isolate for analysis:

> There may be nothing to say about writable texts. First of all, where can we find them? Certainly not in reading (or at least very rarely: by accident, fleetingly, and obliquely in certain limit-works): the writable text is not a thing, we would have a hard time finding it in a bookstore ... The writable is the novelistic without the novel, poetry without the poem, the essay without the dissertation, writing without style, production without product, structuration without structure.
>
> (SZ, 4–5; translation modified)

Faced with this problem of exemplification, Barthes decides to turn back to the readable, back to 'Sarrasine'. This move – announced at the very beginning of the seminar of 1967–9 – is not a case of defeat, of letting the readable simply stand; it is, rather, as I will discuss in more detail towards the end of this chapter, the offering of a 'third way' (SDB, 87), a way which deconstructs the easy opposition between *lisible* and *scriptible*. As this 'third way' is pursued through the lexias and a series of digressions, it becomes apparent that Balzac's tale, contrary to first impressions, fails to maintain its status as a classic, readable text. The main enigmas of the text are eventually disclosed, but 'Sarrasine' generates further gaps within its fabric; 'what at first reading seems a seamless garment' is actually torn.[21]

The twenty-ninth lexia, for instance, is a short and apparently simple sentence from near the beginning of Balzac's story. Referring to the curious, haunting figure who appears at the Lantys' party, the narrator reports: 'It was a man.' It would be easy to pass over this phrase, mining it for information and accepting a stable referent; everything seems perfectly clear in the light of those four safe syllables, which, Barthes notes in the session of 28 March 1968, are enunciated from a perspective of anthropological omniscience (SDB, 232). But the sentence, Barthes observes, is actually far from straightforward: the narrator who utters the words in question knows – because he later reveals; because he is able to tell the tale – *that the figure at the party is actually a castrato*, La Zambinella. The apparent anthropological omniscience is undermined, and Barthes is led to pose a series of troubling questions:

> Who is speaking? Is it a scientific voice which from the type 'personage' infers, in passing, a species, 'man', in order later to give it another species, 'castrato'? Is it a phenomenalist voice naming what it notices, the wholly masculine garb of the old man? Here it is impossible to attribute an origin, a point of view, to the enunciation. Now, this impossibility is one of the ways in which the plural of a text can be appreciated. The more indeterminate the origin of an enunciation, the more plural the text ... [I]n the classic text the majority of the utterances are assigned an origin, we can identify their parentage, who is speaking ... [H]owever, it may happen that in the classic text, always haunted by the appropriation of speech, the voice gets lost, as though it had disappeared into a hole in the discourse. The best way to conceive the classic plural is then to listen to the text as a shimmering [*chatoyant*] exchange of multiple voices, posed on different wavelengths [*ondes*] and seized by moments of a sudden *fading*, whose hole permits the enunciation to migrate from one point of view to another, without warning ...
>
> (SZ, 41–2; translation modified)

The readable text – where everything is supposed to hold together and where statements should have firm origins – is undone by undecidability, by fading. Barthes's question about the words 'It was a man' – 'Who is speaking?' – cannot be answered definitively, for the text shimmers with irreconcilable possibilities.[22] The signifiers drift and disavow 'the law of the Signified'. 'The classical text,' Barthes concludes in an interview about *S/Z* and *Empire of Signs*, 'is closed, but only partially' (GV, 73). It has a plurality which, while muted and 'parsimonious', is nonetheless a plurality. The readable and the writable no longer stand in binary opposition: the one fades into the other.

It is precisely this 'retreat of the signified' (GV, 84) before the 'galaxy of signifiers' (SZ, 5) that keeps Barthes reading – or rereading – 'Sarrasine'. The tenacity of the tale springs from its gaps, its moments of *fading*.[23] If everything in a readable text really were grounded, closed off, fixed, what would call us back to its pages? If the readable were genuinely and wholly readable, the mere telling of the tale would inter interest. But if, by way of contrast, the moment of complete closure were deferred, constantly in retreat, rereading would be kindled, desirable, for something would forever slip away from the reader who has been promised coherence and a firm ending.

Barthes's analysis of 'Sarrasine' stresses the significance of rereading, in fact. Near the beginning of *S/Z*, he notes that the practice in question is 'an operation contrary to the commercial and ideological habits of our society, which recommends "throwing away" the story once it has been consumed ("devoured"), so that we can then move on to another story, buy another book' (SZ, 15–16; translation modified). In the preparatory seminar, Barthes links this tendency more explicitly to capitalism, arguing that 'ephemeral reading' or 'reading without return [*retour*] corresponds to the acceleration of consumption' (SDB, 81). But rereading, he insists, is the sign of commitment to difference – in the classroom in February 1968, Barthes even used the term 'revolutionary' (SDB, 81) – for 'those who fail to reread are obliged to read the same story everywhere' (SZ, 16). In their rush to mastery and the next purchase, such satisfied consumers miss 'the magic of the signifier' and fail to linger with the plurality of the text. This very magic means that rereading 'is no longer consumption, but play (that play which is the return of the different)' (SZ, 16), and 'if we agree to reread the text ... it is actually and invariably for a ludic advantage [*profit*]: to multiply the signifiers, not to reach some ultimate signified' (SZ, 165; translation modified). Rereading is possible, pleasurable and productive precisely because the 'ultimate signified' never arrives, but is, rather, kept at a desirable distance by the magic of the signifier. In the imagery of the preparatory seminar, the text is no longer something that is eaten just once and, in that devouring, assimilated (SDB, 82). To reread is not to consume.

Although Barthes's discussion in the classroom on 15 February 1968 proposes that the ideology of consumption and disdain for rereading reaches its peak in cinema – 'film, *concretely*, can be seen only once' (SDB, 81) – I want in what remains of this chapter to borrow the approach to (re)reading developed in *S/Z* and *Sarrasine de Balzac* for an analysis of Hitchcock's *Under Capricorn*. This is not entirely at odds with Barthes's discussion of cinema and consumption, in fact, for immediately after proposing that film 'can be seen only once', he imagines a '*cultural* (revolutionary) future of cinema' which would depend upon 'the possibility of repeated viewings-readings [*visions-lectures-répétées*]' and the replacement of the 'no return' with 'a new time, that of perpetual rewriting' (SDB, 81). And neither is my filmic direction wholly alien to the *literary* path of Barthes's discussion of 'Sarrasine', for he notes near the end of the preparatory seminar that there is such a thing as 'a readable eye, just as there is a tonal ear' (SDB, 528). Returning to *Under Capricorn* with an eye for undecidability can, I want to suggest, bring out the 'parsimonious' plurality of readable realism. My desire in this interpretation echoes the wish of *S/Z* to appreciate the plural which constitutes the text (SZ, 5). Alfred Hitchcock is evidently not Dreyer, not Antonioni, not Fellini – he is working within the realistic conventions of Hollywood, which means that the oceans of *Lifeboat* (1944) and *To Catch a Thief* (1955), for example, are not the delightfully jarring plastic sheets of Fellini's *Casanova* – but neither is he necessarily quite Hitchcock.[24]

Out of the past

Under Capricorn performed poorly at the box office when it was first released in 1949. Éric Rohmer and Claude Chabrol, in the very first book-length study of the director's films, noted that it had been a 'resounding commercial failure', and John Russell Taylor's authorized biography of Hitchcock describes how the film was 'repossessed by the bank which had financed it, so that it was unseeable for a number of years'.[25] Hitchcock himself, in fact, would later use the term 'mistake' when discussing *Under Capricorn* with François Truffaut, adding that, 'If I were to make another picture set in Australia today, I'd have a policeman hop into the pocket of a kangaroo and yell, "Follow that car!"'[26]

The film nonetheless found favour with early Hitchcock scholars. Rohmer and Chabrol, for instance, after pointing out its commercial failings, went on to put it in the category of Hitchcock's 'most sincere' and 'pure' achievements, and described it as 'one of his later masterpieces'.[27] In the pages of *Cahiers du cinéma*, meanwhile, their fellow New-Wave critic Jean Domarchi declared it to be the director's 'unknown masterpiece', and Robin Wood, working across the Channel, described it as one of the 'obviously "different" films' which show collectively 'the amazing *variety* of [Hitchcock's] work'.[28]

In more recent years, however, *Under Capricorn* has fallen from critical favour. At the turn of the millennium, Florence Jacobowitz called it 'virtually ignored', while Mark Rappaport opened a reappraisal of the film in 2003–4 by describing it as 'the movie no one wants to write about'.[29] Ed Gallafent, commenting shortly after Rappaport, added that *Under Capricorn* has often been seen as 'a footnote to *Rope*', with which it shared a fondness for long takes and the uncertain honour of being one of the two films produced by the short-lived Transatlantic Pictures company established in the late 1940s by Hitchcock and Sidney Bernstein.[30]

Given the relative obscurity of *Under Capricorn* in the present, it seems sensible to offer here a brief, selective plot summary:

> New South Wales, 1831. The Honourable Charles Adare arrives in the colony with his second cousin, the new Governor. Soon after, while visiting a local bank, Adare meets Sam Flusky and wonders why his name sounds familiar. Adare learns that Flusky was sent to Australia as a convict, but his request for information about the crime is refused by Mr Potter, an employee of the bank, who informs Adare that asking such questions about the past is frowned upon. Potter also warns Adare against accepting an invitation to the Fluskys' house, but Charles ignores the advice and finds himself at the mansion the following evening. Here he discovers that the drunk and delirious wife of Mr Flusky was once Lady Henrietta (Hattie) Considine – a family friend from back home in Ireland. After an awkward dinner, Sam informs Charles of the troubles within the marriage: Sam was once a groom employed in the stables of the wealthy Considine family, and his romantic relationship with Hattie led to an incident (he does not provide details) which saw him imprisoned for seven years. Hattie followed him to Australia.

Charles learns that Sam was convicted of murdering Hattie's brother, Dermot, and moves into the Fluskys' house, where he tries to restore Hattie's lost confidence and stature. This leads to a growing romance between Charles and Hattie which causes tensions with Sam. After a public humiliation at a ball hosted by the Governor, Hattie tells Charles the truth about the past: it was actually she who killed Dermot, but Sam took the blame; the truth has been hidden ever since. Just as Charles and Hattie are embracing, Sam returns and orders Charles to leave. Charles takes Sam's horse but returns moments later, saying that the horse has fallen and injured its leg. Sam steps outside and shoots the horse. When he returns, he and Charles struggle over the gun. A shot is fired. Charles falls to the ground.

The wound is not fatal, but the Governor and the Attorney General take a dim view of the event. Sam, because of his criminal past, could face a harsh punishment or even the death penalty. Charles, meanwhile, is to be sent back to Ireland in disgrace. Hattie tells the Governor the truth about the killing of Dermot, but this only means that she will be sent to Ireland to face trial for the crime. Suspecting that Charles and Hattie have engineered a return to Ireland so that they can be together, Sam refuses to corroborate his wife's account of what happened to her brother. This once again puts Sam in danger: the Governor tells him that he could now be charged with shooting Charles.

In the final minutes, however, Charles saves the day when he explains to the authorities how he came to be wounded by a bullet from Sam's gun: it was, he insists, an accident. The Governor is forced to free Sam, and the film ends with Charles leaving Australia for Ireland as Sam and Hattie, reunited as a couple, wave from the edge of the water.[31]

As this account of *Under Capricorn* reveals, the film makes great use of what *Sarrasine de Balzac* and *S/Z* call the hermeneutic code:

> Let us designate as *hermeneutic code* (HER) all the units whose function it is to articulate in various ways a question, its response, and the variety of chance events which can either formulate the question or delay its answer; or even, constitute an enigma and lead to its solution. ... Under the hermeneutic code we list the various (formal) terms by which an enigma can be distinguished, suggested, formulated, held in suspense, and finally disclosed.
>
> (SZ, 17–19; see also SDB, 519–24)

Even the title of Balzac's tale, Barthes observes, enlists the hermeneutic code:

> The title raises a question: *What is Sarrasine?* A noun? A name? A thing? A man? A woman? This question will not be answered until much later, by the biography of the sculptor named Sarrasine. ... Thus, the title *Sarrasine* initiates the first step in a sequence which will not be completed until No. 153.
>
> (SZ, 17)[32]

As he adds in the seminar notes, we find here in the story's title 'the first term of a proposition [*proposition*], the other term of which is in lexia 153'.[33]

From the very outset, that is to say, 'Sarrasine' depends upon a 'question/answer' structure (SDB, 103) which is part of a movement towards the 'discovery of truth' (SDB, 519).[34] Enigmas are created under the hermeneutic code – the preparatory seminar states that the hermeneutic code *is* the code of enigma more forcefully than *S/Z* and the measured deferral of their resolution sustains the desire of the reader to receive answers.[35] And because 'Sarrasine' is a conventional, classic piece of fiction, it must keep its 'promise of response' as part of the 'contract of the readable'; failing to resolve matters would be, Barthes notes in the final session of the seminar, giving the example of Georges Perec's *La Disparition*, 'a sign of modernity' (SDB, 520).[36]

The title of Hitchcock's film does not, I think, have the enigmatic quality of 'Sarrasine', but it is not long before the text, like Balzac's tale, attaches a series of enigmas to a proper name in the form of a question/answer structure. These mysteries are part of what Robin Wood calls, without actually mentioning Barthes, *Under Capricorn*'s 'complex hermeneutic chain'.[37] Around five minutes into the film, Charles Adare visits the bank to discuss his prospects in Australia with Mr Potter, who had introduced himself to Adare during the ceremony to welcome the Governor. During their meeting in an office which looks out onto the main banking hall, an employee enters the room and informs Potter that a Mr Flusky is waiting to see him.

> ADARE (*rising from his seat and turning to look into the banking hall*):   Flusky, Flusky. That's a curious name. It seems to ring a bell somewhere. Flusky, Rusky, Dusky ... Who is he?
> POTTER (*rising to join Adair at the window*):   Uh, one of our most admirable citizens – a large land-owner. He has made some most profitable investments. Rather a financial genius in his way. He owns the

best stud in the colony, and he works like a galley-slave. Uh, that is to say, he works very hard.

ADARE: Flusky, Flusky. Where the devil have I heard that name before?[38]

Where, indeed?

While both men gaze out from the office, their backs are turned to the camera, which never moves or cuts to provide a point-of-view shot. (The entire sequence in the bank is one unbroken shot, in fact.) The scene beyond the window remains indistinct, enigmatic, and it is not even clear at whom they are looking while they discuss the mysterious Flusky, although one man in the hall is slightly more noticeable than the other customers because he is smoking.[39] The form of *Under Capricorn* at this point, that is to say, works to enhance the enigma surrounding the signifier 'Flusky': just as Adare cannot recall why he recognizes the name, the viewer is not permitted to share the gaze which is fixed upon Flusky. We see that Adare and Potter are looking, that something has caught their attention, but the uncutting, unmoving camera withholds for now the subject of their vision.

When Adare learns, as the conversation with Potter continues, that the mysterious Flusky came to Australia as a convict, he asks about the nature of the crime, but Potter refuses to expand: it is not polite in this *terra nova*, he explains, to discuss a man's past.[40] The hermeneutic code is once again at work: to the query about Flusky's crime comes no satisfying response; social propriety demands conveniently that mystery remain, that the truth be suppressed. Adare then asks to be introduced to Flusky, whose subsequent entrance dissolves one element of the overall enigma which has been created during the scene: the viewer now at least knows what he looks like, and this visual disclosure is emphasized when the camera moves in for a close-up on his face. (I presume that this close-up is not meant to stress what Helen Simpson's original novel calls 'a nose pendant after the Jewish manner above a lip that might have lengthened in Wicklow'.[41])

New mystery is soon generated, however, when the conversation turns to Adare's place of origin. In response to a question about his homeland, Adare says, 'Ireland, the west of Ireland', and the camera again closes in on Flusky, with whom this reply has evidently struck a chord. Adare, presumably noticing the reaction (the camera does not let us know for certain), asks if Flusky knows that part of the world. 'I might,' comes the response, hovering cryptically between a 'yes' and a 'no'. In a moment of historical symmetry, Flusky has apparently recognized Adare's surname, for he then asks if Charles is related to 'the Adares of Killeely', to which Charles replies, 'Yes, Lord Killeely is my father. Do you know him?' Flusky turns away without responding to this question – a question which is, of course, searching for an end to the mystery. The long scene in the bank ends with yet another new enigma when, after Flusky has left the office, Potter detains Charles for a moment and advises him not to accept any invitation to Flusky's house. 'Why not?' asks Adare. All that Potter can say before he is interrupted by the sudden return of the other man is, 'A gentleman in your position can't be too careful' – a response which is, of course, no real answer at all.

This early sequence in *Under Capricorn* establishes the enigma – or, to be more precise, the series of enigmas – surrounding the name 'Flusky' which will drive much of the narrative. As in Balzac's 'Sarrasine', there is in Hitchcock's film a gradual movement towards disclosure via delay, snare, equivocation and 'jamming'.[42] For instance, it is not long after the scene in the bank that the viewer receives an answer – a delayed answer – to Adare's query about Flusky's criminal past. As the two men walk along the street, a third man approaches and tries to sell a shrunken human head to Flusky. When Flusky pushes the pedlar to the ground, he finds himself denounced as a murderer (which was, in fact, one of the possibilities raised by Charles in his conversation with Potter). But the answering of this one question (*What was Flusky's crime?*) is followed quickly by the restating of the larger mystery surrounding the figure, for in the very next scene Adare visits the Governor in his official residence and relates his meeting with Potter and Flusky. 'Flusky, Flusky. Odd name,' says the Governor, mirroring Charles's initial response in the bank. He then adds a layer to the mystery when he says, 'Flusky. Had something to do with some woman or other. It can't be the same man.'[43]

But the Governor is wrong: it *is* the same man. This becomes apparent when Charles attends a dinner at Flusky's house. The sequence first answers the enigma, formulated by Potter, surrounding the taboo on accepting such an invitation. When Adare arrives outside the residence, Richard Addinsell's score sounds ominous phrases and the reluctant coachman says, 'There's something *queer* about that place.' He has a point: inside, Charles finds brawling servants, a long line of male guests whose wives have all mysteriously become unable to accompany their husbands to the gathering, and a lady of the house who wanders around drunk and hallucinating.[44] Charles soon discovers that the dishevelled Lady Henrietta Flusky was once Hattie Considine, a friend of his sister from his childhood in Ireland.

While this does not explain why Adare had earlier recognized her married name, 'Flusky', and why the Governor associated it with 'some woman or other', it is not long before the sequence at the Fluskys' house provides a partial explanation. Following the awkward dinner, Sam and Charles walk together outside. The camera joins them when the conversation has already begun, and Sam proceeds to explain how his relationship with Hattie in Ireland had angered her family, for whom he worked as a stable-boy. 'There was bound to be trouble, and trouble there was, alright,' he recalls. 'Her people were determined to get me, and get me they did,' he continues, but then adds, 'We needn't go into how they did it. I was lucky to escape the gallows, but I got seven years' transportation.' The viewer learns here, in other words, that *something* unfortunate happened, and that this *something* led to Sam's conviction and removal to Australia, but the narrative withholds the full story: although it is now clear why the Governor associated Sam's name 'with some woman or other', the finer points of the past remain unknown. In Barthes's language, there has been no more than a 'partial decipherment' (SZ, 149), a 'partial disclosure' (SZ, 209), 'a scrap of an answer' (SZ, 38).

In the next scene, however, comes the missing information. Angry with Charles for his visit to the Flusky house, the Governor says:

> He's the blackguard who eloped with Hattie Considine. He was their stable-boy or something. And there's worse to come. It was hushed up at the time, but he murdered her brother, Dermot, in cold blood. If he'd had justice, he'd have been hanged like a dog. As it was, the jury brought in culpable homicide and he was transported for seven years.

The full truth about the past is out, it seems, and much of the rest of the narrative is concerned with the attempt, led by Charles, to restore Lady Henrietta's wellbeing and confidence, and to make her, in an echo of Hitchcock's earlier *Rebecca* (1940), mistress of the unruly and unwelcoming house. Her appearance changes – so much so, in fact, that Charles says, 'Is that the reflection of Lady Henrietta Considine, or is it not?' as he gazes fondly at her image in the mirror. The use of her old surname here confirms that what Adare calls the 'reincarnation' is underway. 'She's coming back, I tell you,' he says eagerly to Sam.

But something else comes back, too: the *real* events surrounding the death of Lady Henrietta's brother. Shortly after the ball at Government House, she reveals to Charles that the official story about the past is a lie: as the camera closes in upon her face for dramatic emphasis, she explains that the fatal shot was fired by her, not by Sam, and that he took the blame in order to protect her. 'Oh, God, the relief!' she sighs to Sam, having finally dissolved a long lie with truth, with confession.[45]

As it moves towards its final reel, in other words, *Under Capricorn* eventually provides its audience with a genuine answer to the question about Flusky's past. The hermeneutic code, Barthes remarks in Sarrasine *de Balzac*, informs 'a structured process of discovery of the truth' (SDB, 519). The earlier disclosure of historical 'truth' – Sam killed Dermot – is exposed in time as a false revelation, but into the sustaining gap created by this shock steps the authentic version of events. When the film ends, the various mysteries and troubles appear to have been dissolved, Sam and Henrietta seem happy and committed to each other in the warm glow of truth and freedom, and Charles, whose desire for Henrietta had become something of an obstacle to conventional romantic closure, is seen leaving Australia for Ireland as the reunited married couple look on and wave. In the words of *S/Z*, it appears that '[a]ll the enigmas are now dissolved, [and] the vast hermeneutic sentence is closed' (SZ, 209). As a readable Hollywood production, *Under Capricorn* gives the convincing impression of repletion and resolution. Truth, after all, 'is what completes, what closes' (SZ, 76).

The third way; or, 'un *autre* lisible'

One of the most dazzling of achievements of *S/Z* and its preparatory notes of 1967–9 was to undermine such a convenient analysis of the readable text. In the seminar on 'Sarrasine', Barthes asks, beneath the heading 'Sur la lisibilité' ('On Readability'), if, given the Western refusal of writable texts, the only way to subvert readability is with the unreadable (*l'illisible*). '[S]omeone like Sollers,' he replies, would certainly propose this (SDB, 86). For Barthes, however, there is 'a third way [*une troisième voie*]' (SDB, 87): destructive parody of the readable.

The point about parody is not developed at length in the seminar, but it seems to me that the subsequent analysis of 'Sarrasine' – initially and partially in the classroom in 1967–9, and then more extensively in *S/Z* in 1970 – is, in effect, a playful exploration of a 'third way' beyond simple acceptance or outright rejection of the readable. Instead of turning away from Balzac's classic text – instead of rejecting it in favour of an unreadable alternative – Barthes turns back to 'Sarrasine' and, as I noted earlier in this chapter, draws out the strange moments at which the readable fails, exceeds its own rules and limits, blossoms out into plurality. What emerges from this careful analysis is, in the language of the seminar, 'an *other* readable [*un* autre *lisible*]' (SDB, 488), another way of seeing 'Sarrasine'. Balzac's classic fiction is not what it seems.

The same is true of *Under Capricorn*. Hitchcock's film, a mainstream Hollywood production intended for the popular market, appears to obey the conventions of readability, above all in its handling of the enigmas to which I have already turned my attention. Alongside the tendency to dissolve mysteries, to raise and answer questions, there are moments at which the viewer is provided with a privileged position – a position of 'dominant specularity', to take a phrase from Colin MacCabe's classic essay on realism.[46] When Charles tells Hattie that she should take charge of the keys and the kitchen of the house, for instance, only the viewer can see that Milly is observing and listening to the conversation, and that she has presumably just witnessed their intimacies. Later, in the preparations for the ball, Sam suggests that Hattie's dress might be enhanced by a necklace of rubies, but Charles rejects the idea, saying that it would make Hattie 'look like a Christmas tree'. What neither Charles nor Hattie can see, however, but what the camera has allowed the viewer to glimpse by positioning itself to the rear of Sam, is that the latter has been holding a ruby necklace behind his back. With Adare's dismissal of the proposal, he tucks it out of sight. In each case, the composition of the film allows the viewer to see the bigger picture, to see the truth of the situation while characters remain at the level of the partial and the limited.[47]

And yet, this general readability, this obvious movement towards closure and knowledge, is undermined by a strange undecidability which transports *Under Capricorn* in another direction. This rogue element, this disruptive force, emerges shortly after the ball sequence and remains at work until and beyond the final frame of the film. This, as I see it, is the emergence of 'an *other* readable'.

After the argument at the ball, Hattie and Charles return to the Fluskys' home, where she tells Adare the full, true story of her involvement with Sam and her responsibility for the death of Dermot. Just as Charles is urging her to abandon her husband, Sam returns and finds them in an embrace. Adare is asked to leave, and he rides away on Sam's horse, only to return moments later and report that the mare has been injured in a fall. While Charles and Hattie wait inside the house, Sam steps outside and shoots the animal. The camera lingers near the doorway with Charles and Hattie. Sam's returning footsteps grow louder on the gravel. He stops in front of Charles, who has his back to the camera. 'You gentleman!' snarls Sam, invoking the class distinction which has flared up often in the film.[48] 'You bloody murdering gentleman!' The two men wrestle. A shot is heard. Charles falls to the ground.

The authorities in Sydney are poised to take firm legal action against Sam, who, because of his previous conviction, could face the death penalty. At the very end of the film, however, Charles saves the day when he relates to the Governor and Mr Corrigan the events surrounding the shooting. Hattie has already appealed to the Governor and the Attorney General, and now she persuades Charles to tell the truth and to confirm that the gun was not fired deliberately. When Charles begins his narration, his tone is sombre, angry, and he speaks rather slowly. He reaches the point in his story at which Sam returns to the house with the weapon. 'When he came back, I ...' he begins, and then pauses. His delivery now changes significantly: his tone of voice becomes lighter and he speaks more quickly as, in short, he makes light of the shooting:

ADARE: When he came back, I ... (*pause*) took hold of the pistol. It was a large, double-barrelled one. I handled it clumsily and took a charge in my shoulder, that's all.
GOVERNOR: Lady Henrietta said there was a quarrel.
ADARE: Was there? Did she say that? Well, Flusky wasn't exactly delighted at losing his favourite mare. He probably said so. I forget.
GOVERNOR: I may tell you, sir, that I don't believe a word of your story. Not a word.
ADARE: Nevertheless, that will be my evidence.

GOVERNOR: On your word of honour, as a gentleman? Is that all that happened that night?
ADARE: As a gentleman.

In the light of Charles's statement, Sam is released from custody. In the next scene – the very last of the film – Charles is shown leaving Australia for Ireland.

Adare's reconstruction of events brings the married couple back together, removes Sam from danger, and leads to his own withdrawal from the troublesome 'love triangle'. It works, that is to say, towards neat closure. But is Charles's version of events reliable, truthful? Does it represent faithfully what actually happened in the Fluskys' house after the ball? Are we dealing, in other words, with a case of realism, or might this be a moment at which what Barthes called 'an *other* readable' begins to emerge?

Under Capricorn does not allow viewers to answer these questions – questions raised by the film itself – with any degree of certainty. They resonate as open questions, unresolved enigmas, beyond the text's ending, beyond Charles's convenient departure for Ireland. This openness can be traced back to the way in which the text presents the shooting. Because the camera remains behind Adare during the struggle, and because he blocks the viewer's line of sight, it is impossible to see and know precisely what happens when the two men wrestle. We see that Sam is still holding the weapon which he has just used to kill his injured horse, but both figures' hands are obscured during the altercation and at the moment when the trigger is pulled to fire the bullet which wounds Charles. As I observed earlier in this chapter, there are moments in the film at which the camera, operating on the side of the readable, offers the viewer a privileged glimpse of something unseen by other characters (the ruby necklace, for example). There is no such visual access during the struggle between Sam and Charles, however. When Sam hides the jewellery behind his back, the camera isolates his hands for our inspection. But when those same hands hold the gun which wounds Adare, they are hidden from sight; the camera fails here to do what we know it can do, what we know it can do *for us* as curious viewers of *Under Capricorn*.[49] Undecidability therefore hangs over the crucial scene: was it an accident, or did Sam mean to shoot Adare? Is Flusky innocent (as he was in the case of the earlier shooting of Dermot Considine) or guilty?

Charles eventually offers an answer, of course, at the insistence of the Governor: the gun, he says, went off accidentally. But can this account, this piece of 'evidence', as he puts it, be trusted? As I noted above, Adare's description of what happened is presented in a way which makes the crucial part of his narration – *the only part of the story which the viewer does not already know* – seem light, frivolous. We are aware, moreover, that his casual response to the Governor's statement about there having been a quarrel that night – 'Was there?' – is effacing something, for we witnessed the argument to which the Governor has referred, and we know that Charles was involved. What is more, the final part of Adare's response to the Governor's comment make his account, offered here to the representatives of law and authority, strikingly weak: 'I forget,' he says, precisely when he meant to remember.

The Governor suspects that Charles's account (or the crucial part of it, at least) is fabricated: 'I don't believe a word of your story,' he replies. 'Not a word.' Charles's immediate reaction is curious: he does not defend himself by asserting this veracity of his narration, but merely says instead, 'Nevertheless, that will be my evidence.' Has he, realizing Hattie's love for Sam in the shadow of death, done the honourable thing by lying to save Sam and to remove himself from the traumatic love triangle? Has he broken the code of the gentleman but done so, effectively, to restore that code on a higher level?

Because these questions, like the other questions surrounding the shooting, are never answered by the text, what *S/Z* calls 'the vast hermeneutic sentence' is never closed in *Under Capricorn*. Like 'Sarrasine' in Barthes's 'microanalysis' (GV, 69), the text ends on a note of suspension, not resolution. Sam's final remarks to Charles, spoken at the edge of the water, at the edge of Australia, allude to a future encounter, even though Adare is leaving for the other side of the world: 'We've got a lot to make up to you,' says Flusky, before adding to the sense of unfinished business with the line, 'Goodbye for now, sir.' For now, but not forever. This hint that the present will inform the unknown future recurs when Charles says to Hattie, 'I won't ever forget you.' And the land to which Charles is returning – the land mentioned explicitly during this farewell – is, he informed Potter near the beginning of the film, a land where bygones can never be bygones.

What the final scene of *Under Capricorn* leaves open as a possibility, in other words, is a meeting in the future between Charles, Sam and Hattie – a recreation of the troublesome triangle which Adare's departure apparently dismantles. If Charles has lied about the past, and if the falsified past has a habit in the film of returning to trouble its players with a call for the outing of truth, then it seems to me that *Under Capricorn* gestures towards unknown and unseen revelations which lie beyond its limits, beyond the words 'THE END' which appear upon a map of Australia as the credits begin to roll. The typographic placement of the two signifiers is strangely telling, in fact: the final letter, 'D', spills out beyond the edge of the land into the sea, even though both words could have fitted quite neatly within the territory, within the borders. The entire film has taken place within the colony, but 'THE END' – as a formal feature and a simple phrase – leaves the land and, like Charles, lights out for another territory.[50] Where we might, because this is a Hollywood film, expect to find resolution and closure, we encounter *ambivalence*, to use a term which is more significant in Sarrasine *de Balzac* than it is in *S/Z*.[51]

* * *

In a section of *Roland Barthes: Au lieu de la vie* entitled 'Barthes ne «va» pas au cinéma' ('Barthes does not "go" to the cinema'), Marie Gil proposes that the author's relationship to film was 'richer than he let on at the end of his life'.[52] Gil makes her case by looking back over Barthes's long career at the range and number of his various writings on cinema. I am persuaded by her account, but I have sought in this chapter to problematize Barthes's resistance to cinema in a rather different manner. (There is more than one way to resist resistance.) While there is just one reference to Alfred Hitchcock in Barthes's entire published *oeuvre*, and while that body of work has little time for the commercial realism of Hollywood, it is possible to see, by returning to *Under Capricorn* with *S/Z* and the seminar on 'Sarrasine' in mind, how Barthes's work can enable an analysis of mainstream film which appreciates plurality (however parsimonious), ambivalence and undecidability, not closure and conformity. When the posthumously published Sarrasine *de Balzac* reopens the case of realism with a sense of urgency, it at once names and navigates a 'third way' which exceeds the crude critical opposition between acceptance and rejection, between the readable and the writable. If we are to honour the afterlives of Roland Barthes, if we are to rise to their challenges, if we are to put Barthes to work and not merely summarize his words, we might wish to travel and read this way. *Then the great light of the South West begins.*

Notes

1 Ali Smith, *Artful* (London: Penguin, 2013), 103. I thank Nicholas Royle for bringing this book to my attention.
2 Examples of these references can be found in the following works by Barthes: Eisenstein (RF, 41–62 and 89–97), Fellini (CL, 115–16), Dreyer (RF, 96–7), Antonioni (DAN), Chaplin (MY, 35–7), Mankiewicz (MY, 15–18), Pasolini (OC IV, 944–6), Kazan (ET, 39–41), Buñuel (LD, 139), Bresson (ADP) and Chabrol (OC I, 943–5). This list is merely representative, not exhaustive.
3 See, for example, the references to Fellini's *Satyricon* (1969) in *The Neutral* (N, 191) and *The Preparation of the Novel* (PN, 119), and also to the director's *Casanova* (1976) in the latter volume (PN, 106, 108). The notes from the 'discours amoureux' seminar, meanwhile, feature two references to Buñuel (DA, 140, 482); Dreyer's *Ordet* figures briefly in the 'Journal-Moisson' on the voice (LA, 355–6); and the 'Evenings in Paris' section of *Incidents* contains a reference to Barthes seeing 'the film by Pialat on teenagers' in September 1979 (IN, 168). No title for the latter is given in the text, but, given the date, I presume this to have been *Passe ton bac d'abord* (dir. by Maurice Pialat, 1978), which is usually known in English as *Graduate First*. Claude Coste comes to the same conclusion, in fact, in his *Bêtise de Barthes* (Paris: Klincksieck, 2011), 168. I have excluded the volumes of seminar notes on *Le Lexique de l'auteur* and *Sarrasine de Balzac* from this particular chronology because they were published after the *Mourning Diary*'s reference to Hitchcock came to light.
4 For an excellent historical account of Hitchcock's fame and status, see Robert E. Kapsis, *Hitchcock: The Making of a Reputation* (Chicago and London: University of Chicago Press, 1992).
5 In *Roland Barthes, le métier d'écrire* (Paris: Seuil, 2006), Éric Marty relates a visit to the cinema with Barthes to see *The 39 Steps*, but explains that this was one of the remakes, not Hitchcock's version (53). Marty does not specify *which* remake was showing that evening, but, given the period covered by his memoir, I suspect that it was Don Sharp's version of 1978 (released as *The Thirty-Nine Steps*), not the Ralph Thomas remake of 1959.
6 I take the notion of Barthes's 'cinephobia' from Colin Gardner, 'Roland Barthes', in *Film and Philosophy: The Key Thinkers*, ed. Felicity Colman (Abingdon and New York: Routledge, 2014), 109. Gardner's essay offer a fine overview of Barthes's various writings on cinema.
7 Rachel Gabara, *From Split to Screened Selves: French and Francophone Autobiography in the Third Person* (Stanford, CA: Stanford University Press, 2006), 66. Gabara is referring here to Barthes's 'The Third Meaning:

Research Notes on Several Eisenstein Still', which was first published in 1970 (RF, 41–62).
8   So much so, in fact, that Philip Watts has claimed that Barthes's texts exhibit 'a European literary scholar's mistrust of an art form that he saw as primarily a commodity and a popular spectacle'. Philip Watts, 'Roland Barthes's Cold-War Cinema', *SubStance* 34, vol. 3 (2005): 17. *The Afterlives of Roland Barthes* went into production before the publication of Watts's *Roland Barthes' Cinema* (New York: Oxford University Press, 2016), so I was not able to engage with this work.
9   As Philip Watts has pointed out ('Roland Barthes's Cold-War Cinema': 18), the critique of Mankiewicz's film was written at a time when Barthes was 'actively promoting a Brechtian theatrical aesthetic' – an aesthetic far removed from that of *Julius Caesar*.
10 Marlon Brando, the star of *On the Waterfront*, comes in for further criticism in the later essay 'Diderot, Brecht, Eisenstein' for his self-serving 'mannerisms of the Actors' Studio' and his 'grimacing in *Last Tango in Paris*' (RF, 95).
11 This is particularly clear in the brief text entitled 'Au cinémascope' which appeared in February 1954. Here, as so often, the choice is between history (*Battleship Potemkin*) and myth (*The Robe*). Although this piece was one of Barthes's mythologies, it was not included in *Mythologies* itself in 1957, but can be found as a distinct piece in the *Oeuvres complètes* (OC I, 456–7) and, in English, as 'On CinemaScope' (OCS).
12 Barthes's account of the sequence in Dreyer's film contains a small error: the corpse's eyes are not closed. I do not think that this can be attributed simply to the author's 'resistance to cinema': he makes a related textual slip in his summary of Balzac's 'Sarrasine', after all, when he suggests, in his analysis of lexia 220, that the statue becomes broken (SZ, 112).
13 Jean-François Lyotard, 'Answer to the Question: What is the Postmodern?', in *The Postmodern Explained to Children: Correspondence 1982–1985*, trans. Don Barry et al. (London: Turnaround, 1992), 9–25.
14 See Chapter 1 of David Bordwell, Janet Staiger and Kristin Thompson, *The Classical Hollywood Cinema: Film Style & Mode of Production to 1960* (London: Routledge, 1985).
15 Barthes actually uses the term from *S/Z* in 'Diderot, Brecht, Eisenstein' to describe art which is 'metaphysical, i.e., signifying, readable, representative' (RF, 97).
16 Colin Gardner concludes ('Roland Barthes', 116) that 'Buñuel and Antonioni are rare beacons in Barthes' already threadbare cinematic pantheon'.
17 Although I was not aware of it consciously at the time, I can now see that this frustration motivated much of my book *Hitchcock's Magic* (Cardiff: University of Wales Press, 2011), in which I enlisted the work of Barthes to argue for the

seductive power of Hitchcock's films as being a matter of the 'magic of the signifier'.

18 Hélène Cixous, *Manhattan: Lettres de la préhistoire* (Paris: Galilée, 2002), 34: 'J'ai toujours resisté durement à mes resistances' ('I have always resisted fiercely my resistances').

19 SZ, vi. A brief note on the dates given here by Barthes. The published version of the teaching notes carries the dates 1967–8 and 1968–9, as these are the academic years covered by the seminar on 'Sarrasine'. The initial session of the first year did not, however, take place until 8 February 1968, which probably explains the dates given at the beginning of *S/Z*.

20 Richard Miller's English translation of *S/Z* renders the two French terms in question as 'readerly' and 'writerly'. I find this imprecise and prefer 'readable' and 'writable', which I will use instead throughout this chapter.

21 Andrew Brown, *Roland Barthes: The Figures of Writing* (Oxford: Clarendon Press, 1992), 168.

22 In the preparatory seminar on 'Sarrasine', it becomes apparent that '*What* is speaking?' would be an appropriate question to pose at this point in Balzac's tale, for Barthes proposes, in the session of 28 March 1968, that 'the hermeneutic code, the code of enigma' is what speaks in lexia 29, in order to trick the reader, defer revelation and maintain narrative desire (SDB, 234). The corresponding analysis in *S/Z* does not present matters in quite this way (see SZ, 41–2).

23 A more lengthy discussion of *fading* can be found in the figure of that name in the session of the 'discours amoureux' seminar dated 20 February 1975 (DA, 160–7). See also LD, 112–16.

24 In pointing out here that Hitchcock uses water instead of jarringly unrealistic plastic sheets for his oceans, I am not ignoring the fact that he nonetheless often employs rear-projected or painted scenery whose artificiality is inescapable. See, for instance, Chapter 6 of Lesley Brill, *The Hitchcock Romance: Love and Irony in Hitchcock's Films* (Princeton, NJ: Princeton University Press, 1988). I think that such critics are right about this element of Hitchcock, but I also think that the disruption to realism is far more severe in a film like Fellini's *Casanova*.

25 Éric Rohmer and Claude Chabrol's *Hitchcock: The First Forty-Four Films*, trans. Stanley Hochman (New York: Ungar, 1979), 97; John Russell Taylor discusses the film's financial failure and repossession in *Hitch: The Life and Work of Alfred Hitchcock* (London: Abacus, 1981), 189. Rohmer and Chabrol's book first appeared in French in 1957.

26 See François Truffaut, *Hitchcock*, updated edn (London: Paladin, 1978), 224–30, where Hitchcock's comments about the film are consistently negative. He refers

twice to his making a 'mistake' with the film (224, 226) and also to his 'error' (226). The remark about the kangaroo can be found on 229.

27 Rohmer and Chabrol, *Hitchcock*, 36 and 56. The description of the film as one of Hitchcock's 'later' works only makes sense when it is remembered that Rohmer and Chabrol were writing in the late 1950s.

28 Jean Domarchi, 'Le chef-d'oeuvre inconnu', *Cahiers du cinéma* 39 (1954): 33–8; Robin Wood, *Hitchcock's Films Revisited*, rev. edn (New York: Columbia University Press, 2002), 65. Wood's book first appeared simply as *Hitchcock's Films* in 1965 and then went through various revisions as *Hitchcock's Films Revisited*. The description of *Under Capricorn* quoted here is taken from the introduction to the original edition. Not all French responses to the film were as positive as those of Domarchi, Rohmer and Chabrol. For an overview, see James M. Vest, *Hitchcock and France: The Forging of an Auteur* (Westport, CT and London: Praeger, 2003), 15. Threaded through Vest's book is an analysis of the place of *Under Capricorn* in the construction of Hitchcock as an auteur.

29 Florence Jacobowitz, '*Under Capricorn*: Hitchcock in Transition', *CineAction* 52 (2000): 18; Mark Rappaport, '*Under Capricorn* Revisited', *Hitchcock Annual* 12 (2003–4): 42.

30 Ed Gallafent, 'The Dandy and the Magdalen: Interpreting the Long Take in Hitchcock's *Under Capricorn* (1949)', in *Style and Meaning: Studies in the Detailed Analysis of Film*, ed. John Gibbs and Douglas Pye (Manchester and New York: Manchester University Press, 2005), 68.

31 Readers wanting a much more thorough plot summary should consult Jane E. Sloan, *Alfred Hitchcock: A Filmography and Bibliography* (Berkeley and Los Angeles: University of California Press, 1995), 224–32.

32 In a section of Sarrasine *de Balzac* which has no equivalent in *S/Z*, Barthes discusses the metalinguistic and commercial elements of the title of a text (SDB, 98–101).

33 SDB, 103. The French term 'proposition' does not translate simply into English. While it can mean 'proposition'/'proposal' (in the logical sense), it can also mean 'clause' (in the grammatical/linguistic sense). The editors of the 'Sarrasine' seminar, Andy Stafford and Claude Coste, point out in a footnote earlier in the volume that Barthes's use of the term embodies both of these possibilities (SDB, 77, n. 2). I thank Andy Stafford for a clarifying conversation about this issue.

34 The remark about the question/answer structure occurs in the seminar of 15 February 1968. Barthes's essay entitled 'The Structural Analysis of Narrative', which was written in 1969 but not published until 1971, also discusses the question/answer phenomenon (SC, 239).

35 SDB, 234: 'What speaks here is the hermeneutic code, the code of enigma.' *S/Z* approaches this clear equation when it refers to 'the hermeneutic (or enigmatic) *genus*' (SZ, 210), but its formulation lacks the directness of the sentence in the teaching notes.
36 Perec's novel, which was first published in French in 1969, is known in English as *A Void*, trans. Gilbert Adair (London: Harvill, 1994).
37 Wood, *Hitchcock's Films Revisited*, 329.
38 The popular novel upon which the film is based makes it much clearer at this point that Adare does not know Flusky's name from his financial success in Australia. When he is told that Flusky is 'Rich; a landowner', he replies 'No, it's not that. Something, somewhere –', and the novel then refers to an 'elusive memory' relating to the name. Helen Simpson, *Under Capricorn* (London: William Heinemann, 1937), 20. For a fine account of the differences between novel and film, see Constantine Verevis, 'Under a Distemperate Star: *Under Capricorn*', in *Hitchcock at the Source: The Auteur as Adaptor*, ed. R. Barton Palmer and David Boyd (Albany, NY: State University of New York Press, 2011), 173–88.
39 The figure is indeed Flusky, but his identity is not apparent at the time; it only becomes known when he enters the office.
40 Helen Simpson's original novel makes more of the desire to break from the past in colonial Australia, which is presented often as a land of and for the future.
41 Simpson, *Under Capricorn*, 21.
42 For Barthes's account of jamming in the readable text, see SZ, 46–7.
43 Helen Simpson's novel is less enigmatic in the equivalent scene: the Governor's reply, 'Something about his wife –' (31), has more precision, less openness and mystery, than the line in Hitchcock's adaptation.
44 As a readable text, to use the language of *S/Z*, *Under Capricorn* allows the viewer to know clearly that Lady Henrietta is imagining things: when she calls Charles up to her room, the camera follows him to reveal that there is nothing on the end of the bed. Helen Simpson's source novel withholds such certainty at the time of the incident (*Under Capricorn*, 41); the moment of revelation, of truth and knowledge, does not come until Adare's later conversation with Sam (44).
45 As part of their reading of Hitchcock as a Catholic *auteur*, Rohmer and Chabrol make much of the place of secrecy and liberating confession in *Under Capricorn* (*Hitchcock*, 97–103). For a similarly Catholic interpretation, see Donald Spoto, *The Dark Side of Genius: The Life of Alfred Hitchcock*, new edn (London: Plexus, 1994), 335.
46 Colin MacCabe, 'Realism and the Cinema: Notes on Some Brechtian Theses', in *Theoretical Essays* (Manchester: Manchester University Press, 1985), 39.

47 See also the moment at which Charles holds a blank invitation to the ball at Mansion House but pretends that it requests the presence of Hattie and Sam. The camera here shows us that there are no names on the card, and Charles can obviously see this as well, but Sam and Hattie are unaware of the truth.

48 For a discussion of class in *Under Capricorn*, see Wood, *Hitchcock's Films Revisited*, 326–35.

49 As one of my students, Jamie Williams, has pointed out to me, Charles's right hand is partly obscured during his reconstruction of the scene, too, because it is tucked inside his jacket.

50 With this in mind, I cannot agree with Robin Wood's claim that *Under Capricorn* has a 'happy ending, one of the most unambiguous in all of Hitchcock' (*Hitchcock's Films Revisited*, 244–5). Wood, it seems to me, is right to propose that the married couple has been brought back together by the departure of Hattie's '"savior"' (245), but he overlooks the uncertain future to which the film points as it ends.

51 See, notably, SDB, 218, where ambivalence is described as a particular class of the parts of the hermeneutic code. *S/Z* does not go quite this far.

52 Gil, *Roland Barthes: Au lieu de la vie*, 457. The phrase 'Barthes ne « va » pas au cinéma' is, Gil explains, an allusion to Patrice Maniglier and Dork Zabunyan's *Foucault va au cinéma* (Paris: Bayard, 2011).

Postscript: Afterlives' Afterlives

And after?

I have trailed and traced the afterlives of Roland Barthes, gone after them, through the chapters of this book. I have done so because it seems to me that the posthumous publications of recent years render earlier scholarship in the field, for all its charm and insights, incomplete and in need of revision. I am not for one moment proposing that we simply ignore or dismiss previous writings on Barthes's work; I have drawn upon some of that research when preparing my pages, and I continue to learn from it. My point, rather, is that the many additions to Barthes's *oeuvre* in the years since his death, particularly this side of the new millennium, call upon us, as responsible writers, as writers who respond, to intervene, to pick up the pen once more, to face new vistas and to reckon with the afterlives of Roland Barthes. If we ignore this call, if we allow knowledge to remain as it has been, we rot in the realm of what Barthes called 'dead repetition' (RB, 71). My aim here has been, by living with the afterlives, to develop new readings, new understandings, new directions.

I am not foolish or arrogant enough to believe that I have now had the last word. First, this book has not engaged in detail with all of the posthumous publications bearing Barthes's name which are in print at present. I have been selective in order to pursue particular points and patterns at suitable length. 'Encyclopedias are impossible,' Barthes noted in a discussion of the information age towards the end of *The Neutral* (N, 203), and I believe that this also holds true when writing about Barthes's *oeuvre*. Second, *all* criticism comes, in time, to need rethinking and updating. The Barthes of 2016 – the Barthes of the moment of my concluding – will no doubt seem partial and quaint to a reader who happens to open this book, should copies still exist, in 2066. There is much unpublished material in the Barthes archive at the Bibliothèque nationale de

France; it is possible that major texts will emerge into print in the future – after my *Afterlives* – and require further critical reconsideration. (Will we ever see all of the notes for *Vita Nova*, for example? Will the many thousands of other *fiches* find a form between covers?)

Roland Barthes by Roland Barthes comes to a close with a short handwritten passage which the preparatory notes for the book linked to the idea of producing an 'Anti-Dictionary' (LA, 342) that would 'differ ideologically' from its conventional counterpart (LA, 125):

> And after?
> – What to write now? Can you still write anything?
> – One writes with one's desire, and I am not through desiring.
>
> (RB, 188; translation modified)

I have written this book with my desire, and I, likewise, am not through desiring, for the simple reason that the work of Roland Barthes will not stop swelling, signifying anew and breathing life into a posthumous anti-dictionary. Even afterlives have afterlives.

Bibliography

Works by Roland Barthes

NB: For an explanation of the abbreviations used in this book in references to works by Roland Barthes, see the preliminary note on abbreviations and translations.

Album: Inédits, correspondances et varia. Ed. Éric Marty and Claude Coste. Paris: Seuil, 2015.
Camera Lucida: Reflections on Photography. Trans. Richard Howard. Rev. edn. New York: Hill and Wang, 2010.
Carnets du voyage en Chine. Paris: Christian Bourgois, 2009.
Critical Essays. Trans. Richard Howard. Evanston, IL: Northwestern University Press, 1973.
'Dear Antonioni'. Trans. Geoffrey Nowell-Smith. Appendix to Geoffrey Nowell-Smith, *L'avventura*, 63–8. London: BFI, 1997.
Le Discours amoureux: Séminaire à l'Ecole pratique des hautes études 1974–1976. Ed. Claude Coste. Paris: Seuil, 2007.
The Eiffel Tower and Other Mythologies. Trans. Richard Howard. Berkeley and Los Angeles: University of California Press, 1979.
Elements of Semiology. Trans. Annette Lavers and Colin Smith. New York: Hill and Wang, 1973.
Empire of Signs. Trans. Richard Howard. New York: Hill and Wang, 1983.
The Fashion System. Trans. Matthew Ward and Richard Howard. Berkeley and Los Angeles: University of California Press, 1990.
The Grain of the Voice: Interviews 1962–1980. Trans. Linda Coverdale. Berkeley and Los Angeles: University of California Press, 1991.
How To Live Together: Novelistic Simulations of Some Everyday Spaces. Trans. Kate Briggs. New York: Columbia University Press, 2013.
Incidents. Trans. Teresa Lavender Fagan. London and New York: Seagull Books, 2010.
Journal de deuil: 26 octobre 1977 – 15 septembre 1979. Ed. Nathalie Léger. Paris: Seuil/IMEC, 2009.
The Language of Fashion. Ed. Andy Stafford and Michael Carter. Trans. Andy Stafford. Oxford and New York: Berg, 2006.

'Lecture: In Inauguration of the Chair of Literary Semiology, Collège de France, January 7, 1977'. Trans. Richard Howard, *Oxford Literary Review* 4, vol. 1 (1979): 31–44.

Le Lexique de l'auteur: Séminaire à l'École pratique des hautes études 1973–1974, suivi de fragments inédits du Roland Barthes par Roland Barthes. Ed. Anne Herschberg Pierrot. Paris: Seuil, 2010.

A Lover's Discourse: Fragments. Trans. Richard Howard. Harmondsworth: Penguin, 1990.

Michelet. Trans. Richard Howard. Oxford: Basil Blackwell, 1987.

Mourning Diary. London: Notting Hill Books, 2011.

Mourning Diary: October 26, 1977 – September 15, 1979. Ed. Nathalie Léger. Trans. Richard Howard. New York: Hill and Wang, 2010.

Mythologies. Rev. edn. Ed. Annette Lavers. Trans. Annette Lavers and Siân Reynolds. London: Vintage, 2009.

The Neutral: Lecture Course at the Collège de France (1977–1978). Ed. Thomas Clerc. Trans. Rosalind E. Krauss and Denis Hollier. New York: Columbia University Press, 2005.

Le Neutre: Notes de cours au Collège de France 1977–1978. Ed. Thomas Clerc. Paris: Seuil/IMEC, 2002.

Oeuvres complètes. Rev edn. Ed. Eric Marty. Paris: Seuil, 2002. 5 vols.

'On CinemaScope'. Trans. Jonathan Rosenbaum, *Jouvert* 3, vol. 3 (1999). Online publication, available online at http://english.chass.ncsu.edu/jouvert/v3i3/barth.htm.

'On Robert Bresson's Film *Les Anges du péché*'. Trans. Richard Howard. In *Robert Bresson*, ed. James Quandt, 211–13. Toronto: Toronto International Film Festival Group, 1998.

Le Plaisir du texte précédé de *Variations sur l'écriture*. Paris: Seuil, 2000.

The Pleasure of the Text. Trans. Richard Miller. New York: Hill and Wang, 1975.

La Préparation du roman: Notes de cours et de séminaires au Collège de France 1978–1979 et 1979–80. New edn. Ed. Nathalie Léger and Éric Marty. Transcriptions by Nathalie Lacroix. Paris: Seuil, 2015.

La Préparation du roman I et II: Notes de cours et de séminaires au Collège de France 1978–1979 et 1979–80. Ed. Nathalie Léger. Paris: Seuil/IMEC, 2003.

The Preparation of the Novel: Lecture Courses and Seminars at the Collège de France (1978–1979 and 1979–1980). Ed. Nathalie Léger. Trans. Kate Briggs. New York: Columbia University Press, 2011.

The Responsibility of Forms: Critical Essays on Music, Art, and Representation. Trans. Richard Howard. Berkeley and Los Angeles: University of California Press, 1991.

Roland Barthes by Roland Barthes. Trans. Richard Howard. London: Papermac, 1995.
The Rustle of Language. Trans. Richard Howard. Oxford: Blackwell, 1986.
Sade, Fourier, Loyola. Trans. Richard Miller. Baltimore and London: Johns Hopkins University Press, 1997.
Sarrasine de Balzac: Séminaires à l'École pratique des hautes études 1967–1968, 1968–1969. Ed. Claude Coste and Andy Stafford. Paris: Seuil, 2011.
'The "Scandal" of Marxism' and Other Writings on Politics. Trans. Chris Turner. London and New York: Seagull Books, 2015.
The Semiotic Challenge. Trans. Richard Howard. Berkeley and Los Angeles: University of California Press, 1994.
'Simply a Particular Contemporary': Interviews, 1970–79. Trans. Chris Turner. London and New York: Seagull Books, 2015.
Sollers Writer. Trans. Philip Thody. London: Athlone Press, 1987.
S/Z. Trans. Richard Miller. Oxford: Blackwell, 1990.
Travels in China. Trans. Andrew Brown. Cambridge: Polity, 2011.
'A Very Fine Gift' and Other Writings on Theory. Trans. Chris Turner. London and New York: Seagull Books, 2015.
Writing Degree Zero. Trans. Annette Lavers and Colin Smith. London: Jonathan Cape, 1967.

Other works

Aciman, André. 'Deliberating Barthes'. In *Roland Barthes: Critical Evaluations in Cultural Theory*, ed. Neil Badmington, 30–7. Abingdon and New York: Routledge, 2010. 4 vols. Vol. 3.
Aeschimann, Éric. 'Désaccords autour des notes posthumes de Roland Barthes'. *Libération* 21 January 2009. Available online at http://www.liberation.fr/culture/2009/01/21/desaccords-autour-des-notes-posthumes-de-roland-barthes_304293.
Alphant, Marianne. '*Presque* un roman'. In *R/B: Roland Barthes*, ed. Marianne Alphant and Nathalie Léger, 125–8. Paris: Seuil/Centre Pompidou/IMEC, 2002.
Aouillé, Sophie. 'Roland Barthes: *Journal de deuil*'. *Essaim* 23, vol. 2 (2009): 173–4.
Attridge, Derek. 'Roland Barthes's Obtuse, Sharp Meaning and the Responsibilities of Commentary'. In *Writing the Image After Roland Barthes*, ed. Jean-Michel Rabaté, 77–89. Philadelphia: University of Pennsylvania Press, 1997.
Bach, Raymond. 'The "Tombeau idéal": Mallarmé's *Tombeau d'Anatole*'. *Dalhousie French Studies* 20 (1991): 3–26.

Badir, Sémir and Dominique Ducard, eds. *Roland Barthes en* Cours *(1977–1980): Un style de vie*. Dijon: Éditions Universitaires de Dijon, 2009.

Badmington, Neil. 'Follow that Vaporetto!'. *Times Literary Supplement*, 11 December 2015: 22.

Badmington, Neil. *Hitchcock's Magic*. Cardiff: University of Wales Press, 2011.

Badmington, Neil. 'Sighs and Citations'. *Times Literary Supplement*, 15 July 2011: 25.

Badmington, Neil, ed. 'Deliberations: The Journals of Roland Barthes'. Special issue of *Textual Practice* 30, vol. 2 (2016).

Badmington, Neil, ed. *Roland Barthes: Critical Evaluations in Cultural Theory*. Abingdon and New York: Routledge, 2010. 4 vols.

Barnes, Julian. *Levels of Life*. London: Jonathan Cape, 2013.

Batchen, Geoffrey, ed. *Photography Degree Zero: Reflections on Roland Barthes's Camera Lucida*. Cambridge, MA and London: MIT Press, 2009.

Bellon, Guilllaume. *Une Parole inquiète: Barthes et Foucault au Collège de France*. Grenoble: ELLUG, 2012.

Bellour, Raymond. '"... *Rait*": Sign of Utopia'. Trans. Jeffrey Boyd. In *Roland Barthes: Critical Evaluations in Cultural Theory*, ed. Neil Badmington, 356–63. Abingdon and New York: Routledge, 2010. 4 vols. Vol. 4.

Benoit, Éric. *Néant sonore: Mallarmé ou la traversée des paradoxes*. Geneva: Droz, 2007.

Binet, Laurent. *La Septième fonction du langage*. Paris: Grasset, 2015.

Birnbaum, Jean. 'La publication d'inédits de Barthes embrase le cercle de ses disciples'. *Le Monde* 21 January 2009. Available online at http://www.lemonde.fr/culture/article/2009/01/21/la-publication-d-inedits-de-barthes-embrase-le-cercle-de-ses-disciples_1144698_3246.html.

Bishop, Ryan and Sunil Manghani, eds. *Barthes/Burgin: Research Notes for an Exhibition*. Edinburgh: Edinburgh University Press, 2016.

Bordwell, David, Janet Staiger and Kristin Thompson. *The Classical Hollywood Cinema: Film Style & Mode of Production to 1960*. London: Routledge, 1985.

Borges, Jorge Luis. 'The Mirror of Ink'. In *Collected Fictions*, trans. Andrew Hurley, 60–2. New York: Penguin, 1998.

Brill, Lesley. *The Hitchcock Romance: Love and Irony in Hitchcock's Films*. Princeton: Princeton University Press, 1988.

Brown, Andrew. *Roland Barthes: The Figures of Writing*. Oxford: Clarendon Press, 1992.

Burgin, Victor. 'Re-reading *Camera Lucida*'. In *Roland Barthes: Critical Evaluations in Cultural Theory*, ed. Neil Badmington, 149–63. Abingdon and New York: Routledge, 2010. 4 vols. Vol. 3.

Burnier, Michel-Antoine and Patrick Rambaud. *Le Roland-Barthes sans peine*. Paris: Balland, 1978.

Calvet, Louis-Jean. *Roland Barthes: A Biography*. Trans. Sarah Wykes. Bloomington and Indianapolis: Indiana University Press, 1995.

Cassegrain, Guillaume. *Roland Barthes ou l'image advenue*. Vanves: Hazan, 2015.

Chateaubriand, François-René de. *Memoirs of Chateaubriand*. Trans. Robert Baldick. Harmondsworth: Penguin, 1965.

Cixous, Hélène. *Manhattan: Lettres de la préhistoire*. Paris: Galilée, 2002.

Comment, Bernard. 'De la pensée comme autofiction'. *Le Magazine littéraire* 482, January 2009: 58–61.

Compagnon, Antoine. *L'Âge des lettres*. Paris: Gallimard, 2015.

Compagnon, Antoine. 'Roland Barthes's Novel'. Trans. Rosalind Krauss. *October* 112 (2005): 23–34.

Compagnon, Antoine. 'Writing Mourning'. Trans. Sam Ferguson. *Textual Practice* 30, vol. 2 (2016): 209–19.

Compagnon, Antoine, ed. *Prétexte: Roland Barthes: Colloque de Cerisy*. Paris: Christian Bourgois, 2003.

Coste, Claude. *Bêtise de Barthes*. Paris: Klincksieck, 2011.

Culler, Jonathan. *Barthes*. London: Fontana, 1983.

Culler, Jonathan. 'Preparing the Novel: Spiraling Back'. *Paragraph* 31, vol. 1 (2008): 109–20.

Culler, Jonathan. *Structuralist Poetics: Structuralism, Linguistics and the Study of Literature*. London: Routledge and Kegan Paul, 1975.

Dante Alighieri. *La Vita Nuova (Poems of Youth)*. Trans. Barbara Reynolds. London: Penguin, 1969.

De Beauvoir, Simone. *The Second Sex*. Trans. Constance Borde and Sheila Malovany-Chevallier. New York: Vintage, 2011.

De Rambures, Jean-Louis. *Comment travaillent les écrivains*. Paris: Flammarion, 1978.

Derrida, Jacques. 'Differance'. In *'Speech and Phenomena' and Other Essays on Husserl's Theory of Signs*, trans. David B. Allison, 129–60. Evanston, IL: Northwestern University Press.

Derrida, Jacques. '*Geschlecht* II: Heidegger's Hand'. Trans. John P. Leavey, Jr. In *Deconstruction and Philosophy: The Texts of Jacques Derrida*, ed. John Sallis, 161–96. Chicago and London: University of Chicago Press, 1987.

Derrida, Jacques. *Of Grammatology*. Trans. Gayatri Chakravorty Spivak. Baltimore: Johns Hopkins University Press, 1976.

Derrida, Jacques. 'Psyche: Invention of the Other'. In *Psyche: Inventions of the Other: Volume I*, trans. Peggy Kamuf and Elizabeth Rottenberg, 1–47. Stanford: Stanford University Press, 2007.

Derrida, Jacques. *The Truth in Painting*. Trans. Geoff Bennington and Ian McLeod. Chicago and London: University of Chicago Press, 1987.

Derrida, Jacques. 'The Word Processor'. In *Paper Machine*, trans. Rachel Bowlby, 19–32. Stanford: Stanford University Press, 2005.

Didi-Huberman, Georges. 'La Chambre claire-obscure'. *Le Magazine littéraire* 482 (January 2009): 87–8.

Doctorow, E. L. *Homer and Langley*. London: Little, Brown, 2010.

Doehlemann, Martin. *Langeweile?: Deutung eines verbreiteten Phänomens*. Frankfurt: Suhrkamp, 1991.

Domarchi, Jean. 'Le chef-d'oeuvre inconnu'. *Cahiers du cinéma* 39 (1954): 33–8.

Emerson, Ralph Waldo. *Emerson's Complete Works*. London: Waverley, 1883–93. 12 vols.

Esponde, Jean. *Roland Barthes, un été (Urt 1978)*. Bordeaux: Éditions Confluences, 2009.

ffrench, Patrick. *The Time of Theory: A History of* Tel Quel *(1960–1983)*. Oxford: Clarendon Press, 1995.

Flaubert, Gustave. *Bouvard and Pécuchet*. Trans. Mark Polizzotti. Normal, IL: Dalkey Archive Press, 2005.

Flaubert, Gustave. *Madame Bovary: Provincial Lives*. Trans. Geoffrey Wall. Harmondsworth: Penguin, 1992.

Forest, Philippe. *Histoire de* Tel Quel *1960–1982*. Paris: Seuil, 1995.

Freud, Sigmund. *The Psychopathology of Everyday Life*. Trans. Anthea Bell. London: Penguin, 2002.

Fried, Michael. 'Barthes's *Punctum*'. *Critical Inquiry* 31, vol. 3 (2005): 539–74.

Gabara, Rachel. *From Split to Screened Selves: French and Francophone Autobiography in the Third Person*. Stanford, CA: Stanford University Press, 2006.

Gallafent, Ed. 'The Dandy and the Magdalen: Interpreting the Long Take in Hitchcock's *Under Capricorn* (1949)'. In *Style and Meaning: Studies in the Detailed Analysis of Film*, ed. John Gibbs and Douglas Pye, 68–84. Manchester and New York: Manchester University Press, 2005.

Garcin, Jérôme. 'Barthes: Le mal de mère'. *Le Nouvel observateur* 29 January–4 February 2009: 48.

Gardner, Calum, ed. 'Roland Barthes and Poetry'. Special issue of *Barthes Studies* 2 (2016).

Gardner, Colin. 'Roland Barthes'. In *Film and Philosophy: The Key Thinkers*, ed. Felicity Colman, 109–18. Abingdon and New York: Routledge, 2014.

Gil, Marie. *Roland Barthes: Au lieu de la vie*. Paris: Flammarion, 2012.

Goodstein, Elizabeth S. *Experience without Qualities: Boredom and Modernity*. Stanford: Stanford University Press, 2005.

Le Grand Robert de la langue française: Dictionnaire alphabetique et analogique de la langue française. 2nd edn. Paris: Dictionnaires Le Robert, 1992. 9 vols.

Haraway, Donna J. 'A Cyborg Manifesto: Science, Technology, and Socialist-Feminism in the Late Twentieth Century'. In *Simians, Cyborgs, and Women: The Reinvention of Nature*, 149–81. London, Free Association Books, 1991.

Harris, Karen. 'This Essay is a 1000-word Bore: Discuss', *Times Higher Education*, 3 September 2015. Available online at https://www.timeshighereducation.com/opinion/the-essay-is-a-one-thousand-word-bore-discuss.

Harvey, William. *The Works of William Harvey, M.D.* Trans. Robert Willis. London: The Sydenham Society, 1847.

Haustein, Katja. *Regarding Lost Time: Photography, Identity, and Affect in Proust, Benjamin, and Barthes*. London: Legenda, 2012.

Haverkamp, Anselm. 'The Memory of Pictures: Roland Barthes and Augustine on Photography'. *Comparative Literature* 45, vol. 3 (1993): 258–79.

Heidegger, Martin. *Parmenides*. Trans. André Schuwer and Richard Rojcewicz. Bloomington and Indianapolis: Indiana University Press, 1992.

Hellman, Lillian. *The Little Foxes*. In *Six Plays by Lillian Hellman*, 147–225. New York: Vintage, 1979.

Iversen, Margaret. 'What is a Photograph?'. In *Photography Degree Zero: Reflections on Roland Barthes's Camera Lucida*, ed. Geoffrey Batchen, 57–74. Cambridge, MA and London: MIT Press, 2009.

Jacobowitz, Florence. '*Under Capricorn*: Hitchcock in Transition'. *CineAction* 52 (2000): 18–27.

Kapsis, Robert E. *Hitchcock: The Making of a Reputation*. Chicago and London: University of Chicago Press, 1992.

Knight, Diana. *Barthes and Utopia: Space, Travel, Writing*. Oxford: Clarendon Press, 1997.

Knight, Diana. 'Idle Thoughts: Barthes's *Vita Nova*'. *Nottingham French Studies* 36, vol. 1 (1997): 88–98.

Knight, Diana. 'Roland Barthes, or the Woman Without a Shadow'. In *Writing the Image After Roland Barthes*, ed. Jean-Michel Rabaté, 132–43. Philadelphia: University of Pennsylvania Press, 1997.

Knight, Diana. 'What Turns the Writer into a Great Writer? The Conversion Narrative of Barthes's "Vita Nova"'. *L'Esprit créateur* 55, vol. 4 (2015): 165–80.

Kristeva, Julia. *About Chinese Women*. Trans. Anita Barrows. New York and London: Marion Boyars, 1986.

Kuhn, Reinhard. *The Demon of Noontide: Ennui in Western Literature*. Princeton, NJ: Princeton University Press, 1976.

Lavers, Annette. *Roland Barthes: Structuralism and After*. London: Methuen, 1982.

Lebrave, Jean-Louis. 'La Genèse de *La Chambre claire*'. *Genesis* 19 (2002): 79–107.

Leca, Diana. 'Roland Barthes and Literary Minimalism'. *Barthes Studies* 1 (2015): 100–22.

Léger, Nathalie. '«Chaque fiche est une figure du chagrin»'. Interview by Valérie Marin La Meslée. *Le Magazine littéraire* 482 (January 2009): 84–6.

Léger, Nathalie, ed. *Roland Barthes au Collège de France 1977–1980* Paris: Éditions de l'IMEC, 2002.

Létourneau, Sophie. 'Le Prince de la jeunesse: Roland Barthes, cet écrivain mineur'. *Études françaises* 46, vol. 3 (2010): 145–57.

Lombardo, Patrizia. *The Three Paradoxes of Roland Barthes*. Athens, GA and London: University of Georgia Press, 1989.

Lorent, Fanny. *Barthes et Robbe-Grillet: Un dialogue critique.* Paris: Les Impressions Nouvelles, 2015.

Lorrain, Dimitri. *Roland Barthes, la mélancolie et la vie*. Paris: Lemieux, 2015.

Lotringer, Sylvère. 'Barthes After Barthes'. *Frieze* 136 (January–February 2011). Available online at http://www.frieze.com/issue/article/barthes-after-barthes.

Lowenstein, Adam. 'The Surrealism of the Photographic Image: Bazin, Barthes, and the Digital *Sweet Hereafter*'. *Cinema Journal* 46, vol. 3 (2007): 54–82.

Lyotard, Jean-François. 'Answer to the Question: What is the Postmodern?'. In *The Postmodern Explained to Children: Correspondence 1982–1985*, trans. Don Barry et al, 9–25. London: Turnaround, 1992.

MacCabe, Colin. 'Realism and the Cinema: Notes on Some Brechtian Theses'. In *Theoretical Essays*, 33–57. Manchester: Manchester University Press, 1985.

Macciocchi, Maria-Antonietta. *Daily Life in Revolutionary China.* New York: Monthly Review Press, 1972.

McGraw, Betty R. 'Public Parks and Private Gardens: Sartre's Nausea and Barthes's Ennui'. In *Signs in Culture: Roland Barthes Today*, ed. Steven Ungar and Betty R. McGraw, 76–95. Iowa City: University of Iowa Press, 1989.

Mallarmé, Stéphane. *Collected Poems*. Trans. Henry Weinfield. Berkeley and Los Angeles: University of California Press, 1994.

Mallarmé, Stéphane. *For Anatole's Tomb*. Trans. Patrick McGuinness. Manchester: Carcanet, 2003.

Mallarmé, Stéphane. *Oeuvres complètes*. Ed. Bertrand Marchal. Paris: Gallimard, 1998/2003. 2 vols.

Mallarmé, Stéphane. *Pour un tombeau d'Anatole*. Ed. Jean-Pierre Richard. Paris: Seuil, 1961.

Maniglier, Patrice and Dork Zabunyan. *Foucault va au cinéma.* Paris: Bayard, 2011.

Marty, Éric. *Roland Barthes, la littérature et le droit à la mort*. Paris: Seuil, 2010.

Marty, Éric. *Roland Barthes, le métier d'écrire*. Paris: Seuil, 2006.

Marx, Karl. 'The Eighteenth Brumaire of Louis Bonaparte'. In *Surveys from Exile: Political Writings, Volume 2*, ed. David Fernbach, 143–249. Harmondsworth: Penguin, 1973.

Marx-Scouras, Danielle. *The Cultural Politics of* Tel Quel: *Literature and the Left in the Wake of Engagement*. University Park, PA: Pennsylvania State University Press, 1996.

Mavor, Carol. 'Black and Blue: The Shadows of *Camera Lucida*'. In *Photography Degree Zero: Reflections on Roland Barthes's* Camera Lucida, ed. Geoffrey Batchen, 211–42. Cambridge, MA and London: MIT Press, 2009.

Milner, Jean-Claude. *Le Pas philosophique de Roland Barthes*. Lagrasse: Éditions Verdier, 2003.

Mondor, Henri. *Vie de Mallarmé*. Paris: Gallimard, 1941.

Moravia, Alberto. *Boredom*. Trans. Angus Davidson. New York: New York Review Books, 1999.

Moravia, Alberto. *L'Ennui*. Trans. unnamed. Paris: Flammarion, 1961.

Moravia, Alberto. *La Noia*. Milan: Bompiani, 1964.

Moriarty, Michael. *Roland Barthes.* Cambridge: Polity, 1991.

Mortimer, Armine Kotin. 'Coïncidence: Reécriture et désécriture de *Roland Barthes*'. *Genesis* 19 (2002): 169–89.

Nachtergael, Magali. *Roland Barthes contemporain*. Paris: Max Milo, 2015.

Narboni, Jean. *La Nuit sera noire et blanche: Barthes,* La Chambre claire, *le cinéma*. Paris: Les Prairies Ordinaires / Capricci, 2015.

North, Michael. 'Authorship and Autography'. *PMLA* 116, vol. 5 (2001): 1377–85.

Noudelmann, François. *The Philosopher's Touch: Sartre, Nietzche, and Barthes at the Piano*. Trans. Brian J. Reilly. New York: Columbia University Press, 2012.

Nunez, Laurent. 'Vie nouvelle, roman virtuel'. *Le Magazine littéraire* 482 (January 2009): 74–5.

Olin, Margaret. 'Touching Photographs: Roland Barthes's "Mistaken" Identification'. *Representations* 80 (2002): 99–118.

O'Meara, Lucy. *Roland Barthes at the Collège de France*. Liverpool: Liverpool University Press, 2012.

O'Meara, Lucy. 'Barthes and Antonioni in China: The Muffling of Criticism'. *Textual Practice* 30, vol. 2 (2016): 267–86.

Païni, Dominique. 'La Résistance au cinéma'. In *R/B: Roland Barthes*, ed. Marianne Alphant and Nathalie Léger, 116–18. Paris: Seuil/Centre Pompidou/IMEC, 2002.

Pearson, Roger. '«Une inaptitude délicieuse à finir»: Mallarmé and the Orthography of Incompletion'. In *Esquisses/Ébauches: Projects and Pre-texts in Ninenteenth-century French Culture*, ed. Sonya Stephens, 211–21. New York: Peter Lang, 2007.

Perec, Georges. *A Void*. Trans. Gilbert Adair. London: Harvill, 1994.

Pierrot, Anne Herschberg. 'Présence de *Bouvard et Pécuchet* chez Roland Barthes'. *Oeuvres & Critiques* 34, vol. 1 (2009): 33–42.

Pint, Kris. *The Perverse Art of Reading: On the Phantasmatic Semiology in Roland Barthes' Cours au Collège de France*. Trans. Christopher M. Gemerchak. Amsterdam and New York: Rodopi, 2010.

Pleynet, Marcelin. *Le Voyage en Chine: Chroniques du journal ordinaire 11 avril – 3 mai 1974 – extraits*. Paris: Hachette, 1980.

Proust, Marcel. *Selected Letters: 1880–1903*. Ed. Philip Kolb. Trans. Ralph Manheim. London: Collins, 1983.

Proust, Marcel. *The Way by Swann's*. Trans. Lydia Davis. Harmondsworth: Penguin, 2002.

Rabaté, Jean-Michel. 'Le Roman de Roland Barthes'. In *Barthes après Barthes: une actualité en questions*, ed. Catherine Coquio and Régis Salado, 7–14. Pau: Publications de l'Université de Pau, 1993.

Racine, Jean. *Andromache, Britannicus, Berenice*. Trans. John Cairncross. London: Penguin, 1967.

Rappaport, Mark. '*Under Capricorn* Revisited'. *Hitchcock Annual* 12 (2003–4): 42–66.

Richard, Jean-Pierre. *L'Univers imaginaire de Mallarmé*. Paris: Seuil, 1961.

Roger, Philippe. *Roland Barthes, roman*. Paris: Grasset, 1986.

Rohmer, Éric and Claude Chabrol. *Hitchcock: The First Forty-Four Films*. Trans. Stanley Hochman. New York: Ungar, 1979.

Samoyault, Tiphaine. *Roland Barthes: Biographie*. Paris: Seuil, 2015.

Samuel, Henry. 'Roland Barthes' brother publishes philosopher's personal notes, "violating his intimacy"'. *Daily Telegraph* 21 January 2009. Available online at http://www.telegraph.co.uk/news/worldnews/europe/france/4309295/Roland-Barthes-brother-publishes-philosophers-personal-notes-violating-his-intimacy.html.

Sartre, Jean-Paul. *Nausea*. Trans. Robert Baldick. Harmondsworth: Penguin, 1965.

Saussure, Ferdinand de. *Course in General Linguistics*. Ed. Charles Bally, Albert Sechehaye and Albert Reidlinger. Trans. Wade Baskin. London, Fontana, 1974.

Schaeffer, Jean-Marie. *Lettre à Roland Barthes*. Vincennes: Éditions Thierry Marchaisse, 2015.

Shawcross, Nancy M. *Roland Barthes on Photography: The Critical Tradition in Perspective*. Gainesville, FL: University Press of Florida, 1997.

Simpson, Helen. *Under Capricorn*. London: William Heinemann, 1937.

Sloan, Jane E. *Alfred Hitchcock: A Filmography and Bibliography*. Berkeley and Los Angeles: University of California Press, 1995.

Smith, Ali. *Artful*. London: Penguin, 2013.

Sollers, Philippe. *L'Amitié de Roland Barthes*. Paris: Seuil, 2015.

Spoto, Donald. *The Dark Side of Genius: The Life of Alfred Hitchcock*. New edn. London: Plexus, 1994.

Stafford, Andy. *Roland Barthes*. London: Reaktion, 2015.
Stafford, Andy. 'Roland Barthes's Travels in China: Writing a Diary of Dissidence within Dissidence?'. *Textual Practice* 30, vol. 2 (2016): 287–304.
Stendhal. *The Life of Henry Brulard*. Trans. John Sturrock. Harmondsworth: Penguin, 1995.
Stiénon, Valérie and Laurent Demoulin. 'Roland Barthes, ethnographe de lui-même: fiches, carnets et notes inédits'. *Culture: le magazine culturel de l'Université de Liège*, June 2009: 1–7.
Svendsen, Lars. *A Philosophy of Boredom*. Trans. John Irons. London: Reaktion, 2005.
Taylor, John Russell. *Hitch: The Life and Work of Alfred Hitchcock*. London: Abacus, 1981.
Thody, Philip. *Roland Barthes: A Conservative Estimate*. London: Macmillan, 1977.
Thomas, Chantal. *Pour Roland Barthes*. Paris: Seuil, 2015.
Toohey, Peter. *Boredom: A Lively History*. New Haven and London: Yale University Press, 2011.
Truffaut, François. *Hitchcock*. Updated edn. London: Paladin, 1978.
Ungar, Steven. 'Persistence of the Image: Barthes, Photography, and the Resistance to Film'. In *Critical Essays on Roland Barthes*, ed. Diana Knight, 236–49. New York: G.K. Hall & Co., 2000.
Ungar, Steven. *Roland Barthes: The Professor of Desire*. Lincoln, NE: University of Nebraska Press, 1984.
Verevis, Constantine. 'Under a Distemperate Star: *Under Capricorn*'. In *Hitchcock at the Source: The Auteur as Adaptor*, ed. R. Barton Palmer and David Boyd, 173–88. Albany, NY: State University of New York Press, 2011.
Verlaine, Paul. *Choix de poésies*. Paris: Larousse, 1973.
Vest, James M. *Hitchcock and France: The Forging of an Auteur*. Westport, CT and London: Praeger, 2003.
Vial, André. *Mallarmé: Tétralogie pour un enfant mort*. Paris: Corti, 1976.
Wahl, François. 'Ouf!'. In *R/B: Roland Barthes*, eds. Marianne Alphant and Nathalie Léger, 107–10. Paris: Seuil/Centre Pompidou/IMEC, 2002.
Watt, Adam. 'Reading Proust in Barthes's *Journal de deuil*'. *Nottingham French Studies* 53, vol. 1 (2014): 102–12.
Watts, Philip. 'Roland Barthes's Cold-War Cinema'. *SubStance* 34, vol. 3 (2005): 17–32.
Watts, Philip. *Roland Barthes' Cinema*. New York: Oxford University Press, 2016.
Wharton, Edith. *A Backward Glance*. London: Century, 1987.
Wolfe, Cary. *Animal Rites: American Culture, the Discourse of Species, and Posthumanist Theory*. Chicago and London: University of Chicago Press, 2003.
Wood, Robin. *Hitchcock's Films Revisited*. Rev. edn. New York: Columbia University Press, 2002.

Worrell, William H. 'Ink, Oil and Mirror Gazing Ceremonies in Modern Egypt'. *Journal of the American Oriental Society* 36 (1916): 37–53.

Yacavone, Kathrin. *Benjamin, Barthes and the Singularity of Photography*. London: Continuum, 2012.

Zhang, Dora. 'The Sideways Gaze: Roland Barthes's Travels in China', *Los Angeles Review of Books*, 23 June 2012. Available online at https://lareviewofbooks.org/essay/the-sideways-gaze-roland-barthess-travels-in-china.

Index

Aciman, André 55 n.9
Addinsell, Richard 123
Aeschimann, Éric 30 n.11
Alphant, Marianne 58 n.30
Antonioni, Michelangelo 109, 113, 118
Aouillé, Sophie 55–7
arrogance 72–5, 95–6
Attridge, Derek 55 n.9, 60 n.39
Augustine, Saint 32 n.23

Bach, Raymond 13, 31 n.14
Badir, Sémir 11
Balzac, Honoré de 7–8, 110, 111, 114–18, 121, 123, 126
Barnes, Julian 15
Barthes, Henriette 13–39, 41–60
Barthes, Roland (*works by*)
   Album 2, 23, 25, 32 n.20, 37 n.53, 78 n.7, 81 n.28, 85, 102 n.7
   'An Almost Obsessive Relation to Writing Instruments' 63–4, 66–7, 79 n.15, 89
   'À propos du numéro spécial de «Confluences» sur les problèmes du roman' 85
   Camera Lucida 3, 6, 22–3, 27, 28, 31 n.14, 41–60, 78 n.7
   'Ça prend' 57 n.16
   'Compte rendu du voyage en Chine' 7, 88, 89, 91, 104 n.23, 105 n.31, 105 n.33, 106 n.40, 106 n.42, 106 n.47
   'The Death of the Author' 29
   'Deliberation' 31 n.17, 33 n.28, 37 n.52, 37 n.54, 39 n.64, 39 n.65
   'Diderot, Brecht, Eisenstein' 112, 132 n.10, 132 n.15
   Le Discours amoureux (seminar) 15, 60 n.36, 109, 133 n.23
   Elements of Semiology 71, 93
   Empire of Signs 16, 63, 66, 69, 71, 106 n.47, 107 n.50, 117

   'Esquisse d'une société sanatoriale' 102 n.8
   The Fashion System 104 n.22
   How to Live Together 16, 80 n.23, 101 n.5, 105–6 n.37
   Incidents 1, 3, 109, 131 n.3
   'Introduction to the Structural Analysis of Narratives' 134
   'Journal-Moisson' 32 n.20, 131 n.3
   'Leaving the Movie Theater' 57 n.24
   'Lecture: In Inauguration of the Chair of Literary Semiology, Collège de France, January 7, 1977' 35–6 n.50
   Le Lexique de l'auteur 15, 35–6 n.50, 39 n.67, 71, 79 n.16
   'Longtemps, je me suis couché de bonne heure…' 23–4, 25
   A Lover's Discourse 2, 3, 15, 32 n.20, 67, 77–8 n.7, 133 n.23
   Michelet 85
   Mourning Diary 5–6, 7, 8, 13–39, 41–60, 109–10
   Mythologies 66, 70, 71, 81 n.29, 93, 111–12
   The Neutral 6, 35 n.44, 36 n.50, 38 n.59, 38 n.61, 62, 63, 64, 67–82, 95–6, 105 n.36, 109, 131 n.3, 137
   'Objective Literature' 101
   'On CinemaScope' 132 n.11
   'On Photography' 47
   The Pleasure of the Text 7, 85, 98
   The Preparation of the Novel 2, 6, 9, 15, 24, 25, 27, 29, 36–7 n.52, 38 n.58, 44, 54, 57 n.16, 58 n.27, 60 n.41, 65, 67, 80 n.23, 83–4, 90, 101 n.1, 102 n.11, 106 n.47, 106 n.48, 112
   Roland Barthes by Roland Barthes 3, 47, 57 n.24, 66, 71, 79 n.15, 79 n.16, 82 n.33, 86–7, 93, 94, 102 n.12, 106 n.46, 106–7 n.48, 137, 138
   Sade, Fourier, Loyola 67

Sarrasine *de Balzac* 7–8, 104 n.22, 110–11, 113–30
The Semiotic Challenge 71, 81 n.28
'So, How Was China?' 88–9, 92, 104 n.22
Sollers Writer 39 n.67, 67, 77 n.5
'Sur l'«Oedipe» d'André Boucourechliev' 15, 32 n.20
'Sur sept phrases de *Bouvard et Pécuchet*' 78 n.7
S/Z 4, 7–8, 29, 57 n.24, 71, 81 n.28, 93, 110–11, 112, 113–30
'Ten Reasons to Write' 39 n.63
'The Third Meaning' 42–3, 46
Travels in China 6–7, 83–108
'La Vaccine de l'avant-garde' 85
'Variations sur l'écriture' 6, 64, 65, 67, 73, 75, 82 n.39
Vita Nova 3, 6, 14, 23–9, 43, 138
'Writing' 65, 90–1
Writing Degree Zero 9, 78 n.7
Bataille, Georges 32 n.23, 87
Batchen, Geoffrey 11, 41–2, 58 n.30
Beckett, Samuel 98
Bellon, Guillaume 11
Bellour, Raymond 55 n.9
Benoit, Éric 29, 34 n.33, 34 n.37
Bergman, Ingrid 51, 52
Bernstein, Sidney 119
Berry, Walter 14
Binet, Laurent 2, 61, 92
Bishop, Ryan 10
Bordwell, David 132 n.14
boredom 7, 83–108
Borges, Jorge Luis 71
Boucourechliev, André 15, 21, 32 n.30
Brecht, Bertolt 8, 71
Bresson, Robert 109
Briggs, Kate 35 n.45, 35 n.47
Brill, Lesley 133 n.24
Brøndal, Viggo 81 n.27
Brown, Andrew 55 n.9, 58 n.30, 62, 78 n.8, 78 n.10, 133 n.21
Buñuel, Luis 109, 131 n.3
Burgin, Victor 58 n.30
Burnier, Michel-Antoine 78 n.10
Butor, Michel 35 n.50, 36 n.51, 67

Calvet, Louis-Jean 80 n.24, 102 n.8
Camus, Renaud 106 n.45
Cassegrain, Guillaume 2
Chabrol, Claude 109, 118–19, 135 n.45
Chaplin, Charles 109
Chateaubriand, François-René de 1, 98
China, People's Republic of 83–108
Cixous, Hélène 113
Comment, Bernard 58 n.30
Compagnon, Antoine 2, 3, 15, 18, 27, 31 n.19, 32 n.23, 37 n.57, 38 n.60, 39 n.64, 43, 53, 57 n.22, 58 n.28, 58 n.30, 59 n.31, 62
Confucius 91–2
Convert, Pascal 1
Coste, Claude 58 n.30, 78 n.7, 90, 101 n.1, 103 n.21, 104 n.22, 131 n.33
Culler, Jonathan 72, 82 n.40

Dante Alighieri 23, 26, 36 n.31
De Beauvoir, Simone 33 n.27
Degas, Edgar 98
Demoulin, Laurent 48
De Rambures, Jean-Louis 63, 66, 68
Derrida, Jacques 60 n.45, 71, 76, 81 n.28, 82 n.36, 95
Didi-Huberman, Georges 55 n.9
Doehlemann, Martin 101
Domarchi, Jean 119
doxa 7, 42, 46, 67, 72, 75, 92, 93, 96, 107 n.57
Dreyer, Carl Theodor 109, 112–13, 118, 131 n.3, 132 n.12
Dreyfus, Robert 65
Druet, Roger 65
Ducard, Dominique 11

Eisenstein, Sergei 8, 109, 111, 112
Emerson, Ralph Waldo 41
ennui 7, 83–108
Esponde, Jean 10 n.2

Fellini, Federico 52–3, 60 n.41, 109, 118, 131 n.3, 133 n.24
ffrench, Patrick 103 n.19
film 7–8, 41–60, 109–36
Flaubert, Gustave 62, 77 n.7, 78 n.8, 102 n.11
Forest, Philippe 103 n.17, 103 n.19

Freud, Sigmund 69
Fried, Michael 55 n.9
Fry, Christopher 85

Gabara, Rachel 58 n.25, 111
Gallafent, Ed 119
Garcin, Jérôme 55 n.7
Gardner, Calum 10 n.4
Gardner, Colin 131 n.6, 132 n.16
Gide, André 71
Gil, Marie 23, 32 n.20, 35 n.46, 39 n.67, 58 n.30, 64, 102 n.8, 103 n.17, 130
Goncharov, Ivan 98
Goodstein, Elizabeth S. 98
Grégoire, Herman 65
Greimas, Algirdas 70, 80 n.24

Haraway, Donna J. 76
Harris, Karen 8–9
Harvey, William 41
Haustein, Katja 31 n.19
Haverkamp, Anselm 55 n.9
Haydn, Joseph 68
Heidegger, Martin 75–6
Hellman, Lillian 57 n.19
Hitchcock, Alfred 7–8, 51–2, 109–36
Hopper, Edward 98

Iversen, Margaret 58 n.30

Jacobowitz, Florence 119
Jakobson, Roman 37 n.54
Janouch, Gustav 68

Kafka, Franz 68
Kanters, Robert 67
Kapsis, Robert E. 131 n.4
Kazan, Elia 109, 111
Kierkegaard, Søren 100
Knight, Diana 34 n.40, 35 n.43, 59 n.34, 81 n.27
Kristeva, Julia 88, 103 n.19, 105 n.35, 106 n.41
Kuhn, Reinhard 98, 99–100, 108 n.61

Lacan, Jacques 88, 92
La Meslée, Valerie Marin 56 n.10
Lang, Jack 61
Lao-tzu 69

Lavers, Annette 3, 81 n.27
Lebrave, Jean-Louis 42, 56 n.13, 56–7 n.15, 57 n.23, 59 n.32, 78 n.10
Leca, Diana 104 n.24, 107 n.49, 107 n.55
Lederer, Ernst 68
Léger, Nathalie 11, 23, 33 n.24, 48, 56 n.10, 90
Létourneau, Sophie 86
Lin Biao 91–2
Lombardo, Patrizia 81 n.27
Lorent, Fanny 2
Lorrain, Dimitri 2
Lotringer, Sylvère 9
Lowenstein, Adam 55 n.9
Lyotard, Jean-François 112

MacCabe, Colin 126
Macciocchi, Maria-Antonietta 88, 103 n.17
Maistre, Joseph de 68, 69
Mallarmé, Anatole 13–39
Mallarmé, Stéphane 5–6, 13–39
Manghani, Sunil 10
Maniglier, Patrice 136 n.51
Mankiewicz, Joseph L. 109, 111, 132 n.9
Mann, Thomas 35 n.50
Mao Zedong 88, 89, 90, 91, 94, 95, 96, 103 n.17
Mapplethorpe, Robert 8
Marchal, Bertrand 30 n.4
Marty, Éric 14, 15, 25, 30 n.9, 31 n.17, 31 n.19, 32 n.20, 32 n.23, 35 n.48, 42–3, 48, 56 n.14, 57 n.20, 58 n.30, 59 n.33, 62, 85, 131 n.5
Marx, Karl 61, 62, 71, 77 n.5
Marx-Scouras, Danielle 103 n.19
Maupomé, Claude 49
Mavor, Carol 58 n.30
McEwan, Ian 2
McGraw, Betty R. 99
McGuinness, Patrick 18–19, 21–2
Michelet, Jules 36 n.51, 74, 87, 94
Miller, Jacques-Alain 3
Milner, Jean-Claude 60 n.36, 71, 96–7
Mondor, Henri 30 n.3, 30 n.8
Moravia, Alberto 83, 102 n.11
Moriarty, Michael 58 n.30
Mortimer, Armine Kotin 104 n.26
mourning 5–6, 13–39, 41–60

Nachtergael, Magali 1, 2
Narboni, Jean 2, 55 n.9, 57 n.15, 58 n.26,
    60 n.37
North, Michael 55 n.9
Noudelmann, François 32 n.20
Nunez, Laurent 58 n.30

Olin, Margaret 59 n.34
O'Meara, Lucy 11, 34 n.40, 102 n.12,
    103 n.21, 106 n.47
Ossola, Carlo 78 n.11, 79 n.12

Païni, Dominique 58 n.25
Pascal, Blaise 100
Pasolini, Pier Paolo 109
Pearson, Roger 34 n.37
Perec, Georges 121
Perros, Georges 79 n.14
photography 41–60, 61
Pialat, Maurice 131 n.3
Pierrot, Anne Herschberg
    78 n.7, 89
Pint, Kris 11 n.14
Pivot, Bernard 68
Plato 98
Pleynet, Marcelin 88, 103 n.19, 104 n.23,
    105 n.33, 105 n.37, 106 n.47,
    107 n.56
Proust, Marcel 5, 15, 23, 31–2 n.19, 44–5,
    61, 65, 77 n.3, 79 n.14

Rabaté, Jean-Michel 55 n.9, 58 n.30
Racine, Jean 101 n.1
Rambaud, Patrick 78 n.10
Rappaport, Mark 119
readable/writable texts 8, 106 n.47, 110,
    112, 114–18, 121–8, 130
realism 7–8, 109–36
Rebeyrol, Philippe 56 n.14, 84–5
Richard, Jean-Pierre 13, 29 n.2, 29–30 n.3,
    30 n.4, 30 n.6, 30 n.8, 31 n.14,
    32 n.20, 32 n.22
Robbe-Grillet, Alain 3
Roger, Philippe 102 n.8
Rohmer, Éric 118–19, 135 n.45
Rousseau, Jean-Jacques 68, 69

Samoyault, Tiphaine 2, 10, 31 n.14,
    32 n.20, 35 n.44, 57 n.20, 59 n.33,
    61, 71, 77 n.2, 78 n.9, 80 n.24,
    102 n.8, 103 n.17, 104 n.25
Samuel, Henry 30 n.11
Sarduy, Severo 56 n.14, 88
Sartre, Jean-Paul 71, 98, 99, 101 n.3
Saussure, Ferdinand de 37 n.54, 38 n.60,
    67, 69–72, 80 n.21, 80 n.24,
    81 n.27, 93
Schaeffer, Jean-Marie 2
Shawcross, Nancy M. 58 n.30
Sheringham, Michael 1
signifier, signified 9, 21, 22, 28, 38 n.60,
    43, 47, 57 n.24, 70, 71, 72, 73, 76,
    81 n.28, 92–3, 97, 100, 106 n.40,
    106 n.42, 106 n.46, 106 n.47, 110,
    114–15, 117, 132–3 n.17
Simpson, Helen 122, 135 n.38, 135 n.40,
    135 n.43
Singevin, Charles 80 n.24
Sloan, Jane E. 134 n.31
Sollers, Philippe 2, 56 n.13, 88, 91, 92,
    102 n.7, 106 n.39, 125
Spoto, Donald 135 n.45
Stafford, Andy 2, 102 n.8, 103 n.21,
    134 n.33
Staiger, Janet 132 n.14
Stendhal 32 n.23, 79 n.14
Stiénon, Valérie 48
Svendsen, Lars 98. 107–8 n.59, 108 n.64
Swedenborg, Emanuel 68

Taylor, John Russell 133 n.25
Tesson, Philippe 91
Thody, Philip 3
Thomas, Chantal 2, 66, 107 n.54, 107 n.57
Thompson, Kristin 132 n.14
Tolstoy, Leo 68, 69
Toohey, Peter 98, 108 n.64
Truffaut, François 118–19
Turner, Chris 79 n.13

Ungar, Steven 7, 55 n.9, 58 n.25, 98

Valéry, Paul 101 n.1
Van Der Zee, James 52
Verevis, Constantine 135 n.38
Verlaine, Paul 32 n.19
Vest, James M. 134 n.28
Vial, André 34 n.37

Wahl, François 3, 14, 47, 88, 97, 102 n.13
Watt, Adam 15
Watts, Philip 132 n.8, 132 n.9
Wharton, Edith 14
Winnicott, D.W. 59–60 n.35
Wolfe, Cary 82 n.36
Wood, Robin 119, 121, 136 n.48, 136 n.50

Worrell, William H. 81–2 n.30
writing instruments 61–82, 89–91
Wyler, William 44–5, 57 n.17

Yacavone, Kathrin 55 n.9, 59 n.34

Zabunyan, Dork 136 n.52
Zhang, Dora 3

Lightning Source UK Ltd.
Milton Keynes UK
UKHW01f0234010518
321918UK00003B/89/P